Dictionary of Banking

Dictionary of Banking

B. Nandhakumar
Assistant Professor, Department of MBA
Hindusthan College of Arts and Science
Coimbatore

ATLANTIC
PUBLISHERS & DISTRIBUTORS (P) LTD

Published by

ATLANTIC

PUBLISHERS & DISTRIBUTORS (P) LTD

7/22, Ansari Road, Darya Ganj, New Delhi-110002
Phones : +91-11-40775252, 23273880, 23275880, 23280451
Fax : +91-11-23285873
Web : www.atlanticbooks.com
E-mail : orders@atlanticbooks.com

Branch Office
5, Nallathambi Street, Wallajah Road, Chennai-600002
Phones : +91-44-64611085, 32413319
E-mail : chennai@atlanticbooks.com

Printed in India at Glorious Printers, A-13, D.S.I.D.C., Jhilmil Industrial Area, Delhi-110095

Dedicated to

Sri Ramakrishna, Sri Sarada Devi
and
Swami Vivekananda

Preface

Banking is one of the most important sectors of business and finance that assists the world of commerce to keep on running. Without banks and the banking services that they provide, commerce and trade would collapse and credit would become virtually extinct. As time passes, many new concepts are introduced in banking, making it apt to successfully fulfill the emerging needs of trade, commerce finance and businesses.

The changes in the banking industry over the last decade have resulted in a greatly expanded vocabulary. More than 3,500 key terms related to banking, electronic commerce, finance, money management, and legal regulations have been defined clearly and concisely in the book. This glossary presented in alphabetical order provides understandable explanations of terms and phrases commonly encountered in banking. It also includes abbreviations and acronyms of important terms.

The book covers topics relating to general banking, retail banking, corporate banking, development banking, government business, treasury, trade and finance, international banking, Forex, money and capital markets, debt markets, bonds, securities, credit, risk management, ATM cards, monitory policy, IS Audit, mergers & acquisitions, global finance, Euro markets, offshore banking, among others. The entries cover both Indian and global banking practices.

It is an indispensable reference manual for banking and finance professionals, students, business owners, and consumers, and an aid to understanding banking practices and getting the best banking service. The book will be of great use to bankers, business and management professionals, IT professionals, consultants, attorneys, investors, NRIs, and students and teachers of commerce, banking and economics. In addition, it will be very useful for those working in the banks or in finance companies. It will also be useful for those preparing for competitive examinations for bank jobs, as well as those undergoing training in a bank or doing an inductive course on banking.

An effort has been made to explain all the primary concepts in simple language and lucid manner for easy understanding by the readers.

B. Nandhakumar

Acknowledgements

I wish to express my sincere thanks and indebtedness to Dr. S. Senbaganathan for his invaluable guidance in completing this book.

I also express my heartiest thanks to my friends and family members for their help and co-operation to complete this work successfully.

I am thankful to Atlantic Publications for the interest evinced in publishing this book.

B. Nandhakumar

Contents

A

AAA. Letters that show how reliable a particular share, bond or company is considered to be.

ABA. Abbr. American Bankers Association.

Abandonment. An act of giving up voluntarily something that you own, such as an option or the right to a property.

Abatement. An act of reducing.

Above par. To a share with a market price higher than its par value.

Above the line. 1. Companies forming part of normal income and expenditure before tax. 2. To revenue items in a government budget. 3. To advertising for which payment is made (such as an ad in a magazine or a stand at a trade fair) and for which a commission is paid to an advertising.

Absolute. Complete or total.

Absolute monopoly. A situation where only one producer produces or only one supplier supplies something.

Absorb. To take in a small item so that it forms part of a larger one.

Absorption. The process of making a smaller business part of a larger one, so that the smaller company in effect no longer exists.

Absorption costing. A form of costing for a product that includes both the direct costs of production and the indirect overhead costs as well.

Absorption rate. A rate at which overhead costs are absorbed into each unit of production.

Abstract. A short form of a report or document.

Ac and acc. Abbr. Account.

Accelerate. 1. To make something go faster. 2. To reduce the amount of time before a maturity date.

Accelerated depreciation. A system of depreciation which reduces the value of assets at a high rate in the early years to encourage companies, as a result of tax advantages, to invest in new equipment.

Acceleration. The act of making an unpaid balance or bond repayment become payable immediately.

Accept. 1. To take something this is being offered. 2. To say 'yes' or to agree to something.

Acceptable. Which can be accepted.

Acceptance. 1. The act of signing a bill of exchange to show that you agree to pay it. 2. The act of agreeing to an offer. 3. A bill which has been accepted. 4. The act of accepting an offer of new shares for which you have applied.

Acceptance credit. An arrangement of credit from a bank, where the bank accepts bills of exchange drawn on the bank by the debtor: the bank then discounts the bills and is responsible for paying them when they mature; the debtor owes the bank for the bills but these are covered by letters of credit.

Acceptance sampling. The process of testing a small sample of a batch to see if the whole batch is good enough to be accepted who accepts a bill of exchange by signing it, thus making a commitment to pay it by a specified date.

Access. To be able to obtain or reach something.

Access fee. A fee charged to bank customers for using online services.

Access time. The time taken by a computer to find data stored in it.

Accident insurance. Insurance which will pay the insured person when an accident takes place.

Accident policy. An insurance contract which provides a person with accident insurance.

Accommodation. 1. Money lent for a short time. 2. To agree terms for settlement with creditors.

Accommodation address. An address used for receiving messages, but which is not the real address of the company.

Accordance. In agreement or conformity with, as a result of what someone has said should be done.

Accord and satisfaction. The payment by a debtor of (part of) a debt.

Accordingly. In agreement with what has been decided.

According to. 1. In accordance with. 2. As stated or shown by someone.

Account. 1. A record of financial transactions over a period of time, such as money paid, received, borrowed or owed. 2. (in a shop) an arrangement which a customer has to buy goods and pay for them at a later date, usually the end of the month. 3. A part of a total bill. 4. A customer who does a large amount of business with a firm and has an account with it. 5. To write each sum of money in the account book. 6. Stock exchange a period during which shares are traded for credit, and at the end of which the shares bought must be paid for. 7. Notice.

Account aggregation. A service for online banking customers, which allows them to group various accounts, including credit card accounts, together.

Accountancy. The work of an accountant.

Accountant. A person who keeps a company's accounts or deals with an individual person's tax affairs.

Accountant's opinion. A report of the audit of a company's books, carried out by a certified public accountant.

Account book. A book with printed columns which is used to record sales and purchases.

Account day. A day on which shares which have been bought must be paid for (usually a Monday ten days after the end of an account). Also called settlement day.

Account end. End of an accounting period.

Account executive. 1. An employee who looks after customers or who is the link between customers and the company. 2. An employee of an organisation such as a bank, public relations firm or advertising agency who is responsible for looking after particular clients and handling their business with the organisation.

Accounting. The work of recording money paid, received, borrowed or owed.

Accounting period. A period of time at the end of which the firm's accounts are made up.

Accounting Standards Board. A committee set up by British accounting institutions to monitor methods used in accounting.

Account number. A special number given to an account, either a bank account (in which case it appears on cheques) or a customer account.

Account reconcilement. Same as bank reconciliation.

Accounts department. A department in a company which deals with money paid, received, borrowed or owed.

Accounts manager. The manager of an accounts department.

Accounts payable. Money owed by a company.

Accounts receivable. Money owed to a company.

Account statement. A written document from a bank showing the balance of an account at the end of a period.

Account trading. Buying shares and selling the same shares during an account, this means that the dealer has only to pay the difference between the price of the shares bought and the price obtained for them when they are sold.

Accrete. To have something added to it, especially (of a fund) to have interest added to it.

Accretion. The process of adding interest to a fund over a period of time.

Accrual. 1. The act of noting financial transactions when they take place, and not when payment is made. 2. A gradual increase by addition.

Accruals basis Or Accruals concept. A method of preparing accounts in which revenues and costs are both reported during the period to which they refer and not during the period when payments are received or made.

Accrue. To increase and be due for payment at a later date.

Accrued dividend. A dividend earned since the last dividend was paid.

Accrued interest. Interest which has been earned by an interest-bearing investment.

Acct. Abbr. Account.

Accumulate. To grow in quantity by being added to, or to get more of something over a period of time.

Accumulated depreciation. The total amount by which an asset has been depreciated since it was purchased.

Accumulated profit. A profit which is not paid as dividend but is taken over into the accounts of the following year.

Accumulated reserves. Reserves which a company has put aside over a period of years.

Accumulation. The process of growing larger by being added to, or of getting more and more of something.

Accumulation unit. A type of unit in a unit trust, which produces dividends which are used to form more units. (as opposed to an income unit, which produces dividends which the investor receives as income)

Achieve. To succeed in doing something, to do something successfully.

Acid test ratio. Same as liquidity ratio.

Acquire. To buy.

Acquirer. A person or company which buys something.

Acquisition. Something bought.

Acquisition accounting. A full consolidation, where the assets of a subsidiary company which has been purchased are included in the parent company's balance sheet and the premium paid for the goodwill is written off against the year's earnings.

Across-the-board. Applying to everything or everyone.

Across-the-board tariff increase. An increase in duty which applies to a whole range of items.

Act. A law passed by parliament which must be obeyed by the people.

ACT. Abbr. Advance Corporation Tax.

Action. 1. A thing which has been done. 2. To do something (usually to go on strike) to show that you are not happy with conditions at work. 3. A case in a law court where a person or company sues another person or company.

Active. Involving many transactions or activities.

Active account. An account, such as a bank account or investment account, which is used (i.e. money is deposited and withdrawn) Frequently.

Active partner. A partner who works in a company that is a partnership.

Activity. The fact of being active or busy.

Activity chart. A plan showing work which has been done, made so that it can be compared to a previous plan showing how much work should be done.

Actual. Real or correct.

Actual price. A price for a commodity which is for immediate delivery.

Actuarial. Calculated by an actuary.

Actuarial tables. Lists showing how long people of certain ages are likely to live, used to calculate life assurance premiums and annuities.

Actuary. A person employed by an insurance company or other organisation to calculate the risk involved in an insurance, and therefore the premiums payable by people taking out insurance.

Adaptable. Able to change or be changed.

Adaptation. The process of changing something, or of being changed, to fit new conditions.

Add. To put figures together to make a total.

Added value. An amount added to the value of a product or service, equal to the difference between its cost and the amount received when it is sold. Wages, taxes, etc. are deducted from the added value to give the profit.

Addition. An act of putting numbers together.

Additional. Extra which is added.

Additional borrowing. Extra borrowing in addition to money already borrowed.

Additional premium. A payment made to cover extra items in an existing insurance.

Addressing machine. A machine which puts addresses on envelopes automatically.

Address list. A list of names and addresses of people and companies.

Add up. 1. To put several figures together to make a total. 2. To make sense.

Add up to. To make a total of.

Adequacy. The fact of being large enough or good enough for something.

Adequate. Large or good enough.

Adjudicate. To give a judgement between two parties in law or to decide a legal problem.

Adjudication. The act of giving a judgement or of deciding a legal problem.

Adjudication of bankruptcy. A legal order making someone bankrupt.

Adjudication tribunal. A group which adjudicates in industrial disputes.

Adjudicator. A person who gives a decision on a problem.

Adjust. To change something to fit new conditions.

Adjustable. Which can be adjusted.

Adjustable peg. A method of pegging one currency to another, which allows the exchange rate to be adjusted from time to time.

Adjustable rate mortgage. A mortgage where the interest rate changes according to the current market rates. Abbr. ARM.

Adjustable rate preferred stock. A preference shares on which dividends are paid in line with the interest rate on Treasury bills. Abbr. ARPS.

Adjusted balance. A balance in a bank account which is adjusted to take account of debits and credits during a period. This balance can then be used as a basis for calculating bank charges.

Adjusted gross income. A person's total annual income less expenses, pension contributions, capital losses, etc., used as a basis to calculate income tax. Abbr. AGI

Adjuster. A person who calculates losses for an insurance company.

Adjustment. 1. The act of adjusting. 2. A slight change. 3. An entry in accounts which does not represent a receipt or payment, but which is made to make the accounts correct. 4. A change in the exchange rates, made to correct a balance of payment deficit.

Adjustment trigger. A factor such as a certain level of inflation which triggers an adjustment in exchange rates.

Administer. To organise, manage or direct the whole of an organisation or part of one.

Administered price. A price fixed by a manufacturer which cannot be varied by a retailer. The India term is resale price maintenance.

Administration. 1. The action of organising, controlling or managing a company. 2. A person or group of people who manage or direct an organisation. 3. An appointment by a court of a person to manage the affairs of a company.

Administration costs Or Administration expenses. The costs of management, not including production, marketing or distribution costs.

Administration order. 1. An order by a court, by which a debtor repays his debts in instalments. 2. An order by a court to appoint an administrator for a company.

Administrative receiver. A person appointed by a court to administer the affairs of a company.

Administrator. 1. A person who directs the work of other employees in a business. 2. A person appointed by a court to manage the affairs of someone who dies without leaving a will.

Admission charge. The price to be paid before going into an area or building, e.g. to see an exhibition.

Ad valorem. It meaning 'according to value', showing that a tax is calculated according to the value of the goods taxed.

Ad valorem duty. The duty calculated on the sales value of the goods.

Ad valorem tax. Tax calculated according to the value of the goods taxed.

Advance. 1. Money paid as a loan or as a part of a payment to be made later. 2. An increase. 3. Early, before something happens. 4. To make something happen earlier.

Adverse. Unfavourable.

Adverse balance of trade. A situation in which a country imports more than it exports.

Adverse trading conditions. Bad conditions for trade.

Adverse action. A decision which has unfavourable consequences for employees.

Advertising agency. An office which plans designs and manages advertising for other companies.

Advertising budget. Money planned for spending on advertising.

Advice. 1. An opinion as to what action to take. 2. According to what is written on the advice note. 3. Advising that a bill of exchange has been drawn.

Advise. 1. To tell someone what has happened. 2. To suggest to someone what should be done.

Advise against. To suggest that something should not be done.

Advisor. A person who suggests what should be done.

Advisory board. A group of advisors.

Advisory funds. Funds placed with a financial institution to invest on behalf of a client, the institution investing them at its own discretion.

Affect. To cause some change in something, especially to have a bad effect on something.

Affiliate. A company which partly owns another company, or is partly owned by the same holding company as another.

Affiliated. Connected with or owned by another company.

Affinity card. A credit card where a percentage of each purchase made is given by the credit card company to a stated charity.

Affluent society. A type of society where most people are rich.

Afford. To be able to pay for or buy something.

After date. A bill of exchange payable at a date later than that on the bill.

Aftermarket. A market in new shares, which starts immediately after trading in the shares begins. (i.e. a secondary market)

After tax. After tax has been paid.

After tax profit. Profit after tax has been deducted.

Against. 1. Preposition. 2. Compared with.

Aged debtors analysis Or Ageing schedule. A list which analyses a company's debtors, showing the number of days their payments are outstanding.

Agency. 1. An office or job of representing another company in an area. 2. An office or business which arranges things for other companies.

Agency bank. A bank which does not accept deposits, but acts as an agent for another (usually foreign) bank.

Agency bill. A bill of exchange drawn on the local branch of a foreign bank.

Agency broker. A dealer who acts as the agent for an investor, buying and selling for a commission.

Agent. 1. A person who represents a company or another person in an area. 2. A person in charge of an agency.

Agent bank. A bank which uses the credit card system set up by another bank.

Agent's commission. Money, often a percentage of sales, paid to an agent.

Aggregate. Total, with everything added together.

Aggregate demand. Total demand for goods and services from all sectors of the economy, such as individuals, companies and the government.

Aggregate risk. The risk which a bank runs in lending to a customer.

Aggregate supply. All goods and services on the market.

AGI. Abbr. Adjusted gross Income Or Annual gross income.

Agio. 1. A charge made for changing money of one currency into another, or for changing banknotes into cash. 2. The difference between two values, such as between the interest charged on loans made by a bank and the interest paid by the bank on deposits, or the difference between the values of two currencies, or between a gold coin and paper currency of the same face value.

AGM. Abbr. Annual General Meeting.

Agree. 1. To decide and approve something together with another person or other people. 2. To come to a decision that is acceptable to everyone about something. 3. To say that you accept something that is suggested.

Agreed. Which has been accepted by everyone.

Agreed price. A price which has been accepted by both the buyer and seller.

Agreed takeover bid. A takeover bid which is accepted by the target company and recommended by its directors to its shareholders.

Agreement. A spoken or written contract between people or groups which explains how they will act.

Agreement among underwriters. A document which forms a syndicate of underwriters, linking them to the issuer of a new share issue.

Agree with. To say that your opinions are the same as someone else's.

AIM. Abbr. Alternative investment market.

Air carrier. A company which sends cargo or passengers by air.

Air forwarding. The process of arranging for goods to be shipped by air.

Air freight. The transportation of goods in aircraft, or goods sent by air.

Air freight charges Or Air freight rates. Money charged for sending goods by air.

Airmail. A postal service which sends letters or parcels by air.

Airmail envelope. A very light envelope for sending airmail letters.

Airmail sticker. A blue sticker with the words 'air mail', which can be stuck on an envelope or parcel to show that it is being sent by air.

Airmail transfer. An act of sending money from one bank to another by airmail.

Airport tax. A tax added to the price of an air ticket to cover the cost of running an airport.

All-in policy. An insurance policy which covers all risks.

All-in rate. 1. A price which covers all the costs connected with a purchase, such as delivery, tax and insurance, as well as the cost of the goods themselves. 2. A wage which includes all extra payments, such as bonuses and merit pay.

Allocate. 1. To provide a particular amount from a total sum of money for a particular purpose. 2. To divide something in various ways and share it out.

Allocation. The process of providing sums of money for particular purposes, or a sum provided for a purpose.

Allocation rate. The percentage of a payment that is actually invested in a fund after initial charges have been taken into account.

All Or none. A buying order which stipulates that the whole order has to be bought at a certain price and no parts of the order can be executed separately. Abbr. AON.

Allot. To allot shares to give a certain number of shares to people who have applied for them.

Allotment. 1. The process of sharing out something, especially money between various departments, projects or people. 2. The act of giving shares in a new company to people who have applied for them.

Allow. 1. To say that someone can do something. 2. To give. 3. To agree to or accept legally.

Allowable. Legally accepted.

Allowable expenses. Business expenses which can be claimed against tax.

Allowance. 1. Money which is given for a special reason. 2. Part of an income which is not taxed. 3. Money removed in the form of a discount.

Allowance for bad debt. Provision made in a company's accounts for debts which may never be paid.

Allow for. 1. To give a discount for something, or to add an extra sum to cover something. 2. To include something in your calculations.

All-risks policy. An insurance policy which covers risks of any kind, with no exclusions.

Alpha. 1. An anticipated performance of a share, compared to the market in general. 2. A rate of return on a unit trust or mutual fund, compared with typical returns for that category of trust.

Alternate account. A bank account where the several signatories can each sign cheques without asking another to validate their signature.

Alternative. Which can take the place of something.

Alternative order. An order to do one of two things (such as buy or sell stock at certain prices).

American Stock Exchange. The smaller of the two Stock Exchanges based in New York (the other is the New York Stock Exchange or NYSE). Abbr. Amex.

Amortisable. Which can be amortised.

Amortize. 1. To repay a loan by regular payments, most of which pay off the interest on the loan at first, and then reduce the principal as the repayment period progresses. 2. To depreciate or to write down the capital value of an asset over a period of time in a company's accounts.

Amount. A quantity of money.

Amount paid up. An amount paid for a new issue of shares, either the total payment or the first instalment, if the shares are offered with instalment payments.

Amount to. To make a total of.

Analogue computer. A computer which works on the basis of electrical impulses representing numbers.

Analyze. To examine someone or something in detail.

Analysis. A detailed examination and report.

Analyst. A person who analyses.

Angel network. A network of backers, organised through a central office which keeps a database of suitable investors and puts them in touch with entrepreneurs who need financial backing.

Annual. For one year.

Annual accounts. The accounts prepared at the end of a financial year.

Annual depreciation. A reduction in the book value of an asset at a particular rate per year.

Annual General Meeting. An annual meeting of all shareholders of a company, when the company's financial situation is presented by and discussed with the directors, when the accounts for the past year are approved and when dividends are declared and audited. Abbr. AGM.

Annual gross income. Total annual income before any deductions or exclusions. Abbr. AGI.

Annual income. Money received during a calendar year.

Annualised. Shown on an annual basis.

Annualised percentage rate. A yearly percentage rate, calculated by multiplying the monthly rate by twelve.

Annually. Each year.

Annual management charge. A charge made by the financial institution which is managing an account.

Annual management fee. An annual charge made for running a fund, usually calculated as a percentage of the amount invested.

Annual percentage yield. The annual rate of compound interest earned by an account. Abbr. APY.

Annual report. A report of a company's financial situation at the end of a year, sent to all the shareholders.

Annual rest system. A system by which extra payments or overpayments made to reduce the amount borrowed on a mortgage are credited to the account only once a year.

Annual return. An official report which a registered company has to make each year to the Registrar of Companies.

Annuitant. A person who receives an annuity.

Annuity. Money paid each year to a retired person, usually in return for a lump-sum payment. The value of the annuity depends on how long the person lives, as it usually cannot be passed on to another person. Annuities are fixed payments, and lose their value with inflation, whereas a pension can be index-linked.

Note: When a person retires, he or she is required by law to purchase a 'compulsory purchase annuity' with the funds accumulated in his or her pension fund. This provides a taxable income for the rest of his or her life, but usually it is a fixed income which does not change with inflation.

Annuity certain. An annuity that provides payments for a certain number of years, regardless of life or death of the annuitant.

Anticipate. To expect something to happen.

Anticipated balance. A balance which is forecast from a deposit when it matures.

Anti-dumping. Which protects a country against dumping.

Anti-inflationary. Which tries to restrict inflation.

Anti-trust. Attacking monopolies and encouraging competition.

Applicant. A person who applies for something.

Application. 1. The act of asking for something, usually in writing, or a document in which someone asks for something, e.g. a job. 2. Effort or diligence.

Application form. A form to be filled in when applying for a new issue of shares or for a job.

Apply. 1. To ask for something, usually in writing. 2. To affect or to relate to.

Appoint. To choose someone for a job.

Appointment. The act of being appointed to a job, or of appointing someone to a job.

Apportion. To share out something, e.g. costs, funds or blame.

Apportionment. The sharing out of costs.

Appraisal. A calculation of the value of someone or something.

Appraise. To assess or to calculate the value of something or someone.

Appraise. An employee who is being appraised by his or her manager in an appraisal interview.

Appreciate. 1. To notice how good something is. 2. (of currency, shares, etc.) to increase in value.

Appreciation. 1. An increase in value. Also called capital appreciation 2. The act of valuing something highly.

Appropriation. The act of putting money aside for a special purpose.

Appropriation account. The part of a profit and loss account which shows how the profit has been dealt with, e.g., how much has been given to the shareholders as dividends and how much is being put into the reserves.

Approval. 1. The act of saying or thinking that something is good. 2. On approval in order to be able to use something for a period of time and check that it is satisfactory before paying for it.

Approve. 1. To think something is good. 2. To agree to something officially.

Approved securities. State bonds which can be held by banks to form part of their reserves.

Approximate. Not exact, but almost correct.

Approximately. Not quite exactly, but close to the figure shown.

Approximation. A rough calculation.

APR. Abbr. Annual Percentage Rate.

APY. Abbr. Annual Percentage Yield.

Arbitrage. The business of making a profit from the difference in value of various assets, e.g. by: selling foreign currencies or commodities on one market and buying on another at almost the same time to profit from different exchange rates; buying currencies forward and selling them forward at a later date, to benefit from a difference in prices; buying a security and selling another security to the same buyer with the intention of forcing up the value of both securities.

Arbitrage fund. A fund which tries to take advantage of price discrepancies for the same asset in different markets.

Arbitrage syndicate. A group of people who together raise the capital to invest in arbitrage deals.

Arbitrager. A person whose business is arbitrage.

Note: Arbitrageurs buy shares in companies which are potential takeover targets, either to force up the price of the shares before the takeover bid, or simply as a position while waiting for the takeover bid to take place. They also sell shares in the company which is expected to make the takeover bid, since one of the consequences of a takeover bid is usually that the price of the target company rises while that of the bidding company falls. Arbitrageurs may then sell the shares in the target company at a profit, either to one of the parties making the take overbid, or back to the company itself.

Arbitration. The settling of a dispute by an outside party agreed on by both sides.

Area manager. A manager who is responsible for a company's work in a specific part of the country.

ARM. Abbr. Adjustable Rate Mortgage.

Arm's length transaction. A transaction which is carried out by two parties with no connection between them (resulting in a fair market value for the item sold).

Arrangement fee. A charge made by a bank to a client for arranging credit facilities.

Arrears. 1. Money which is owed, but which has not been paid at the right time. 2. Owing money which should have been paid earlier.

Arrive. To reach a place.

Arrive at. To work out and agree on something.

Article. 1. A product or thing for sale. 2. A section of a legal agreement such as a contract or treaty.

Articles of association. A document which lays down the rules for a company regarding such matters as the issue of shares, the conduct of meetings and the appointment of directors.

Articles of incorporation. A document which sets up a company and lays down the relationship between the shareholders and the company.

Note: The term is also called Memorandum of Association.

A shares. Ordinary shares with limited voting rights or no voting rights at all.

Note: A company may be set up with two classes of share: 'A' shares, which are available to the general investor, and 'B' shares which are only bought by certain individuals, such as the founder and his family. Such division of shares is becoming less usual nowadays.

Asian Currency Unit. A unit of account for dollar deposits held in Singapore and other Asian markets. Abbr. ACU.

Asian Development Bank. A bank set up by various Asian countries, with other outside members, to assist countries in the region with money and technical advice. Abbr. ADB.

Asked price. A price at which a commodity or stock is offered for sale by a seller (also called 'offer price' in the UK).

Asking price. A price which the seller is hoping will be paid for the item being sold.

Assay mark. A mark put on gold or silver items to show that the metal is of the correct quality.

Assess. To calculate the value of something or someone.

Assessment. A calculation of value.

Assessor. A person who advises a tribunal.

Asset. Something which belongs to a company or person, and which has a value.

Note: A company's balance sheet will show assets in various forms: current assets, fixed assets, intangible assets, etc.

Asset allocation. The work of deciding how much money should be spent on the purchase of different types of investment, such as growth units or income units, depending on the particular needs of the individual investor.

Asset-backed securities. Shares which are backed by the security of assets.

Asset backing. A support for a share price provided by the value of the company's assets.

Asset management account. An account with a stockbroker which also acts as a bank account, and has credit card facilities as well. Also called central assets account.

Asset play. A share which seems to be undervalued based on its asset value and so is an attractive buy.

Asset stripper. A person who buys a company to sell its assets.

Asset stripping. The practice of buying a company at a lower price than its asset value, and then selling its assets.

Asset value. The value of a company calculated by adding together all its assets.

Assign. 1. To give something to someone by means of an official legal transfer. 2. To give someone a job of work to do and make him or her responsible for doing it.

Assignation. A legal transfer.

Assignee. A person who receives something which has been assigned to him or her.

Assignment. 1. The legal transfer of a property or right. 2. A particular task given to someone.

Assignor. A person who assigns something to someone.

Assigns. People to whom property has been assigned.

Associate. 1. Linked. 2. A person who works in the same business as someone. 3. A person or company linked to another in a takeover bid.

Associate bank. A bank which is part of a group such as Visa or Master Card.

Associate company. A company which is partly owned by another company.

Associated company. A company which is partly owned by another company (though less than 50%), which exerts some management control over it or has a close trading relationship with it.

Associate director. A director who attends board meetings, but has not been elected by the shareholders.

Association. A group of people or companies with the same interest.

Assumption. 1. The act of taking for yourself. 2. The transfer of the rest of a mortgage to someone.

Assurance. A type of insurance which pays compensation for an event that is certain to happen at some time, especially for the death of the insured person. Also called life assurance, life insurance.

Assure. To insure someone, or someone's life, so that the insurance company will pay compensation when that person dies.

Assuror. An insurer or a company which insures.

At call. Immediately available.

ATM. Abbr. Automated Teller Machine.

ATM alliance. a group of banks whose cards can be used at the same ATMs.

ATS. Abbr. Automatic Transfer Service.

Attachment order. An order from a court to hold a debtor's property to prevent it being sold until debts are paid.

Attract. To make someone want to join or come to something.

Attractive prices. A prices which are cheap enough to make buyers want to buy.

Attractive salary. A good salary to make high-quality applicants apply for the job.

Attributable profit. A profit which can be shown to come from a particular area of the company's operations.

Auction. 1. A method of selling goods where people want to buy compete with each other by saying how much they will offer for it, and the item is sold to the person who makes the highest offer. 2. A method of selling government stock, where all stock on issue will be sold, and the highest price offered will be accepted (as opposed to tendering, where not all the stock may be sold if the tender prices are too low) to sell something at an auction.

Auction system. A system where prices are agreed as the result of market makers offering stock for sale on the trading floor (as opposed to a quote system, where prices are quoted on a computerised screen).

Audit. 1. The examination of the books and accounts of a company. 2. A detailed examination of something in order to assess it.

Auditing. The work of examining the books and accounts of a company.

Auditor. A person who audits.

Note: Auditors are appointed by the company's directors and voted for by the AGM.

Auditors' fees. Fees paid to a company's auditors, which are approved by the shareholders at an AGM.

Auditors' qualification. A form of words in a report from the auditors of a company's accounts, stating that in their opinion the accounts are not a true reflection of the company's financial position. Also called qualification of accounts.

Auditors' report. A report written by a company's auditors after they have examined the accounts of the company.

Note: If the auditors are satisfied, the report certifies that, in their opinion, the accounts give a 'true and fair' view of the company's financial position.

Audit trail. The records that show all the stages of a transaction, e.g. a purchase, a sale or a customer complaint, in the order in which they happened.

Note: An audit trail can be a useful tool for problem solving and, in financial markets, may be used to ensure that the dealers have been fair and accurate in their proceedings.

Authenticate. To say that something is true or genuine, especially to state that gold is of a correct quality.

Authentication. 1. An action of checking that something is true, such as an instruction sent to a bank by email. 2. A method of proving the identity of a person or company.

Note: Authentication is particularly important on the Internet where you do not actually see the person or premises of a company when making a purchase. If Company X wants to prove to Internet customers that they are really Company X and not a fraudster, they must ask an independent authenticator to issue them with a unique certificate of authentication.

A visitor to the Company X website can ask to see this certificate and will be shown the unique number supplied by the trustworthy independent authenticator. Authentication is normally only used on commercial web sites that are selling goods.

Authorization. Permission or power to do something.

Authorize. 1. To give permission for something to be done. 2. To give someone the authority to do something.

Authorised capital. An amount of capital which a company is allowed to have, as stated in the memorandum of association.

Authorised dealer. A person or company (such as a bank) that is allowed by the country's central bank to buy and sell foreign currency.

Authorised stock. Same as authorised capital.

Authorities. The government, the people in control.

Authority to purchase. A bill drawn up and presented with shipping documentation to the purchaser's bank, allowing the bank to purchase the bill.

Automated screen trading. A system where securities are bought, sold and matched automatically by computer. Abbr. AST.

Automated teller machine. A machine which gives out money when a special card is inserted and special instructions given. Abbr. ATM.

Automatic. Which works or takes place without any person making it happen.

Automatically. Without a person giving instructions.

Automatic data processing. Data processing done by a computer.

Automatic transfer service. A service by which money can be transferred automatically from a customer's savings account to cover an overdraft in a current account. Abbr. ATS.

Automatic vending machine. A machine which provides drinks, cigarettes etc., when a coin is put in.

Automation. The use of machines to do work with very little supervision by people.

Availability. The fact of being easy to obtain.

Availability float. 1. A time between the moments a cheque is deposited and the time the money will have cleared. 2. The amount of money in an account represented by deposits which have not yet cleared.

Available. Which can be obtained or bought.

Available capital. Capital which is ready to be used.

Available funds. Funds held by a bank which it can use for loans or other investments.

AVC. Abbr. Average variable cost.

Average. 1. A number calculated by adding several figures together and dividing by the number of figures added. 2. In general. 3. The sharing of the cost of damage or loss of a ship between the insurers and the owners.

Average adjustment. A calculation of the share of the cost of damage or loss of a ship that an insurer has to pay.

Average balance. The balance in an account calculated over a period.

Average daily balance. The balance in an account calculated by taking the final balances for each day, and averaging them.

Note: The average daily balance is used for the purpose of calculating interest or bank charges.

Average due date. The average date when several different payments fall due.

Average out. To come to a figure as an average.

Averaging. Buying or selling shares at different times and at different prices to establish an average price.

Avoidance. The act of trying not to do something or not to pay something.

Award. Something given by a court, tribunal or other official body, especially when settling a dispute or claim.

Away. Not here, somewhere else.

B

B2B. To advertising or marketing that is aimed at other businesses rather than at consumers.

Note: The word is most commonly used of business to business dealings conducted over the Internet.

B2C. To advertising or marketing that is aimed at consumers rather than at other businesses.

Note: The word is most commonly used of business to consumer dealings conducted over the Internet.

Back. 1. The opposite side to the front. 2. To help someone, especially financially. 3. To sign a bill promising to pay it if the person it is addressed to is not able to do so.

Back and filling. To a market where prices rise and fall slightly.

Backdate. 1. To put an earlier date on a document such as a cheque or an invoice. 2. To make something effective from an earlier date than the current date.

Back door. By buying a listed company on order to acquire a listing on a Stock Exchange (which is cheaper than applying for a new listing).

Back-end load. A management charge or commission which is levied when the investor sells out of the fund.

Back-end loaded. An insurance or investment scheme where commission is charged when the investor withdraws his or her money from the scheme.

Backer. 1. A person or company that backs someone. 2. The person who backs a bill.

Backhander. A bribe or money given to persuade someone to do something for you.

Backing. Especially financial support.

Back interest. Interest which has not yet been paid.

Backlog. An amount of work, or of items such as orders or letters, which should have been dealt with earlier but is still waiting to be done.

Back office. 1. The part of a broking firm where the paperwork involved in buying and selling shares is processed. 2. The part of a bank where cheques are processed, statements of account drawn up and other administrative tasks are done. 3. The general administration department of a company.

Back orders. Orders received and not yet fulfilled, usually because the item is out of stock.

Back out. To stop being part of a deal or an agreement.

Back pay. A salary which has not been paid.

Back payment. 1. A payment which is due but has not yet been paid. 2. The act of paying money which is owed.

Back rent. A rent due but not paid.

Back tax. Tax which is owed.

Back to back credit. 1. Credit facilities for the purchase of goods, where the credit is asked for by the purchaser, but is granted to a middleman, who buys the goods, then sells them on to the final purchaser, and uses the credit as a basis for obtaining further credit facilities. 2. Credit in a currency allowed to a foreign trader on the basis of credit which has been granted by a bank in the trader's own country.

Back to back loan. A loan from one company to another in one currency arranged against a loan from the second company to the first in another currency. Also called parallel loan.

Note: Back to back loans are used by international companies to get round exchange controls.

Back up. 1. To support or help. 2. To go into reverse. 3. To sell long-term bonds and replace them by short-term bonds.

Backup. Supporting or helping.

Backup copy. A copy of a computer disk to be kept in case the original disk is damaged.

Backup credit. Credit provided by banks for a euro currency note.

Backup line. Credit provided by banks against the security of commercial bills of exchange which are about to mature.

Back wages. Same as back pay.

Backward integration. A process of expansion in which a business which deals with the later stages in the production and sale of a product acquires a business that deals with an earlier stage in the same process, usually a supplier. Also called vertical integration.

Bad bargain. Item which is not worth the price asked.

Bad buy. A thing bought which was not worth the money paid for it.

Bad cheque. A cheque, which is returned to the drawer for any reason.

Bad debt. A debt which will not be paid, usually because the debtor has gone out of business, and which has to be written off in the accounts.

Bad debt provision. Money put aside in accounts to cover potential bad debts.

Bail out. 1. To rescue a company which is in financial difficulties. 2. To pay money to a court as a guarantee that someone will return to face charges.

Bail-out. A rescue of a company in financial difficulties.

Balance. 1. The amount which has to be put in one of the columns of an account to make the total debits and credits equal. 2. The rest of an amount owed.

a) Balance in hand. Cash held to pay small debts.

b) Balance brought down or forward. The closing balance of the previous period used as the opening balance of the current period.

c) Balance carried down or forward. The closing balance of the current period.

Balance due to us. The amount owed to us which is due to be paid.

1. To be equal (i.e. the assets owned must always equal the total liabilities plus capital). 2. To calculate the amount needed to make the two sides of an account equal. 3. To plan a budget so that expenditure and income are equal.

Balance certificate. A share certificate given to an investor who has sold part of his or her shareholding and shows the number of shares which he or she has retained.

Balanced budget. A budget where expenditure and income are equal.

Balance of payments. A comparison between total receipts and payments arising from a country's international trade in goods, services and financial transactions. Abbr. BOP.

Balance of payments deficit. A situation when a country imports more than it exports.

Balance of payments surplus. A situation where a country sells more to other countries than it buys from them.

Balance of trade. A record of the international trading position of a country in merchandise, excluding invisible trade. Also called trade balance.

Balance sheet. It a statement of the financial position of a company at a particular time, such as the end of the financial year or the end of a quarter, showing the company's assets and liabilities.

Note: The balance sheet shows the state of a company's finances at a certain date. The profit and loss account shows the movements which have taken place since the end of the previous accounting period. A balance sheet must balance, with the basic equation that assets (i.e. what the company owns, including money owed to the company) must equal liabilities (i.e. what the company owes to its creditors) plus capital (i.e. what it owes to its shareholders).

Balancing item and Balancing figure. An item introduced into a balance sheet to make the two sides balance.

Ballot. 1. An election where people vote for someone by marking a cross on a paper with a list of names. 2. A selection made by taking papers at random out of a box.

Ballot box. A sealed box into which ballot papers are put.

Ballot paper. A paper on which the voter marks a cross to show who they want to vote for.

Band. A range of figures with an upper and a lower limit, to which something, e.g. the amount of someone's salary or the exchange value of a currency, is restricted but within which it can move.

Bank. A business which holds money for its clients, lends money at interest, and trades generally in money.

Bankable. Which a bank will accept as security for a loan.

Bankable paper. A document which a bank will accept as security for a loan.

Bank account. An account which a customer has with a bank, where the customer can deposit and withdraw money.

Bank balance. The state of a bank account at any particular time.

Bank base rate. A basic rate of interest, on which the actual rate a bank charges on loans to its customers, is calculated.

Bank bill. A bill of exchange by one bank telling another bank (usually in another country) to pay money to someone.

Bank book. A book, given by a bank, which shows money which you deposit or withdraw from your savings account (also called a 'passbook').

Bank borrowing. Money borrowed from a bank.

Bank card. A credit card or debit card issued to a customer by a bank for use instead of cash when buying goods or services.

Note: There are internationally recognized rules that govern the authorization of the use of bank cards and the clearing and settlement of transactions in which they are used.

Bank charges. Charges which a bank makes for carrying out work for a customer.

Bank charter. An official government document allowing the establishment of a bank.

Bank cheque. A bank's own cheque, drawn on itself and signed by a bank official.

Bank clerk. A person who works in a bank, but is not a manager.

Bank credit. Loans or overdrafts from a bank to a customer.

Bank deposits. All money placed in banks by private or corporate customers.

Bank discount rate. A rate charged by a bank for a loan where the interest charges are deducted when the loan is made.

Bank draft. An order by one bank telling another bank, usually in another country, to pay money to someone.

Banker. A person who is in an important position in a bank.

Banker's acceptance. A bill of exchange guaranteed by a bank.

Banker's bill. An order by one bank telling another bank, usually in another country, to pay money to someone.

Banker's draft. A draft payable by a bank in cash on presentation.

Banker's lien. The right of a bank to hold some property of a customer as security against payment of a debt.

Banker's order. An order written by a customer asking a bank to make a regular payment.

Banker's reference. Details of a company's bank, account number, etc., supplied so that a client can check if the company is a risk.

Bank for International Settlements. A bank which acts as the clearing bank for the central banks of various countries through which they settle their currency transactions and which also acts on behalf of the IMF. Abbr. BIS.

Bank identification number. Internationally organized six-digit number which identifies a bank for charge card purposes. Abbr. BIN.

Banking account. An account, which a customer has with a bank.

Banking code. A voluntary code of practice adopted by banks and building societies in their dealings with their customers.

Banking hours. The hours when a bank is open for its customers.

Banking service. The various ways in which a bank can help a customer, such as operating accounts, making transfers, paying standing orders and selling foreign currency.

Bank line. Same as line of credit.

Bank loan. A loan made by a bank to a customer, usually against the security of a property or asset.

Bank manager. The person in charge of a branch of a bank.

Bank mandate. A written order to a bank, asking it to open an account and allow someone to sign cheque on behalf of the account holder, and giving specimen signatures and relevant information.

Bank of England. The British central bank, owned by the state, which, together with the Treasury, regulates the nation's finances.

Note: The Bank of England issues banknotes which carry the signatures of its officials. It is the lender of last resort to commercial banks and supervises banking institutions in the UK Its Monetary Policy Committee is independent of the government and sets interest rates. The Governor of the Bank of England is appointed by the government.

Bank of Japan. The central bank of Japan. Abbr. BOJ.

Bank on. To feel sure that something will happen.

Bank rate. 1. Discount rate of a central bank. 2. Formerly, the rate at which the Bank of India lent to other banks (then also called the Minimum Lending Rate (MLR), and now called the base rate)

Bank reconciliation. The act of making sure that the bank statements agree with the company's ledgers.

Bank reserves. Cash and securities held by a bank to cover deposits.

Bank return. A regular report from a bank on its financial position.

Bankroll. To provide the money that enables something or someone to survive.

Bankrupt. A person who has been declared by a court not to be capable of paying his or her debts and whose affairs are put into the hands of a receiver.

Bank statement. A written statement from a bank showing the balance of an account at a specific date.

Bank syndicate. A group of major international banks which group together to underwrite a massive loan.

Bank transfer. An act of moving money from a bank account to another account.

Bar chart. A chart where values or quantities are shown as columns of different heights set on a base line, the different lengths expressing the quantity of the item or unit. Also called bar graph, histogram.

Bar code. A system of lines printed on a product which, when read by a computer, give a reference number or price.

Bargain. 1. An agreement on the price of something. 2. Something which is cheaper than usual 3. A sale and purchase of one lot of shares on the Stock Exchange to try to reach agreement about something, especially a price, usually with each person or group involved putting forward suggestions or offers which are discussed until a compromise is arrived at.

Bargain hunter. A person who looks for cheap deals.

Bargain hunting. Looking for cheap goods or shares, which no one has noticed.

Bargaining. The act of trying to reach agreement about something, e.g. a price or a wage increase for workers.

Bargaining position. The offers or demands made by one group during negotiations.

Bargaining power. The strength of one person or group when discussing prices or wage settlements.

Bargain offer. The sale of a particular type of goods at a cheap price.

Bargain sale. The sale of all goods in a store at cheap prices.

Bargains done. The number of deals made on the Stock Exchange during a day.

Barrels per day. A figure used to show the output of an oilfield.

Barren. To money which is not earning any interest.

Barrier. Anything which makes it difficult for someone to do something, especially to send goods from one place to another.

Barrier to entry. A factor that makes it impossible or unprofitable for a company to try to start selling its products in a particular market.

Note: Barriers to entry may be created, for example, when companies already in a market have patents that prevent their goods from being copied, when the cost of the advertising needed to gain a market share is too high, or when an existing product commands very strong brand loyalty.

Barter. 1. A system in which goods are exchanged for other goods and not sold for money. 2. A system in which advertising space or time is exchanged for goods from the advertiser to exchange goods for other goods and not for money.

Barter agreement. An agreement to exchange goods by barter.

Bartering. The act of exchanging goods for other goods and not for money.

Base. 1. The lowest or first position. 2. A place where a company has its main office or factory, or a place where a businessperson's office is located.

Based on. 1. Calculating from. 2. To set up a company or a person in a place.

Base currency. A currency against which exchange rates of other currencies are quoted.

Base rate. Same as bank base rate.

Base-weighted index. An index which is weighted according to the base year.

Base year. The first year of an index, against which changes occurring in later years are measured.

Basic. 1. Normal. 2. Most important. 3. Simple, or from which everything starts.

Basic balance. The balance of current account and long-term capital accounts in a country's balance of payments.

Basic banking service. Basic service offered by banks to their customers, in connection with operating their accounts.

Basic commodities. Ordinary farm produce, produced in large quantities, e.g. corn, rice or sugar.

Basic discount. A normal discount without extra percentages.

Basic industry. The most important industry of a country, e.g. coal, steel or agriculture.

Basic pay. A normal salary without extra payments.

Basic product. The main product made from a raw material.

Basic rate tax. The lowest rate of income tax.

Basics. Simple and important facts or principles.

Basic salary and Basic wage. Same as basic pay.

Basis. 1. A point or number from which calculations are made. 2. The general terms of agreement or general principles on which something is decided or done.

Basis point. One hundredth of a percentage point (0.01%), the basic unit used in measuring market movements or interest rates.

Basis price. 1. The price agreed between buyer and seller on the over-the- counter market. 2. The price of a bond shown as its annual percentage yield to maturity.

Basis swap. The exchange of two financial instruments, each with a variable interest calculated on a different rate.

Batch. 1. A group of items which are made at one time. 2. A group of documents which are processed at the same time.

Batch number. A number attached to a batch.

Batch processing. A system of data processing where information is collected into batches before being loaded into the computer.

Batch production. Production in batches.

Bear. In stock exchange a person who sells shares, commodities or currency because he or she thinks their price will fall and it will be possible to buy them again more cheaply later.

Note: The opposite is bull.

Bear covering. In stock exchange a point in a market where dealers who sold stock short, now buy back (at lower prices) to cover their positions.

Bearer. A person who holds a cheque or certificate.

Bearer bond or bearer security. A bond which is payable to the bearer and does not have a name written on it.

Bearing. Which bears, which produces.

Bearish. To a factor which tends to make market prices fall.

Bear market. A period when share prices fall because shareholders are selling since they believe the market will fall further.

Note: The opposite is a bull market.

Bear position. In stock exchange a short position, that is, selling shares which you do not own (you will buy them later at a lower price so as to be able to settle).

Bear raid. Selling large numbers of shares to try to bring down prices.

Bear squeeze. 1. An action by banks to raise exchange rates, forcing currency bear sellers to buy back currency at a loss (i.e. at a higher price). 2. An operation by market makers to increase the price of shares, so as to force bears to buy at higher prices than they intended.

Bed and breakfast deal. Formerly, an arrangement where shares were sold one day and bought back the following day, in order to establish a profit or loss for tax declaration.

Note: This is no longer possible, since a period of thirty days has to elapse between the sale and repurchase of the same shares to allow a new price to be established.

Bed-pepping. An arrangement by which you sell existing investments and put the resulting cash into PEP. This establishes any gains on the investments, so that you can calculate whether you should pay capital gains tax.

Behavioural finance. A psychological view of the way people take financial decisions.

Below par. To a share with a market price lower than its par value.

Below the line. Part of a budget referring to receipts from redeemed debts and from expenditure covered by borrowings.

Below-the-line expenditure. 1. Payments which do not arise from a company's normal activities, e.g. redundancy payments. 2. Extraordinary items which are shown in the profit and loss account below net profit after taxation, as opposed to exceptional items which are included in the figure for profit before taxation.

Benchmark. A point in an index which is important, and can be used to compare with other figures.

Beneficial interest. A situation where someone is allowed to occupy or receive rent from a house without owning it.

Beneficial occupier. A person who occupies a property but does not own it fully.

Beneficial owner. A person who owns a property which is being used by someone else.

Beneficiary. A person who gains money from something.

Benefit. 1. Payments which are made to someone under a national or private insurance scheme. 2. Something of value given to an employee in addition to their salary.

Benefit in kind. A benefit other than money received by an employee as part of his or her total compensation package, e.g. a company car or private health insurance. Such benefits are usually subject to tax.

Bequest. Something, e.g. property or money (but not freehold land), given to someone in a will.

Best practice. The most effective and efficient way to do something or to achieve a particular aim.

Note: In business, best practice is often determined by benchmarking, that is by comparing the method one organization uses to carry out a task with the methods used by other similar organizations and determining which method is most efficient and effective.

Best-selling. Which sells better than any other.

Bet. An amount deposited when you risk money on the result of a race or of a game to risk money on the result of something.

Beta. A measurement of the return on investment in a certain stock compared against a one percentage point return on the stock market.

Bid. 1. An offer to buy something at a specific price. 2. An offer to sell something or do a piece of work at a specific price.

Bid basis. The pricing of unit trusts at a lower bid price to encourage buyers.

Bidder. A person who makes a bid, usually at an auction.

Bidding. The act of making offers to buy, usually at an auction.

Bid market. A market where there are more bids to buy than offers to sell.

Note: The opposite is an offered market.

Bid-offer price. A price charged by unit trusts to buyers and sellers of units, based on the bid-offer spread.

Bid-offer spread. The difference between buying and selling prices (i.e. between the bid and offer prices).

Bid price. A price at which investors sell shares or units in a unit trust.

Note: The opposite, i.e. the buying price, is called the offer price; the difference between the two is the spread.

Bid rate. A rate of interest offered on deposits.

Big Bang. 1. The change in practices on the London Stock Exchange, with the introduction of electronic trading on October 27th 1986. 2. A similar change in financial practices in another country.

Note: The changes included the abolition of stock jobbers and the removal of the system of fixed commissions. The Stock Exchange trading floor closed and deals are now done by phone or computer or on the Internet.

Bilateral. Between two parties or countries.

Bilateral clearing. The system of annual settlements of accounts between certain countries, where accounts are settled by the central banks.

Bilateral credit. Credit allowed by banks to other banks in a clearing system (to cover the period while cheque is being cleared).

Bilateral netting. The settlement of contracts between two banks to give a new position.

Bill. 1. A written list of charges to be paid. 2. A list of charges in a restaurant. 3. A written paper promising to pay money. 4. A draft of a new law which will be discussed in Parliament. 5. A small poster.

Bills payable (BP). Especially bills of exchange, which a company will have to pay to its creditors.

Bills receivable (BR). Especially bills of exchange, which are due to be paid by a company's debtors.

Bill broker. A discount house, a firm which buys and sells bills of exchange for a fee.

Billing. The work of writing invoices or bills.

Billing error. A mistake in charging a sum to a credit card.

Bill of exchange. A document, signed by the person authorizing it, which tells another person or a financial institution to pay money unconditionally to a named person on a certain date.

Note: Bills of exchange are usually used for payments in foreign currency. To accept a bill to sign a bill of exchange to show that you promise to pay it. To discount a bill to buy or sell a bill of exchange at a lower price than that written on it in order to cash it later.

Comment: A bill of exchange is a document raised by a seller and signed by a purchaser, stating that the purchaser accepts that he owes the seller money, and promises to pay it at a later date. The person raising the bill is the 'drawer'; the person who accepts it is the 'drawee'. The seller can then sell the bill at a discount to raise cash. This is called a 'trade bill'. A bill can also be accepted (i.e. guaranteed) by a bank and in this case it is called a 'bank bill'.

Bill of lading. A list of goods being shipped, which the transporter gives to the person sending the goods to show that the goods have been loaded.

Bill of sale. A document which the seller gives to the buyer to show that the sale has taken place.

BIN. Abbr. Bank Identification Number.

Bind. 1. To tie or to attach. 2. To make it a legal duty for someone or something to act in a particular way.

Binder. 1. A stiff cardboard cover for papers. 2. A temporary agreement for insurance sent before the insurance policy is issued.

Binding. Which legally forces someone to do something.

BIS. Abbr. Bank for International Settlements.

Black economy. Goods and services which are paid for in cash, and therefore not declared for tax. Also called hidden economy, parallel economy and shadow economy.

Blackleg. An employee who continues working when there is a strike.

Black list. 1. A list of goods, people or companies which have been blacked. 2. A list of people considered by an employer to be too dangerous or disruptive to employ.

Blacklist. To put goods, people or a company on a black list.

Black market. The buying and selling of goods or currency in a way which is not allowed by law.

Black market prices. To pay high prices to get items which are not easily available.

Blank. With nothing written on it a space on a form which has to be completed.

Blank cheque. A cheque with the amount of money and the payee left blank, but signed by the drawer.

Blank endorsement. An endorsement which consists of a signature, and no other details.

Blanket agreement. An agreement which covers many different items.

Blind trust. A trust set up to run a person's affairs without the details of any transaction being known to the person concerned.

Blip. Bad economic figures (a higher inflation rate, lower exports, etc.), which only have a short-term effect.

Block. 1. A series of items grouped together. 2. A series of buildings forming a square with streets on all sides.

Block booking. Booking of several seats or rooms at the same time.

Blocked account. A bank account which cannot be used, usually because a government has forbidden its use.

Blocked currency. A currency which cannot be taken out of a country because of government exchange controls.

Block trading. Trading in very large numbers of shares.

Blue chip. A very safe investment, a risk-free share in a good company.

Blue-chip investments Or blue-chip shares. Low-risk shares in good companies.

Blue-collar union. A trade union formed mainly of blue-collar workers.

Blue-collar worker. A manual worker in a factory.

Bluetooth. Trademark a type of technology allowing for communication between mobile phones, computers and the Internet.

Board. 1. Board of directors. 2. A group of people who run an organisation, trust or society. 3. On a ship, plane or train. 4. A screen on which share prices are posted (on the wall of the trading floor in a Stock Exchange).

Board meeting. A meeting of the directors of a company.

Board of directors. 1. A group of directors elected by the shareholders to run a company. 2. A group of people elected by the shareholders to draw up company policy and to appoint the president and other executive officers who are responsible for managing the company.

Board order. An order to a stockbroker to buy or sell at a particular price.

Boardroom. A room where the directors of a company meet.

Boardroom battle. An argument between directors.

Boiler room. A room in which telephone sales executives try to sell securities to potential investors.

Bombay Stock Exchange. The main stock exchange in India. Abbr. BSE.

Bona fide. Trustworthy, which can be trusted.

Bonanza. Great wealth, or a source of great wealth.

Bond. 1. A contract document promising to repay money borrowed by a company or by the government at a certain date, and paying interest at regular intervals. 2. Goods (held) in bond goods held by customs until duty has been paid. 3. A form of insurance fund which is linked to a unit trust, but where there is no yield because the income is automatically added to the fund.

Note: Bonds are in effect another form of long-term borrowing by a company or government. They can carry a fixed interest or a floating interest, but the yield varies according to the price at which they are bought; bond prices go up and down in the same way as share prices.

Bonded warehouse. A warehouse where goods are stored until excise duty has been paid.

Bond market. A market in which government or municipal bonds are traded.

Bond rating. A rating of the reliability of a company or government or local authority which has issued a bond.

Bond yield. Income produced by a bond, shown as a percentage of its purchase price.

Bonus. An extra payment in addition to a normal payment.

Bonus issue. A scrip issue or capitalisation issue, where a company transfers money from reserves to share capital and issues free extra shares to the shareholders (the value of the company remains the same, and the total market value of shareholders' shares remains the same, the market price being adjusted to account for the new shares). Also called share split or stock dividend or stock split.

Bonus share. An extra share given to an existing shareholder.

Book. 1. A company's books the financial records of a company 2. To have a list of shares which he or she is prepared to buy or sell on behalf of clients.

Note: The books of account record a company's financial transactions. These are: sales (sales day book and sales returns book); purchases (purchases day book and purchases returns book); cash payments and receipts (cash book) and adjustments (journal). These books are commonly known as the 'books of prime entry', but in addition, a company's accounting records usually include the ledger accounts (nominal ledger, sales ledger and purchases ledger) which may also be referred to as 'books of account'.

Book debts. Trade debts as recorded in a company's accounts.

Bookkeeper. A person who keeps the financial records of a company or an organisation.

Bookkeeping. The work of keeping the financial records of a company or an organisation.

Bookkeeping transaction. A transaction (such as the issue of bonus shares) which involves changes to a company's books of accounts, but does not alter the value of the company in any way.

Book sales. Sales as recorded in the sales book.

Book-squaring. The process of reducing the dealer's exposure to the market to nil.

Book value. The value of an asset as recorded in the company's balance sheet.

Bookwork. The keeping of financial records.

Boom. 1. A time when sales, production or business activity are increasing. 2. A time when anything is increasing.

Boom industry. An industry which is expanding rapidly.

Booming. Which is expanding or becoming prosperous.

Boom share. A share in a company which is expanding.

Boost. Help given to increase something.

BOP. Abbr. Balance of Payments.

Borderline case. A worker who may or may not be recommended for a particular type of treatment, such as for promotion or dismissal.

Border tax adjustment. A deduction of indirect tax paid on goods being exported or imposition of local indirect tax on goods being imported.

Borrow. 1. To take money from someone for a time, possibly paying interest for it, and repaying it at the end of the period. 2. To buy at spot prices and sell forward at the same time.

Borrowing. The action of borrowing money.

Borrowing costs. The interest and other charges paid on money borrowed.

Borrowing power. The amount of money which a company can borrow.

Borrowings. Money borrowed.

Borrow short. To borrow for a short period.

Bottom. The lowest part or point.

Bottom feeder. A someone who tries to buy shares when they are falling or have fallen substantially, in the hope that they will rise again (informal.).

Bottom fishing. The act of buying shares when they are falling or have fallen substantially, in the hope that they will rise again (informal).

Bottom line. 1. The last line on a balance sheet indicating profit or loss. 2. The final decision on a matter.

Bought deal. A method of selling shares in a new company or selling an issue of new shares in an existing company, where securities houses guarantee to buy all the shares on offer at a fixed price.

Bought ledger. A book in which purchases are recorded.

Bought ledger clerk. An office worker who deals with the bought ledger or the sales ledger.

Bounce. To be returned by the bank to the person who has tried to cash it, because there is not enough money in the payer's account to pay it.

Boutique. 1. A section of a department store selling up-to-date clothes. 2. A small financial institution offering specialist advice or services.

Box number. A reference number used when asking for mail to be sent to a post office or when asking for replies to an advertisement to be sent to the newspaper's offices.

Boycott. A refusal to buy or to deal in certain products.

Bracket. A group of items or people taken together.

Bracket together. To treat several items together in the same way.

Branch. The local office of a bank or large business, or a local shop which is part of a large chain.

Branch manager. A person in charge of a branch of a company.

Branch office. A less important office, usually in a different town or country from the main office.

Brand loyalty. The feeling of trust and satisfaction that makes a customer always buy the same brand of product.

Brand name. A name of a particular make of product.

Breach. A failure to carry out the terms of an agreement.

Breach of contract. The failure to do something which has been agreed in a contract.

Breach of trust. A situation where a person does not act correctly or honestly when people expect him or her to.

Breach of warranty. 1. The act of supplying goods which do not meet the standards of the warranty applied to them. 2. A failure to do something which is a part of a contract.

Break. 1. A sharp fall in share prices. 2. A lucky deal or good opportunity. 3. To fail to carry out the duties of a contract. 4. To cancel a contract.

Break down. 1. To stop working because of mechanical failure. 2. To stop. 3. To show all the items in a total list of costs or expenditure.

Breakdown. 1. An act of stopping working because of mechanical failure. 2. An act of stopping talking. 3. An act of showing details item by item.

Breakeven point. A point at which sales cover costs, but do not show a profit.

Break-out. A movement of a share price above or below its previous trading level.

Breakpoint. A level of deposits in an account that triggers a new higher level of interest.

Break up. To split something large into small sections.

Break-up value. 1. The value of the material of a fixed asset. 2. The value of various parts of a company taken separately.

Bribe. Money given secretly and usually illegally to someone in authority to get them to help.

Bricks-and-mortar. 1. Conducting business in the traditional way in buildings such as shops and warehouses and not being involved in e-commerce. 2. Referring to the fixed assets of a company, especially its buildings.

Bridge finance: Loans to cover short-term needs.

Bring. To come to a place with someone or something.

Bring down. To reduce.

Bring forward. 1. To make something take place earlier. 2. To take an account balance from the end of the previous period as the starting point for the current period.

Bring in. To earn an amount of interest.

Brisk. Characterised by a lot of activity.

Broker. 1. A dealer who acts as a middleman between a buyer and a seller. 2. (Stock) broker a person or firm that buys and sells shares or bonds on behalf of clients.

Brokerage. 1. Payment to a broker for a deal carried out. 2. Same as broking.

Brokerage firm Or Brokerage house. A firm which buys and sells shares for clients.

Brokerage rebates. The percentage of the commission paid to a broker which is returned to the customer as an incentive to do more business.

Broker-dealer. A dealer who makes a market in shares (i.e. buys shares and holds them for resale) and also deals on behalf of investor clients.

Broker's commission. The payment to a broker for a deal which he or she has carried out.

Broking. The business of dealing in stocks and shares.

BSE Index. An index of prices on the Indian Stock Exchange. Full form Bombay Stock Exchange Index.

Budget. 1. A plan of expected spending and income for a period of time. 2. The annual plan of taxes and government spending proposed by a finance minister.

Budget account. A bank account where you plan income and expenditure to allow for periods when expenditure is high, by paying a set amount each month.

Budgetary. Referring to a budget.

Budgetary control. Controlled spending according to a planned budget.

Budgetary policy. The policy of planning income and expenditure.

Budgetary requirements. The rate of spending or income required to meet the budget forecasts.

Budget deficit. 1. A deficit in a country's planned budget, where income from taxation will not be sufficient to pay for the government's expenditure. 2. A deficit in personal finances where a household will borrow to finance large purchases which cannot be made out of income alone.

Budget department. A department in a large store which sells cheaper goods.

Budgeting. The preparation of budgets to help plan expenditure and income.

Budget surplus. A situation where there is more revenue than was planned for in the budget.

Budget variance. The difference between the cost as estimated for a budget and the actual cost.

Buffer stocks. Stocks of a commodity bought by an international body when prices are low and held for resale at a time when prices have risen, with the intention of reducing sharp fluctuations in world prices of the commodity.

Building society. A financial institution which accepts and pays interest on deposits, and lends money to people who are buying property against the security of the property which is being bought.

Build into. To include something in something which is being set up.

Build up. 1. To create something by adding pieces together. 2. To expand something gradually.

Bulk buying. The act of buying large quantities of goods at low prices.

Bulk carrier. A ship which carries large quantities of loose goods such as corn or coal.

Bulk purchase. An act of buying a large quantity of goods at low prices.

Bull. In stock exchange a person who believes the market will rise, and therefore buys shares, commodities or currency to sell at a higher price later.

Bullet. A repayment of the capital of a loan when it matures.

Bullish. Optimistic, feeling that prices of shares will rise.

Bull market. A period when share prices rise because people are optimistic and buy shares.

Bull position. In stock exchange a strategy of buying shares in the hope that they will rise.

Bundle. To make a lot of money (informal).

Bundling. The action of selling various financial services together as a package, such as a mortgage and house insurance.

Buoyant. Referring to a market where share prices are rising continuously.

Bureau de change. An office where you can change foreign currency.

Business. 1. Work in buying, selling or doing other things to make a profit. 2. A commercial company. 3. Affairs discussed.

Business address. The details of number, street and town where a company is located.

Business call. A visit to talk to someone about business.

Business card. A card showing a businessperson's name and the name and address of the company he or she works for.

Business centre. The part of a town where the main banks, shops and offices are located.

Business correspondence. Letters concerned with a business.

Business correspondent. A journalist who writes articles on business news for newspapers.

Business cycle. The period during which trade expands, slows down and then expands again. Also called trade cycle.

Business day. A day (a normal weekday) when banks and stock exchanges are open for business.

Business expenses. Money spent on running a business, not on stock or assets.

Business hours. The time when a business is open, usually 9.00 a.m. to 5.30 p.m.

Business magazine. A magazine dealing with business affairs.

Business plan. A document drawn up to show how a business is planned to work, with cash flow forecasts, sales forecasts, etc., often used when trying to raise a loan, or when setting up a new business.

Business-to-business. Full form of B2B.

Business-to-consumer. Full form of B2C.

Business transaction. An act of buying or selling.

Buy. To get something by paying money.

Buy back. 1. To buy something which you sold earlier. 2. To buy its own shares.

Buyback. 1. A type of loan agreement to repurchase bonds or securities at a later date for the same price as they are being sold. 2. An international trading agreement where a company builds a factory in a foreign country and agrees to buy all its production. 3. The continuation of a life assurance cover after a claim has been paid on critical illness under a policy that provides cover against both critical illness and death.

Buyer. 1. A person who buys. 2. A person who buys stock on behalf of a trading organisation for resale or for use in production.

Buyer's market. A market where products are sold cheaply because there are few people who want to buy them.

Buy forward. To buy foreign currency before you need it, in order to be sure of the exchange rate.

Buy in. 1. (of a seller at an auction) to buy the thing which you are trying to sell because no one will pay the price you want. 2. To buy stock to cover a position. 3. (of a company) to buy its own shares.

Buying. The act of getting something for money.

Buying department. The department in a company which buys raw materials or goods for use in the company.

Buying power. The ability to buy.

Buyout. The purchase of a controlling interest in a company.

Buy to let. A situation where a property is bought as an investment to rent out rather than live in.

By-product. A product made as a result of manufacturing a main product.

C

CA. Abbr. Chartered Accountant.

Cable. 1. A telegram, a message sent by telegraph. 2. A spot exchange rate for the dollar and sterling to send a message or money by telegraph.

CAD. Abbr. Cash Against Documents.

Cage. The part of a broking firm where the paperwork involved in buying and selling shares is processed.

Calculate. 1. To find the answer to a problem using numbers. 2. To estimate.

Calculation. The answer to a problem in mathematics.

Calculator. An electronic machine which does calculations such as adding, subtracting and multiplying.

Calendar. 1. A book or set of sheets of paper showing the days and months in a year, often attached to pictures. 2. A list of dates, especially a list of dates of new share issues.

Calendar month. A whole month as on a calendar, from the 1st to the 30th or 31st.

Calendar year. A year from the 1st January to 31st December.

Call. 1. A conversation on the telephone. 2. A demand for repayment of a loan by a lender. 3. A demand to pay for new shares which then become paid up. 4. A price established during a trading session 5. A visit.

Callable bond. A bond which can be redeemed before it matures.

Callable capital. The part of a company's capital which has not been called up.

Call-back pay. Pay given to an employee who has been called back to work after their normal working hours.

Called up capital. A share capital in a company which has been called up but not yet paid for.

Call in. To ask for a debt to be paid.

Call loan. A bank loan repayable at call.

Call money. Money loaned for which repayment can be demanded without notice. Also called money at call, money on call.

Call option. An option to buy shares at a future date and at a specific price.

Call-over price. A price which is applied when selling is conducted by a chairman, and not by open outcry.

Call price (In Stock Exchange). A price to be paid on redemption of a bond.

Call purchase or Call sale. A transaction where the seller or purchaser can fix the price for future delivery.

Call rate. 1. The number of calls per day or per week which a salesperson makes on customers. 2. A rate of interest on money at call.

Call rule. A price fixed on a Stock Exchange at the end of a day's trading and which remains valid until trading starts again the next day.

Call up. To ask for share capital to be paid.

Calm. Quiet, not excited.

Cancel. 1. To stop something which has been agreed or planned. 2. To stop payment of a cheque which has been signed.

Cancellation. The act of stopping something which has been agreed or planned.

Cancellation clause. A clause in a contract which states the terms on which the contract may be cancelled.

Cancel out. (of two things) To balance each other or act against each other so that there is no change in the existing situation.

Candlestick chart. A chart similar to a bar chart, but showing the opening and close as well as the high and low figures for a particular period. These are shown as lines standing up on top of the body of the chart or hanging down beneath it, so that they look a little like the wick on a candle.

Cap. 1. An upper limit placed on something, such as an interest rate (the opposite, i.e. a lower limit, is a 'floor'). 2. Same as capitalization.

Capacity. 1. The amount which can be produced, or the amount of work which can be done. 2. The amount of space. 3. Ability. 4. (of a borrower.) the ability to pay back a loan. 5. Speaking officially.

Capacity utilization. The fact of using something as much as possible.

Cap and collar. An agreement giving both an upper and a lower limit to a loan.

Capital. 1. The money, property and assets used in a business. 2. Money owned by individuals or companies, which they use for investment.

Capital account. 1. An account of dealings such as money invested in or taken out of the company by the owners of a company. 2. Items in a country's balance of payments which do not refer to the buying and selling merchandise, but refer to investments. 3. The total equity in a business.

Capital adequacy or Capital adequacy ratio. The amount of money which a bank has to have in the form of shareholders' capital, shown as a percentage of its assets. Also called capital-to-asset ratio.

Note: The amount is internationally agreed at 8%.

Capital allowances. The allowances based on the value of fixed assets which may be deducted from a company's profits and so reduce its tax liability.

Note: Under current Indian law, depreciation is not allowable for tax on profits, whereas capital allowances, based on the value of fixed assets owned by the company, are tax-allowable.

Capital asset pricing model. Method of calculating the expected return on a share, by showing what percentage of future return is dependent on the movements of the stock market taken as a whole. Abbr. CAPM.

Capital assets. The property, machines and other assets, which a company owns and uses but which it does not buy and sell as part of its regular trade. Also called fixed assets.

Capital base. The capital structure of a company (shareholders' capital plus certain loans and retained profits) used as a way of assessing the company's worth.

Capital bonus. An extra payment by an insurance company which is produced by a capital gain.

Capital commitments. Expenditure on assets which has been authorized by directors, but not yet spent at the end of a financial period.

Capital employed. An amount of capital consisting of shareholders' funds plus the long-term debts of a business.

Capital equipment. Which a factory or office uses to work.

Capital expenditure. Money spent on fixed assets (property, machines and furniture). Also called capital investment, capital outlay.

Capital exports. The movement of capital out of a country (into overseas investments, or into loans to overseas countries).

Capital flow. The movement of investment capital from one country to another. Also called capital movement.

Capital gains. Money made by selling a fixed asset or by selling shares.

Note: If the asset is sold for less than its purchase price, the result is a capital loss. In India capital gains tax is payable on the sale of assets, in particular shares and properties, above a certain minimum level.

Capital gains tax. A tax paid on capital gains. Abbr. CGT.

Capital goods. Machinery, buildings and raw materials which are used to make other goods.

Capital-intensive industry. An industry which needs a large amount of capital investment in plant to make it work.

Capitalization. The value of a company calculated by multiplying the price of its shares on the stock exchange by the number of shares issued. Also called market capitalization.

Capitalization issue. Same as bonus issue.

Capitalization of reserves. The issuing free bonus shares to shareholders.

Capitalize. 1. To invest money in a working company. 2. To convert reserves or assets into capital.

Capitalize on. To make a profit from.

Capitalism. The economic system in which each person has the right to invest money, to work in business and to buy and sell, with no restrictions from the state.

Capitalist. Working according to the principles of capitalism.

Capitalist economy. An economy in which each person has the right to invest money, to work in business and to buy and sell, with no restrictions from the state.

Capital levy. A tax on the value of a person's property and possessions.

Capital loss. A loss made by selling assets.

Capital market. An international market where money can be raised for investment in a business.

Capital movement. Same as capital flow.

Capital outlay. Same as capital expenditure.

Capital profit. A profit made by selling an asset.

Capital-protected fund. A fund which guarantees the investor's capital and at the same time gives some growth.

Capital ratio. Same as capital adequacy ratio.

Capital requirements. 1. The amount of capital which a firm needs to operate normally. 2. The amount of liquid assets needed by a bank to fulfill its obligations.

Capital reserves. 1. Money from profits, which forms part of the capital of a company and can be used for distribution to shareholders only when a company is wound up. Also called un distributable reserves. 2. The share capital of a company which comes from selling assets and not from normal trading.

Capital shares. (on the Stock Exchange) shares in a unit trust which rise in value as the capital value of the units rises, but do not receive any income.

Note: The other form of shares in a split-level investment trust are income shares, which receive income from the investments, but do not rise in value.

Capital structure. The way in which a company's capital is made up from various sources.

Capital transfer tax. Formerly, a tax on gifts or bequests of money or property.

CAPM. Abbr. Capital Asset Pricing Model.

Capped floating rate note. A floating rate note which has an agreed maximum rate.

Capped rate. A mortgage rate which is guaranteed not to go above a certain level for a set period of time, although it can move downwards.

Captive market. A market where one supplier has a monopoly and the buyer has no choice over the product which he or she must purchase.

Capture. To take or get control of something.

Carat. 1. A measure of the quality of gold (pure gold being 24 carat). 2. A measure of the weight of precious stones.

Note: Pure gold is 24 carats and is too soft to make jewellery. Most jewellery and other items made from gold are not pure, but between 19 and 22 carats. 22 carat gold has 22 parts of gold to two parts of alloy.

Card. A small piece of cardboard or plastic, usually with information printed on it.

Cardholder. A person who holds a credit card or bank cash card.

Card index. A series of cards with information written on them, kept in special order so that the information can be found easily.

Carriage. The transporting of goods from one place to another.

Carriage forward. A deal where the customer pays for transporting the goods.

Carriage free. The customer does not pay for the shipping.

Carriage paid. A deal where the seller has paid for the shipping.

Carrier. 1. A company which transports goods. 2. A vehicle or ship which transports goods.

Carry. 1. To take from one place to another. 2. To vote to approve. 3. To produce.

Carry forward. To take an account balance at the end of the current period or page as the starting point for the next period or page.

Carry over a balance. To take a balance from the end of one page or period to the beginning of the next.

Carry-over. 1. The stock of a commodity held at the beginning of a new financial year. 2. The fact of not paying an account on settlement day, but later.

Cartel. A group of companies which try to fix the price or to regulate the supply of a product so that they can make more profit.

Cash. Money in the form of coins or notes.

Cashable. Which can be cashed.

Cash account. An account which records the money which is received and spent.

Cash advance. A loan in cash against a future payment.

Cash against documents. A system whereby a buyer receives documents for the goods on payment of a bill of exchange.

Cash and carry. 1. A large store selling goods at low prices, where the customer pays cash and takes the goods away immediately. 2. Buying a commodity for cash and selling the same commodity on the futures market.

Cash balance. A balance in cash, as opposed to amounts owed.

Cash basis. A method of preparing the accounts of a business, where receipts and payments are shown at the time when they are made (as opposed to showing debts or credits which are outstanding at the end of the accounting period). Also called receipts and payments basis.

Cash book. A book which records cash received and paid out.

Cash box. Metal box for keeping cash.

Cash budget. A plan of cash income and expenditure.

Cash card. A plastic card used to obtain money from a cash dispenser.

Cash cow. A product or subsidiary company that consistently generates good profits but does not provide growth.

Cash crop. An agricultural crop grown for sale to other buyers or to other countries, rather than for domestic consumption.

Cash deal. A sale done for cash.

Cash desk. The place in a store where you pay for the goods bought.

Cash discount. A discount given for payment in cash. Also called discount for cash.

Cash dispenser. A machine which gives out money when a special card is inserted and instructions given.

Cash dividend. A dividend paid in cash, as opposed to a dividend in the form of bonus shares.

Cash economy. A black economy, where goods and services are paid for in cash, and therefore not declared for tax.

Cash float. Cash put into the cash box at the beginning of the day or week to allow change to be given to customers.

Cash flow. Cash which comes into a company from sales (cash inflow) or the money which goes out in purchases or overhead expenditure (cash outflow).

Cash flow forecast. A forecast of when cash will be received or paid out.

Cash flow statement. A report which shows cash sales and purchases.

Cashier. 1. A person who takes money from customers in a shop or who deals with the money that has been paid. 2. A person who deals with customers in a bank and takes or gives cash at the counter.

Cash in. To sell shares or other property for cash.

Cash in hand. Money and notes, kept to pay small amounts but not deposited in the bank.

Cash in on. To profit from.

Cash in transit. Cash being moved from one bank or business to another.

Cash items. Goods sold for cash.

Cash limit. 1. A fixed amount of money which can be spent during a certain period. 2. A maximum amount someone can withdraw from an ATM using a cash card.

Cash market. The gilt-edged securities market (where purchases are paid for almost immediately, as opposed to the futures market).

Cash offer. An offer to pay in cash, especially an offer to pay cash when buying shares in a takeover bid.

Cash on delivery. Payment in cash when goods are delivered. Abbr. COD.

Cash payment. Payment in cash.

Cash position. A state of the cash which a company currently has available.

Cash positive. Having cash in hand, as opposed to having debts and overdrafts.

Cash price. A lower price or better terms which apply if the customer pays cash.

Cash purchase. A purchase made for cash.

Cash register. A machine which shows and adds the prices of items bought, with a drawer for keeping the cash received.

Cash reserves. A company's reserves in cash deposits or bills kept in case of urgent need.

Cash sale. A transaction paid for in cash.

Cash-strapped. Short of money.

Cash terms. Lower terms which apply if the customer pays cash.

Cash transaction. A transaction paid for in cash.

Cash transfer hatch. A small door in an outside wall, allowing cash to be passed through.

Cash up. To add up the cash in a shop at the end of the day.

Cash voucher. A piece of paper which can be exchanged for cash.

Cash with order. Terms of sale showing the payment has to be made in cash when the order is placed. Abbr. CWO.

Casting vote. A vote used by the chairman in the case where the votes for and against a proposal are equal.

Casual. Not permanent, or not regular.

Casual labour. Workers who are hired for a short period.

Casual work. Work where the workers are hired for a short period.

Casual worker. A worker who can be hired for a short period.

Catalogue price. A price as marked in a catalogue or list.

CCA. Abbr. Current Cost Accounting.

CD. Abbr. Certificate of Deposit.

Ceiling. The highest point that something can reach, e.g. the highest rate of a pay increase.

Example: Output reached its ceiling in June and has since fallen back.

Ceiling price. The highest price that can be reached.

Central. Organized from one main point.

Central assets account. Same as asset management account.

Central bank. The main government-controlled bank in a country, which controls that country's financial affairs by fixing main interest rates, issuing currency, supervising the commercial banks and trying to control the foreign exchange rate.

Central bank discount rate. The rate at which a central bank discounts bills, such as treasury bills.

Central bank intervention. An action by a central bank to change base interest rates, to impose exchange controls or to buy or sell the country's own currency in an attempt to influence international money markets.

Centralization. The organization of everything from a central point.

Central office. The main office which controls all smaller offices.

Central purchasing. Purchasing organized by a central office for all branches of a company.

Centre. 1. An important town. 2. A group of items in an account.

CEO. Abbr. Chief Executive Officer.

Certain annuity. An annuity which will be paid for a certain number of years only.

Certificate. An official document which shows that something is owned by someone or that something is true.

Certificated bankrupt. A bankrupt who has been discharged from bankruptcy with a certificate to show that he or she was not at fault.

Certificate of approval. A document showing that an item has been approved officially.

Certificate of authentication. A unique number supplied to a company by an independent source (an 'authenticator') to prove that the company is who they claim to be.

Certificate of authority. A certificate showing that someone has the authority to do something, such as sign a cheque.

Certificate of deposit. A document from a bank showing that money has been deposited at a certain guaranteed interest rate for a certain period of time. Abbr. CD.

Certificate of incorporation. A document issued by Companies House to show that a company has been legally set up and officially registered.

Certificate of origin. A document showing where imported goods come from or were made.

Certificate of quality. A certificate showing the grade of a soft commodity.

Certificate of registration. A document showing that an item has been registered.

Certificate of tax deducted. A document issued by a financial institution showing that tax has been deducted from interest payments on an account.

Certified accountant. An accountant who has passed the professional examinations and is a member of the Chartered Association of Certified Accountants.

Certified cheque or Certified check. A cheque which a bank says is good and will be paid out of money put aside from the payer's bank account.

Certify. To make an official declaration in writing.

Cession. Giving up property to someone (especially a creditor).

CF. Abbr. Carried Forward.

CFO. Abbr. Chief Financial Officer.

Chairman. A person who presides over the board meetings of a company.

Chairman and managing director. A managing director who is also chairman of the board of directors.

Chamber of Commerce. A group of local business people who meet to discuss problems which they have in common and to promote commerce in their town.

Change. 1. Money in coins or small notes. 2. Money given back by the seller, when the buyer can pay only with a larger note or coin than the amount asked. 3. (of a business, property, etc.) to be sold to a new owner.

Change machine. A machine which gives small change for a note or larger coin.

Changer. A person who changes money.

Channel. To send in a certain direction.

Channel of distribution. Same as distribution channel.

Charge. 1. Money which must be paid, or the price of a service. 2. A debit on an account. 3. A guarantee of security for a loan, for which assets are pledged. 4. Being formally accused in a court.

Chargeable. Which can be charged.

Chargeable gains. Gains made by selling an asset, such as shares, on which capital gains will be charged.

Charge account. An arrangement which a customer has with a store to buy goods and to pay for them at a later date, usually when the invoice is sent at the end of the month.

Note: The customer will make regular monthly payments into the account and is allowed credit of a multiple of those payments.

Charge card. A type of credit card (such as American Express) for which a fee is payable, but which does not allow the user to take out a loan (he or she has to pay off the total sum charged at the end of each month).

Charges forward. Charges which will be paid by the customer.

Charging period. A period of time during which charges are made to a credit card before they are charged to the cardholder.

Chart. A diagram displaying information as a series of lines, blocks, etc.

Charter. The action or business of hiring transport for a special purpose.

Chartered. 1. To a company which has been set up by charter, and not registered under the Companies Act. 2. A ship, bus or plane which has been hired for a special purpose.

Chartered accountant. An accountant who has passed the professional examinations and is a member of the Institute of Chartered Accountants. Abbr. CA.

Chartered Institute of Bankers. A professional association of bankers, providing training, professional examinations and qualifications which are recognized worldwide. Abbr. CIB.

Charter flight. A flight in an aircraft which has been hired for that purpose.

Charter value. The value of a bank's being able to continue do business in the future, reflected as part of its share price.

Charting. The work of using charts to analyze stock market trends and forecast future rises or falls.

Chattel mortgage. Money lent against the security of an item purchased, but not against real estate.

Cheap. Ad not costing a lot of money or not expensive.

Cheaply. Without paying much money.

Cheap money. Money which can be borrowed at a low rate of interest.

Cheap rate. A rate which is not expensive.

Cheat. To trick someone so that he or she loses money.

Check. 1. A sudden stop. 2. Investigation or examination.

Check digit. The last digit of a string of computerized reference numbers, used to validate the transaction.

Check off. A system where union dues are automatically deducted by the employer from a worker's pay cheque.

Check out. To go through a checkout and pay for the goods bought.

Checkout. The place where goods are paid for in a shop or supermarket.

Check sample. A sample to be used to see if a consignment is acceptable.

Cheque. A note to a bank asking them to pay money from your account to the account of the person whose name is written on the note.

Cheque book. A booklet with new blank cheques.

Cheque card or Cheque guarantee card. A plastic card from a bank which guarantees payment of a cheque up to a certain amount, even if the user has no money in his account.

Cheque requisition. An official note from a department to the company accounts staff asking for a cheque to be written.

Cheque to bearer. A cheque with no name written on it, so that the person who holds it can cash it.

Chief executive officer. The most important director in charge of a company. Abbr. CEO.

Chief financial officer. An executive in charge of a company's financial operations, reporting to the CEO. Abbr. CFO.

Chief operating officer. A director in charge of all a company's operations (same as a 'managing director'). Abbr. COO.

Chronological order. The arrangement of records such as files and invoices in order of their dates.

Churning. 1. A practice employed by stockbrokers, where they buy and sell on a client's discretionary account in order to earn their commission (the deals are frequently of no advantage to the client). 2. A practice employed by insurance salesmen where the salesman suggests that a client should change his insurance policy solely in order to earn the salesman a commission.

CIB. Abbr. Chartered Institute of Bankers.

CIF. Abbr. Cost, insurance and freight.

Circular. 1. Sent to many people. 2. A leaflet sent by a broker to clients, with information about companies and shares.

Circularize. To send a circular.

Circular letter of credit. A letter of credit sent to all branches of the bank which issues it.

Circulate. 1. (of money) to move about without restriction by the government. 2. To send or to give out without restrictions. 3. To send information.

Circulating capital. Capital in the form of cash or debtors, raw materials, finished products and work in progress which a company requires to carry on its business.

Circulation of capital. A movement of capital from one investment to another.

Circumstances. A general situation, especially insofar as it influences what a person can do or the way in which something happens.

Civil action. A court case brought by a person or a company against someone who has done them wrong.

Civil law. Laws relating to people's rights and to agreements between individuals.

Claim. 1. An act of asking for something that you feel you have a right to. 2. An act of stating that something is a fact. 3. An act of asking for money from an insurance company when something you insured against has taken place.

Claim back. To ask for money to be paid back.

Claim form. A form which has to be filled in when making an insurance claim.

Claims department. A department of an insurance company which deals with claims.

Claims reserve. Money set aside by an insurance company to meet costs of claims incurred but not yet settled.

Classified directory. A list of businesses grouped under various headings such as computer shops or newsagents.

Classify. To put into classes or categories according to specific characteristics.

Clause. A section of a contract.

Claw back. To take back money which has been allocated.

Clean bill of lading. A bill of lading with no note to say the shipment is faulty or damaged.

Clean float. An act of floating a currency freely on the international markets, without any interference from the government.

Clear. (of a period of time) free, total.

Clearance certificate. A document showing that goods have been passed by customs.

Clearance sale. A sale of items at low prices to get rid of stock.

Cleared date. A date on which a cheque has cleared and funds have been removed from the account.

Clearing. 1. Passing of goods through customs. 2. An act of passing of a cheque through the banking system, transferring money from one account to another.

Clearing house. A central office where clearing banks exchange cheques, or where stock exchangé or commodity exchange transactions are settled.

Clearing member. A member firm of a stock exchange which is also a member of the stock exchange clearing house.

Clear off a debt. To pay all of a debt.

Clear profit. Profit after all expenses have been paid.

Clear title. Title to property without any charges or other encumbrances.

Clicks-and-mortar. Conducting business both through e-commerce and also in the traditional way in buildings such as shops and warehouses.

Client. A person with whom business is done or who pays for a service.

Clients' account. An account with a bank for clients of a solicitor.

Close. The end of a day's trading on the stock exchange.

Close a position. 1. To arrange your affairs so that you no longer have any liability to pay (e.g. by selling all your securities or when a purchaser of a futures contract takes on a sales contract for the same amount to offset the risk). 2. To bring something to an end.

Close company. A privately owned company controlled by a few shareholders where the public may own a small number of the shares.

Closed. 1. Not open for business, or not doing business. 2. Restricted.

Closed economy. A type of economy where trade and financial dealings are tightly controlled by the government.

Closed-end mortgage. A mortgage where the borrower cannot use the property as security for other borrowings, such as a second mortgage, and cannot repay the mortgage early either.

Closed fund. A fund, such as an investment trust, where the investor buys shares in the trust and receives dividends (as opposed to an open-ended trust, such as a unit trust, where the investor buys units, and his investment is used to purchase further securities for the trust).

Closed market. A market where a supplier deals only with one agent or distributor and does not supply any others direct.

Close down. 1. To shut a shop, factory or service for a long period or forever. 2. (of a shop, factory or service) to stop doing business or operating.

Closed shop. A system where a company agrees to employ only union members for specific jobs.

Close-ended or Closed-end. To an investment which has a fixed capital, such as an investment trust.

Closely held. To shares in a company which are controlled by only a few shareholders.

Close off. Come to the end of an accounting period and make up the profit and loss account.

Close out. To end a futures contract by selling the relevant commodity or financial instrument.

Closing. 1. Final or coming at the end. 2. At the end of an accounting period.

Example: At the end of the quarter the bookkeeper has to calculate the closing balance.

Closing bell. A bell which is rung when a stock exchange closes for business.

Closing bid. The last bid at an auction, the bid which is successful.

Closing costs. The costs involved in finalizing a deal, especially a mortgage or other bank loan.

Closing date. The last date.

Closing-down sale. Sale of goods when a shop is closing for ever.

Closing out. The ending of a futures contract by selling the relevant commodity.

Closing price. The price of a share at the end of a day's trading.

Closing statement. A statement of all charges and fees involved in a mortgage, made just before the mortgage is signed.

Closing stock. The details of stock at the end of an accounting period.

Closing time. The time when a shop or office stops work.

CN. Abbr. Credit Note.

Co. 1. Working or acting together. 2. Care of.

Co-creditor. A person who is a creditor of the same company as you are.

COD. Abbr. Cash on delivery.

Code. 1. A system of signs, numbers or letters which mean something. 2. A set of rules.

Code of practice. 1. Rules drawn up by an association which the members must follow when doing business. 2. The formally established ways in which members of a profession agree to work.

Co-director. A person who is a director of the same company as you.

Co-financing. The act of arranging finance for a project from a series of sources.

Coincident indicator. An indicator which coincides with economic activity (as opposed to leading indicators and lagging indicators).

Co-insurance. An insurance policy where the risk is shared among several insurers.

Cold start. The act of beginning a new business or opening a new shop with no previous turnover to base it on.

Collapse. 1. A sudden fall in price. 2. A sudden failure.

Collar. 1. Purchasing fixed minimum and maximum rates of interest, dividends or repayments at the same time.

Note: If a company has money in variable rate investments and wants to protect its income, it will buy a floor; instead of paying the premium for this purchase it will simultaneously sell a cap, so effectively creating a 'collar' round its investments.

Collateral. Used to provide a guarantee for a loan security, such as negotiable instruments, shares or goods, used to provide a guarantee for a loan.

Collateral loan. A loan secured on assets.

Colleague. A person who works in the same organization as another.

Collect. 1. To get money which is owed to you by making the person who owes it pay. 2. To take things away from a place.

Collecting agency. An agency which collects money owed to other companies for a commission.

Collection. 1. The act of getting money together, or of making someone pay money which is owed. 2. The fetching of goods.

Collection charge or Collection rate. A charge for collecting something.

Column. A series of numbers arranged one underneath the other.

COMEX. Abbr. New York Commodity Exchange.

Commerce. The buying and selling of goods and services.

Commercial. 1. To business. 2. Profitable.

Commercial bank. A bank which offers banking services to the public, as opposed to a merchant bank.

Commercial bill. A bill of exchange issued by a company (a trade bill) or accepted by a bank (a bank bill) (as opposed to Treasury bills which are issued by the government)

Commercial directory. A book which lists all the businesses and business people in a town.

Commercialization. The act of making something into a business run for profit.

Commercialize. To make something into a business.

Commercial law. The laws regarding business.

Commercially. In a business way.

Commercial mortgage. A mortgage on commercial property, such as offices, shops and factories.

Commercial mortgage-backed Securities. Shares which are backed by the security of a commercial mortgage. Abbr. CMBS.

Commercial port. A port which has only goods traffic and no passengers.

Commercial property. A building, or buildings, used as offices or shops.

Commercial value. The value that a thing would have if it were offered for sale. These goods are intended only as a sample and would not be worth anything if sold.

Commission. 1. Money paid to a salesperson or agent, usually a percentage of the sales made. 2. A group of people officially appointed to examine some problem.

Commission agent. An agent who is paid a percentage of sales.

Commission broker. A stockbroker who works for a commission.

Commissioner. An important official appointed by a government or other authority, or a member of a commission.

Commission sale. A sale where the salesperson is paid a commission.

Commit. To guarantee something, especially a loan issue, or to guarantee to do something.

Commitment. An agreement by an underwriting syndicate to underwrite a note issuance facility.

Commitment fee. A fee paid to a bank which has arranged a line of credit which has not been fully used.

Commodity. Something sold in very large quantities, especially a raw material such as a metal or a food such as wheat.

Note: Commodities are either traded for immediate delivery (as 'actual' or 'physicals'), or for delivery in the future (as 'futures'). Commodity markets deal either in metals (aluminum, copper, lead, nickel, silver and zinc) or in 'soft' items, such as cocoa, coffee, sugar and oil.

Commodity exchange. A place where commodities are bought and sold.

Commodity futures. Commodities traded for delivery at a later date.

Commodity market. A place where people buy and sell commodities.

Commodity trader. A person whose business is buying and selling commodities.

Common carrier. A firm which carries goods or passengers, and which anyone can use.

Common dividend. A dividend payable on common stock.

Common equity. Ordinary shares in a company.

Common ownership. A situation where a business is owned by the employees who work in it.

Common pricing. The illegal fixing of prices by several businesses so that they all charge the same price.

Common seal or Company's seal. A metal stamp for stamping documents with the name of the company to show that they have been approved officially.

Common stock. Ordinary shares in a company, giving shareholders a right to vote at meetings and to receive dividends.

Commutation factors. Factors used to calculate the amount of pension to be given up in exchange for a lump sum.

Commute. 1. To travel to work from home each day. 2. To change a right into cash.

Companies Act. An Act of Parliament which regulates the workings of companies, stating the legal limits within which companies may do their business.

Company. A business organization, a group of people organized to buy, sell or provide a service, usually for profit.

Note: A company can be incorporated (with memorandum and articles of association) as a private limited company, and adds the initials 'Ltd' after its name, or as a public limited company, when its name must end in 'Plc'. Unincorporated companies are partnerships such as firms of solicitors, architects, accountants, etc., and they add the initials 'Co.' after their name.

Company director. A person appointed by the shareholders to help run a company.

Company law. Laws which refer to the way companies work.

Company promoter. A person who organizes the setting up of a new company.

Company registrar. The person who keeps the share register of a company.

Company secretary. A person who is responsible for a company's legal and financial affairs.

Compare with. To examine two things to see where they are the same and where they differ.

Compensate. To give someone money to make up for a loss or injury.

Compensating balance. The amount of money which a customer has to keep in a bank account in order to get free services from the bank.

Compensation. Payment for damage done.

Compensation deal. A deal where an exporter is paid (at least in part) in goods from the country to which he is exporting.

Compensation fund. A fund operated by the stock exchange to compensate investors for losses suffered when members of the stock exchange default.

Compensation package. The salary, pension and other benefits offered with a job.

Compensatory financing. Finance from the IMF to help a country in difficulty.

Compete. To try to do better than another person or another company.

Competence framework. The set of duties or tasks performed as part of a job with the standards which should be achieved in these duties.

Competing products. The products from different companies which have the same use and are sold in the same markets at similar prices.

Competition. 1. A situation where companies or individuals are trying to do better than others, e.g. trying to win a larger share of the market, or to produce a better or cheaper product or to control the use of resources. 2. Companies which are trying to compete with your product.

Competitive. 1. Involving competition. 2. Intended to compete with others, usually by being cheaper or better.

Competitive bid. A method of auctioning new securities, where various underwriters offer the stock at competing prices.

Competitive devaluation. A devaluation of a currency to make a country's goods more competitive on the international markets.

Competitively priced. Sold at a low price which competes with the price of similar products from other companies.

Competitive pricing. The practice of putting low prices on goods so as to compete with other products.

Competitive products. Products made to compete with existing products.

Competitor. A person or company that is competing with another.

Completion date. A date when something will be finished.

Compliance. Agreement to do what is ordered.

Compliance department. A department in a stock broking firm which makes sure that the stock exchange rules are followed and that confidentiality is maintained in cases where the same firm represents rival clients.

Comply. To agree to do what is ordered.

Composite. Made up a various parts joined together.

Composite index. An index made from various indices.

Composition. An agreement between a debtor and creditors, where the debtor settles a debt by repaying only part of it.

Compound. 1. To agree with creditors to settle a debt by paying part of what is owed. 2. To add to.

Compounded annual return. A net return on an investment, calculated after adding interest and deducting tax.

Compounded interest rate. An interest rate showing the effect of adding the interest to the capital.

Compounding method. The method used when compounding interest (daily, monthly, quarterly or annually). Abbr. CM.

Compound interest. Interest which is added to the capital and then earns interest itself.

Comprehensive insurance or Comprehensive policy. An insurance policy which covers you against all risks which are likely to happen.

Compromise. An agreement between two sides, where each side gives way a little.

Compulsory. Which is forced or ordered.

Compulsory purchase. The purchase of an annuity with the fund built up in a personal pension scheme.

Computational error. A mistake made in calculating.

Computerize. To change something from a manual system to one using computers.

Computer model. A system for calculating investment opportunities, used by fund managers to see the right moment to buy or sell.

Computer program. Instructions to a computer telling it to do a particular piece of work.

Concealment of assets. The act of hiding assets so that creditors do not know they exist.

Concentration. 1. The action of grouping a large number of things together. Also called market concentration. 2. The action of a bank in lending too much to one single sector of the economy.

Note: It is generally thought that banks should not make more than 10% of their loans to a single sector.

Concert party. An arrangement where several people or companies work together in secret (usually to acquire another company through a takeover bid).

Concession. 1. The right to use someone else's property for business purposes. 2. The right to be the only seller of a product in a place. 3. An allowance, such as a reduction of tax or price.

Conciliation. The practice of bringing together the parties in a dispute with an independent third party, so that the dispute can be settled through a series of negotiations.

Condition. 1. Something which has to be carried out as part of a contract or which has to be agreed before a contract becomes valid. 2. A general state or the general way of life in a certain place.

Conditional. Provided that specific conditions are taken into account.

Conditional offer. An offer to buy provided that specific terms apply.

Conditions of employment. The terms of a contract of employment.

Conditions of sale. Agreed ways in which a sale takes place, e.g. discounts or credit terms.

Confidential report. A secret document which must not be shown to other people.

Confirm. 1. To say again that something agreed before is correct. 2. To say that letters of credit from foreign purchasers are agreed, and that the sellers will be paid for orders placed.

Confirmation. 1. The act of writing to confirm the details of a transaction or agreement. 2. An agreement that orders from foreign purchasers will be paid.

Conflict of interest. A situation where a person or firm may profit personally from decisions taken in an official capacity.

Conglomerate. A group of subsidiary companies linked together and forming a group, each making very different types of products.

Consensus. An opinion which most people agree on.

Conservative. Careful, not overestimating.

Consideration. 1. Serious thought. 2. Something valuable exchanged as part of a contract.

Consignee. A person who receives goods from someone for their own use or to sell for the sender.

Consignment. 1. The sending of goods to someone who will sell them for you. 2. A group of goods sent for sale.

Consignment note. A note saying that goods have been sent.

Consignor. A person who consigns goods to someone.

Note: The goods remain the property of the consignor until the consignee sells or pays for them.

Consolidate. 1. To include the accounts of several subsidiary companies as well as the holding company in a single set of accounts. 2. To group goods together for shipping. 3. To remain at the same level for some time, before moving up again.

Consolidated accounts. Accounts where the financial position of several different companies (i.e. a holding company and its subsidiaries) are recorded together.

Consolidated balance sheet. A balance sheets of subsidiary companies grouped together into the balance sheet of the parent company.

Consolidated fund. Money in the Exchequer which comes from tax revenues and is used to pay for government expenditure.

Consolidated shipment. Goods from different companies grouped together into a single shipment.

Consolidation. 1. The grouping together of goods for shipping. 2. Taking profits from speculative investments and investing them safely in blue-chip companies.

Consortium. A group of companies which work together.

Consular invoice. An invoice stamped by a consul to show that goods being imported have correct documentation and are being shipped legally.

Consult. To ask an expert for advice.

Consultancy. The act of giving specialist advice.

Consultant. A specialist who gives advice.

Consumable goods Or Consumables. Goods which are bought by members of the public and not by companies. Also called consumer goods.

Consumer. A person or company that buys and uses goods and services.

Consumer bank. Same as retail bank.

Consumer council. A group representing the interests of consumers.

Consumer credit. The credit given by shops, banks and other financial institutions to consumers so that they can buy goods.

Consumer credit counselling service. A service which advises people about problems with items bought on credit.

Consumer durables. Items which are bought and used by the public, e.g. washing machines, refrigerators or cookers.

Consumer panel. A group of consumers who report on products they have used so that the manufacturers can improve them or use what the panel says about them in advertising.

Consumer price index. An American index showing how prices of consumer goods have risen over a period of time, used as a way of measuring inflation and the cost of living. Abbr. CPI.

Consumer protection. The activity of protecting consumers against unfair or illegal traders.

Consumer research. Research into why consumers buy goods and what goods they may want to buy.

Consumer resistance. A lack of interest by consumers in buying a new product.

Contested takeover. A takeover bid where the board of the target company does not recommend it to the shareholders and tries to fight it. Also called hostile bid.

Contingency. A possible state of emergency when decisions will have to be taken quickly.

Contingency fund. Money set aside in case it is needed urgently.

Contingency plan. A plan which will be put into action if something happens which no one expects to happen.

Contingent liability. A liability which may or may not occur, but for which provision is made in a company's accounts, as opposed to 'provisions', where money is set aside for an anticipated expenditure.

Continuous compounding. A system where interest is calculated all the time and added to the principal.

Contra. To enter a similar amount in the opposite side of an account.

Contra account. An account which offsets another account, e.g. where a company's supplier is not only a creditor in that company's books but also a debtor because it has purchased goods on credit.

Contract. 1. A legal agreement between two parties. 2. By private legal agreement. 3. An agreement for the supply of a service or goods. 4. (Stock Exchange) a deal to buy or sell shares, or an agreement to purchase options or futures.

Note: A contract is an agreement between two or more parties which creates legal obligations between them. Some contracts are made 'under seal', i.e. they are signed and sealed by the parties; most contracts are made orally or in writing. The essential elements of a contract are: (a) that an offer made by one party should be accepted by the other; (b) consideration (i.e. payment of money); (c) the intention to create legal relations. The terms of a contract may be express or implied. A breach of contract by one party entitles the other party to sue for damages or to ask for something to be done.

Contract law. Laws relating to private agreements.

Contract note. A note showing that shares have been bought or sold but not yet paid for, also including the commission.

Contract of employment. A contract between an employer and an employee stating all the conditions of work.

Contractor. A person or company that does work according to a written agreement.

Contractual liability. A legal responsibility for something as stated in a contract.

Contractual obligation. Something that a person is legally forced to do through having signed a contract to do.

Contractual savings. Savings in the form of regular payments into long-term investments such as pension schemes.

Contra entry. An entry made in the opposite side of an account to make an earlier entry worthless, i.e. a debit against a credit.

Contrarian research. Research that shows you should buy shares against the current trend.

Contribute. To give money or add to money.

Contribution. Money paid to add to a sum.

Contribution of capital. Money paid to a company as additional capital.

Contributory pension scheme. A scheme where the worker pays a proportion of his or her salary into the pension fund.

Control. 1. The power or ability to direct something. 2. The act of restricting or checking something or making sure that something is kept in check.

Controlled economy. An economy where most business activity is directed by orders from the government.

Controlling interest. To own more than 50% of the shares so that you can direct how the company is run.

Convergence. 1. A situation where the economic factors applying in two countries move closer together, e.g. when basic interest rates, or budget deficits become more and more similar. 2. A situation where the price of a commodity on the futures market moves towards the spot price as settlement date approaches.

Conversion. 1. A change. 2. The action of changing convertible loan stock into ordinary shares.

Conversion discount Or Conversion premium. The difference between the price of convertible stock and the ordinary shares into which they are to be converted.

Note: If the convertible stock is cheaper, the difference is a conversion premium; if the stock is dearer, the difference is a conversion discount.

Conversion issue. An issue of new bonds(called 'conversion bonds') timed to coincide with the date of maturity of older bonds, with the intention of persuading investors to reinvest.

Conversion of funds. The act of using money which does not belong to you for a purpose for which it is not supposed to be used.

Conversion period. A time during which convertible loan stock may be changed into ordinary shares.

Conversion price Or Conversion rate. 1. A price at which preference shares are converted into ordinary shares. 2. A rate at which a currency is changed into a foreign currency.

Conversion value. A value of convertible stock, including the extra value of the ordinary shares into which they may be converted.

Convert. 1. To change money of one country for money of another. 2. To use someone else's money for yourself.

Convertible currency. A currency which can easily be exchanged for another.

Convertible debenture. A debenture or loan stock which can be exchanged for ordinary shares at a later date.

Convertible loan stock. Money lent to a company which can be converted into shares at a later date.

Convertibles. Corporate bonds or preference shares which can be converted into ordinary shares at a set price on set dates.

Conveyance. A legal document which transfers a property from the seller to the buyer.

COO. Abbr. Chief operating officer.

Cooperative. Where the profits are shared among the workers.

Cooperative bank. A bank which is owned by its members, who deposit money or who borrow money as loans.

Cooperative society. An organization where customers and workers are partners and share the profits.

Copyright. A legal right which protects the creative work of writers and artists and prevents others from copying or using it without authorization, and which also applies to such things as company logos and brand names.

Copyright notice. A note in a book showing who owns the copyright and the date of ownership.

Corner. 1. Place where two streets or two walls join. 2. A situation where one person or a group controls the supply of a certain commodity.

Corporate. 1. To corporations or companies, or to a particular company as a whole. 2. To business in general.

Corporate finance. The financial affairs of companies.

Corporate governance. A theory of the way companies should be run.

Corporate image. An idea which a company would like the public to have of it.

Corporate loan. A loan issued by a corporation.

Corporate name. The name of a large corporation.

Corporate plan. A plan for the future work of a whole company.

Corporate planning. 1. The process of planning the future work of a whole company. 2. Planning the future financial state of a group of companies.

Corporate raider. A person or company which buys a stake in another company before making a hostile takeover bid.

Corporate resolution. A document signed by the officers of a corporation, naming those persons who can sign cheques, withdraw cash and have access to the corporation's bank account.

Corporate secretary. A person responsible for the corporation's legal and financial affairs.

Corporate spinoffs. Small companies which have been split off from larger organizations.

Corporation. 1. A large company. 2. A company which is incorporated in India. 3. A municipal authority

Note: A corporation is formed by registration with the Registrar of Companies under the Companies Act (in the case of public and private companies) or other Acts of Parliament (in the case of building societies and charities).

Corporation income tax. A tax on profits made by incorporated companies.

Correction. 1. An act of making something correct. 2. A change in the valuation of something that is thought to be overvalued or undervalued which results in its being more realistically valued.

Correspondent bank. A bank which acts as an agent for a foreign bank.

Cost. 1. The amount of money which has to be paid for something. 2. To have as its price.

Cost, insurance, and freight. The estimate of a price, which includes the cost of the goods, the insurance, and the transport charges. Abbr. CIF.

Cost accounting. The process of preparing special accounts of manufacturing and sales costs.

Cost analysis. The process of calculating in advance what a new product will cost.

Cost-benefit analysis. The process of comparing the costs and benefits of various possible ways of using available resources. Also called benefit-cost analysis.

Cost centre. 1. A person or group whose costs can be itemized and to which costs can be allocated in accounts. 2. A unit, a process, or an individual that provides a service needed by another part of an organization and whose cost is therefore accepted as an overhead of the business.

Cost-cutting. Intended to reduce costs.

Cost-effective. Which gives good value when compared with the original cost.

Cost-effectiveness Or Cost efficiency. The quality of being cost-effective.

Cost-income ratio. A ratio between the costs involved in running a business and the income the business produces.

Costing. A calculation of the manufacturing costs, and so the selling price, of a product.

Costly. Costing a lot of money, or costing too much money.

Cost of capital. Interest paid on the capital used in operating a business.

Cost of living. Money which has to be paid for basic items such as food, heating or rent.

Cost-of-living index. A way of measuring the cost of living which is shown as a percentage increase on the figure for the previous year. It is similar to the consumer price index, but includes other items such as the interest on mortgages.

Cost of sales. All the costs of a product sold, including manufacturing costs and the staff costs of the production department, before general overheads are calculated. Also called cost of goods sold.

Cost plus. A system of calculating a price, by taking the cost of production of goods or services and adding a percentage to cover the supplier's overheads and margin.

Cost price. A selling price which is the same as the price, either the manufacturing price or the wholesale price, which the seller paid for the item.

Cost-push inflation. Inflation caused by increased wage demands and increased raw materials costs, which lead to higher prices, which in turn lead to further wage demands. Also called cost inflation.

Council. An official group chosen to run something or to advise on a problem.

Counselling. The act of giving professional advice to others on personal matters.

Count. 1. To add figures together to make a total. 2. To include something.

Counter-claim. A claim for damages made in reply to a previous claim.

Counter-offer. A higher or lower offer made in reply to another offer.

Counter purchase. An international trading deal, where a company agrees to use money received on a sale to purchase goods in the country where the sale was made.

Countersign. To sign a document which has already been signed by someone else.

Counter-trade. A trade which does not involve payment of money, but something such as a barter or a buy-back deal instead.

Countervailing duty. A duty imposed by a country on imported goods, where the price of the goods includes a subsidy from the government in the country of origin. Also called anti-dumping duty.

Coupon. 1. A piece of paper used in place of money. 2. A piece of paper which replaces an order form. 3. a slip of paper attached to a government bond certificate which can be cashed to provide the annual interest.

Coupon ad. An advertisement with a form attached, which you cut out and return to the advertiser with your name and address for further information.

Cover. 1. The proportion of a target audience reached by advertising. 2. The protection guaranteed by insurance. 3. An amount of money large enough to guarantee that something can be paid for.

Covering letter or Covering note. A letter or note sent with documents to say why you are sending them.

Cover note. A letter from an insurance company giving details of an insurance policy and confirming that the policy exists.

CPI. Abbr. Consumer Price Index.

Crash. A financial collapse.

Creation. The process of making something.

Creative. Someone who works in the conceptual or artistic side of a business.

Creative accountancy Or Creative accounting. An adaptation of a company's figures to present a better picture than is correct, usually intended to make a company more attractive to a potential buyer, or done for some other reason which may not be strictly legal.

Note: Creative accounting is the term used to cover a number of accounting practices which, although legal, may be used to mislead banks, investors and shareholders about the profitability or liquidity of a business.

Creative financing. Finding methods of financing a commercial project that is different from the normal methods of raising money.

Credit. 1. A period of time allowed before a customer has to pay a debt incurred for goods or services. 2. An amount entered in accounts to show a decrease in assets or expenses or an increase in liabilities, revenue or capital. In accounts, credits are entered in the right-hand column.

Credit account. An account which a customer has with a shop which allows him or her to buy goods and pay for them later.

Credit balance. A balance in an account showing that more money has been received than is owed.

Credit card. A plastic card which allows you to borrow money and to buy goods without paying for them immediately (you pay the credit card company at a later date).

Credit column. The right-hand column in accounts showing money received.

Credit control. A check that customers pay on time and do not owe more than their credit limit.

Credit entry. An entry on the credit side of an account.

Credit facilities. An arrangement with a bank or supplier to have credit so as to buy goods.

Credit freeze. A period when lending by banks is restricted by the government.

Credit history. A record of how a potential borrower has repaid his or her previous debts.

Credit limit. The largest amount of money which a customer can borrow.

Credit line. An overdraft, the amount by which a person can draw money from an account with no funds, with the agreement of the bank.

Credit note. A note showing that money is owed to a customer. Abbr. CN.

Creditor. A person or company that is owed money, i.e. a company's creditors are its liabilities.

Creditors' meeting. A meeting of all the people to whom an insolvent company owes money, to decide how to obtain the money owed.

Credit rating. An amount which a credit agency feels a customer will be able to repay.

Credit references. Details of persons, companies or banks who have given credit to a person or company in the past, supplied as references when opening a credit account with a new supplier.

Credit refusal. A decision not to give someone credit.

Credit risk. A risk that a borrower may not be able to repay a loan.

Credit scoring. A calculation made when assessing the creditworthiness of someone or something.

Credit side. The right-hand column of accounts showing money received.

Credit threshold. A limit for credit allowed to a customer.

Credit transfer. An act of moving money from one account to another.

Crisis. A serious economic situation where decisions have to be taken rapidly.

Crisis management. 1. Management of a business or a country's economy during a period of crisis. 2. Actions taken by an organization to protect itself when unexpected events or situations occur that could threaten its success or continued operation.

Note: Crisis situations may result from external factors such as the development of a new product by a competitor or changes in legislation, or from internal factors such as a product failure or faulty decision- making, and often involve the need to make quick decisions on the basis of uncertain or incomplete information.

Crore. (in India) ten million

Note: One crore equals 100 lakh.

Cross. To write two lines across a cheque to show that it has to be paid into a bank.

Note: Crossed cheques have the words 'AC payee' printed in the space between the two vertical lines.

Cross-border capital flows. Movements of capital from one country to another.

Crossed cheque. A cheque with two lines across it showing that it can only be deposited at a bank and not exchanged for cash.

Cross holding. A situation where two companies own shares in each other in order to stop either from being taken over.

Cross rate. An exchange rate between two currencies expressed in a third currency.

Cross-selling. The act of selling insurance or other financial services at the same time as a mortgage.

Cum rights. Sold with the right to purchase new shares in a rights issue.

Cumulative. Added to regularly over a period of time.

Cumulative preference share or Cumulative preferred stock. A preference share which will have the dividend paid at a later date even if the company is not able to pay a dividend in the current year.

Currency. 1. Money in coins and notes which is used in a particular country. 2. A foreign currency, the currency of another country.

Currency band. The exchange rate levels between which a currency is allowed to move without full devaluation.

Currency clause. A clause in a contract which avoids problems of payment caused by changes in exchange rates, by fixing the exchange rate for the various transactions covered by the contract.

Currency conversion systems. Computer software used to convert accounts from one currency to another automatically.

Currency futures. Purchases of foreign currency for delivery at a future date.

Currency movements. Changes in exchange rates between countries.

Currency reserves. Foreign money held by a government to support its own currency and to pay its debts.

Currency swap. An agreement to use a certain currency for payments under a contract in exchange for another currency (the two companies involved can each buy one of the currencies at a more favourable rate than the other).

Current. To the present time.

Current account. 1. An account in an bank from which the customer can withdraw money when he or she wants. Current accounts do not always pay interest. Also called cheque account. 2. An account of the balance of payments of a country relating to the sale or purchase of raw materials, goods and invisibles.

Current assets. The assets used by a company in its ordinary work, e.g. materials, finished goods, cash and monies due, and which are held for a short time only.

Current balance. The balance in an account at the start of a day's trading. Also called ledger account.

Current cost accounting. A method of accounting which notes the cost of replacing assets at current prices, rather than valuing assets at their original cost. Abbr. CCA.

Current liabilities. The debts which a company has to pay within the next accounting period. In a company's annual accounts, these would be debts which must be paid within the year and are usually payments for goods or services received.

Current yield. A dividend calculated as a percentage of the current price of a share on the stock market.

Cushion. Money which allows a company to pay interest on its borrowings or to survive a loss.

Custody. Control of a thing under the law, as when holding valuables or share certificates in safekeeping for someone.

Custom. 1. The use of a shop by regular shoppers. 2. A thing which is usually done.

Customer. A person or company that buys goods.

Note: The customer may not be the consumer or end user of the product.

Customer identification file. A computer record which a bank keeps on each customer, containing information about the customer's credit rating. Abbr. CIF.

Customer service department. A department which deals with customers and their complaints and orders.

Customize. To change something to fit the special needs of a customer.

Customs. The government department which organizes the collection of taxes on imports, or an office of this department at a port or airport.

Customs clearance. 1. The act of passing goods through customs so that they can enter or leave the country. 2. A document given by customs to a shipper to show that customs duty has been paid and the goods can be shipped.

Customs declaration. A statement showing goods being imported on which duty will have to be paid.

Customs duty. A tax on goods imported into a country.

Customs entry point. A place at a border between two countries where goods are declared to customs.

Customs seal. A seal attached by a customs officer to a box, to show that the contents have not passed through customs.

Customs tariff. A list of taxes to be paid on imported goods.

Cut. 1. The sudden lowering of a price, salary or the number of jobs. 2. A share in a payment.

Cut down on. To reduce suddenly the amount of something used.

Cutoff date. A date when something is stopped, such as the final date for receiving applications for shares, or the date when the current trading account ends and the next account begins.

Cut-price. Sold at a cheaper price than usual.

Cut-throat competition. Sharp competition which cuts prices and offers high discounts.

CWO. Abbr. Cash with order.

Cycle. A period of time during which something leaves its original position and then returns to it.

Cyclical factors. The way in which a trade cycle affects businesses.

D

Daily. Done every day.

Daily interest. A rate of interest calculated each day and added to the principal.

Daily consumption. An amount used each day.

Daily sales returns. Reports of sales made each day.

Damp down. To reduce.

Data. Information available on computer e.g. letters or figures.

Note: Takes a singular or plural.

Data acquisition. The act of gathering information about a subject.

Data bank. A store of information in a computer.

Database. A set of data stored in an organized way in a computer system.

Data capture or Data entry. Same as data acquisition.

Data mining. The use of advanced software to search online databases and identify statistical patterns or relationships in the data that may be commercially useful.

Data processing. The act of selecting and examining data in a computer to produce information in a special form.

Data stream. Data system available online, giving information about securities, prices, stock exchange transactions, etc.

Date. 1. The number of the day, month and year. 2. Up to now.

Dated. 1. With a date written on it. 2. Out-of-date.

Date draft. A draft which has a certain maturity date.

Date of bill. A date when a bill will mature.

Date of record. The date when a shareholder must be registered to qualify for a dividend.

Date stamp. A stamp with rubber figures which can be moved, used for marking the date on documents.

Dawn raid. A sudden planned purchase of a large number of a company's shares at the beginning of a day's trading.

Note: Up to 15% of a company's shares may be bought in this way, and the purchaser must wait for seven days before purchasing any more shares. Sometimes a dawn raid is the first step towards a takeover of the target company.

Day book. A book with an account of sales and purchases made each day.

Day order. An order to a stockbroker to buy or sell on a certain day.

Day release. An arrangement where a company allows a worker to go to college to study for one or two days each week.

Day shift. A shift worked during the daylight hours (from early morning to late afternoon).

Day trader. A person who buys shares and sells them within the same day.

Dead account. An account which is no longer used.

Dead-cat bounce. A slight rise in a share price after a sharp fall, showing that some investors are still interested in buying the share at the lower price, although further sharp falls will follow.

Deadline. The date by which something has to be done.

Deadlock. A point where two sides in a dispute cannot agree.

Dead loss. A total loss.

Deal. A business agreement, affair or contract.

Dealer. 1. A person who buys and sells. 2. A person or firm that buys or sells on their own account, not on behalf of clients.

Dealer bank. A bank which deals on the stock exchange or which deals in government securities.

Dealing. 1. The business of buying and selling on the stock exchange, commodity markets or currency markets. 2. The business of buying and selling goods.

Dealing floor. 1. An area of a broking house where dealing in securities is carried out by phone, using monitors to display current prices and stock exchange transactions. 2. A part of a stock exchange where dealers trade in securities.

Dealing-only broker. A broker who buys and sells shares for clients, but does not provide any advice and does not manage portfolios (as opposed to a full-service broker).

Dear money. Money which has to be borrowed at a high interest rate, and so restricts expenditure by companies. Also called tight money.

Death benefit. Insurance benefit paid to the family of someone who dies in an accident at work.

Death in service. An insurance benefit or pension paid when someone dies while employed by a company.

Debenture. Agreement to repay a debt with fixed interest using the company's assets as security.

Debenture bond. 1. A certificate showing that a debenture has been issued. 2. An unsecured loan.

Debenture capital. A capital borrowed by a company, using its fixed assets as security.

Debenture holder. A person who holds a debenture for money lent.

Debenture stock. A capital borrowed by a company, using its fixed assets as security.

Debit. An amount entered in accounts which shows an increase in assets or expenses or a decrease in liabilities, revenue or capital. In accounts, debits are entered in the left-hand column.

Debit balance. A balance in an account showing that more money is owed than has been received.

Debit bureau. A centralized system for checking a customer's credit rating when he or she presents a cheque as payment.

Debit card. A plastic card, similar to a credit card, but which debits the holder's account immediately through an EPOS system.

Debit column. The left-hand column in accounts showing the money paid or owed to others.

Debit entry. An entry on the debit side of an account.

Debit interest. An interest on debts, such as overdrafts.

Debit note. A note showing that a customer owes money.

Debits and credits. Money which a company owes and money it receives, or figures which are entered in the accounts to record increases or decreases in assets, expenses, liabilities, revenue or capital.

Debit side. A left-hand column of accounts showing money owed or paid to others.

Debt. Money owed for goods or services.

Debts due. Money owed which is due for repayment.

Debt collection. The act of collecting money which is owed.

Debt collection agency. A company, which collects debts for other companies for a commission.

Debt-convertible bond. A floating-rate bond, which can be converted to a fixed rate of interest.

Debt counselling. The work of advising people who are in debt of the best ways to arrange their finances so as to pay off their debts.

Debt instrument. A document by which someone promises to repay a debt.

Note: Debt instruments include such things as IOUs, CDs and bank notes.

Debtor. A person who owes money.

Debtor side. The debit side of an account.

Debt-service ratio. The debts of a company shown as a percentage of its equity.

Debt servicing. The payment of interest on a debt.

Decelerate. To slow down.

Deciding factor. The most important factor which influences a decision.

Decimal point. A dot which indicates the division between the whole unit and its smaller parts (such as 4.75).

Decimal system. A system of mathematics based on the number 10.

Declaration. An official statement.

Declaration of bankruptcy. An official statement that someone is bankrupt.

Declare. To make an official statement of something,

Declared. Which has been made public or officially stated.

Declared value. The value of goods entered on a customs declaration.

Decline. 1. A gradual falls. 2. The final stage in the life cycle of a product when the sales and profitability are falling off and the product is no longer worth investing in to fall slowly or decrease.

Decrease. A fall or reduction.

Deduct. To take money away from a total.

Deduction. The removing of money from a total, or the amount of money removed from a total.

Deed. A legal document or written agreement.

Deed of assignment. A document which legally transfers a property from a debtor to a creditor.

Deed of covenant. A signed legal agreement by which someone agrees to certain conditions, such as the payment of a certain sum of money each year.

Deed of partnership. Agreement which sets up a partnership.

Deed of transfer. A document which transfers the ownership of shares.

Defalcation. An illegal use of money by someone who is not the owner but who has been trusted to look after it.

Default. 1. A failure to carry out the terms of a contract, especially failure to pay back a debt. 2. Because no one else will act.

Defence. 1. The action of protecting someone or something against attack. 2. The act of fighting a lawsuit on behalf of a defendant.

Defence document. A document published by a company, which is the subject of a takeover bid, saying why the bid should be rejected.

Defend. To fight to protect someone or something that is being attacked.

Defensive shares or Defensive stocks. Shares which are not likely to fall in value because they are in stable market sectors, and which are therefore bought as protection against potential losses in more speculative investments.

Deferment. The act of leaving until a later date.

Deferred coupon note. A bond where the interest is not paid immediately, but only after a certain date.

Deferred creditor. A person who is owed money by a bankrupt but who is paid only after all other creditors.

Deferred equity. A share ownership at a later date (i.e. as part of convertible loan stock).

Deferred payment. 1. Money paid later than the agreed date. 2. Payment for goods by installments over a long period.

Deferred shares or Deferred stock. Shares which receive a dividend only after all other dividends have been paid.

Deferred tax. A tax which may become payable at some later date.

Deficiency. A lack of something, or the amount by which something, e.g. a sum of money, is less than it should be.

Deficit. The amount by which spending is higher than income.

Deficit financing. A type of financial planning by a government in which it borrows money to cover the difference between its tax income and its expenditure.

Defined. With specific aims.

Defined benefit plan or Defined contribution plan. A pension plan set up by corporations for their employees.

Deflation. A general reduction in economic activity as a result of a reduced supply of money and credit, leading to lower prices.

Note: The opposite is inflation.

Deflationary. Which can cause deflation.

Defray. To provide money to pay costs.

Delinquency. The fact of being overdue in payment of an account, an interest payment, etc.

Delinquent. To an account or payment of tax which is overdue.

Deliver. To transport goods to a customer.

Delivered price. A price which includes packing and transport.

Delivery. 1. The transporting of goods to a customer. 2. A consignment of goods being delivered. 3. The transport of a commodity to a purchaser. 4. The transfer of a bill of exchange or other negotiable instrument to the bank which is due to make payment.

Delivery month. A month in a futures contract when actual delivery will take place.

Delivery note. A list of goods being delivered, given to the customer with the goods.

Delivery of goods. The transport of goods to a customer's address.

Delivery order. The instructions given by the customer to the person holding her goods, to tell her where and when to deliver them.

Delivery service. A transport service organized by a supplier or a shop to take goods to customers.

Delivery time. The number of days before something will be delivered.

Delta shares or Delta securities. Shares in about 120 companies listed on the London Stock Exchange, but not on the SEAQ system because they are very rarely traded.

Demand. 1. An act of asking for payment. 2. The need that customers have for a product or their eagerness to buy it.

Demand bill. A bill of exchange, which must be paid when payment is asked for.

Demand deposit. Money in a deposit account, which can be taken out when you want it by writing a cheque.

Demand draft. A draft which is to be paid Immediately.

Demand-led inflation or Demand-pull inflation. Inflation caused by rising demand which cannot be met.

Demand note. A promissory note which must be paid when it is presented.

Demand price. The price at which a quantity of goods will be bought.

Demise. 1. A death. 2. The act of granting a property on a lease.

Demurrage. Money paid to a customer when a shipment is delayed at a port or by customs.

Denomination. A unit of money (on a coin, banknote or stamp).

Department. 1. A specialized section of a large organization. 2. A section of a large store selling one type of product.

Departmental manager. The manager of a department.

Department store. A large store with separate sections for different types of goods.

Deposit. 1. Money placed in a bank for safekeeping or to earn interest money deposited which you can withdraw by giving seven days' notice. 2. Money given in advance so that the thing which you want to buy will not be sold to someone else.

Deposit account. A bank account which pays interest but on which notice has to be given to withdraw money.

Deposit multiplier. A factor by which a bank can increase deposits as a ratio of its reserves.

Depositor. A person who deposits money in a bank, building society, etc.

Depository. A person or company with whom money or documents can be deposited.

Deposit slip. A piece of paper stamped by the cashier to prove that you have paid money into your account.

Deposit-taking institution or Depository institution. An institution such as a building society, bank or friendly society, which is licensed to receive money on deposit from private individuals and to pay interest on it.

Depreciate. 1. To reduce the value of assets in accounts. 2. To lose value.

Note: Various methods of depreciating assets are used, such as the 'straight line method', where the asset is depreciated at a constant percentage of its cost each year and the 'reducing balance method', where the asset is depreciated at a constant percentage which is applied to the cost of the asset after each of the previous years' depreciation has been deducted.

Depreciation. 1. A loss of value. 2. A reduction in value, writing down the capital value of an asset over a period of time in a company's accounts.

Depreciation rate. The rate at which an asset is depreciated each year in the company accounts.

Depress. To reduce something.

Depressed area. A part of a country suffering from depression.

Depressed market. A market where there are more goods than customers.

Depression. A period of economic crisis with high unemployment and loss of trade.

Deregulation. The reduction of government control over an industry.

Derivative instruments or Derivatives. Any forms of traded security, such as option contracts, which are derived from ordinary bonds and shares, exchange rates or stock market indices.

Note: Derivatives traded on stock exchanges or futures exchanges include options on futures or exchange rates or interest rate. While they can be seen as a way of hedging against possible swings in exchange rates or commodity prices, they can also produce huge losses if the market goes against the trader.

Descending tops. A term used by chartists to refer to a falling market, where each peak is lower than the one before.

Detailed account. An account which lists every item.

Determine. To fix, arrange.

Devaluation. A reduction in the value of a currency against other currencies.

Devalue. To reduce the value of a currency against other currencies.

Developing country or Developing nation. A country which is not fully industrialized.

Development. The work of planning the production of a new product and constructing the first prototypes.

Development area or development zone. An area which has been given special help from a government to encourage businesses and factories to be set up there.

Deviation. A change of route or strategy.

Devise. The act of giving freehold land to someone in a will.

Differential. Which shows a difference

Differential tariffs. Different tariffs for different classes of goods as, e.g., when imports from certain countries are taxed more heavily than similar imports from other countries.

Difficulty. A problem or trouble in doing something.

Digital. Converted into a form that can be processed by computers and accurately reproduced.

Digital cash. A form of digital money that can be used like physical cash to make online purchases and is anonymous because there is no way of obtaining information about the buyer when it is used.

Digital money. A series of numbers that has a value equivalent to a sum of money in a physical currency.

Digital wallet. A piece of personalized software on the hard drive of a user's computer that contains, in coded form, such items as credit card information, digital cash, a digital identity certificate, and standardized shipping information, and can be used when paying for a transaction electronically. Also called e-purse, electronic purse.

Dilute. To make less valuable.

Dilution levy. An extra charge levied by fund managers on investors buying or selling units in a fund, to offset any potential effect on the value of the fund of such sales or purchases.

Dilution of shareholding. A situation where the ordinary share capital of a company has been increased, but without an increase in the assets so that each share is worth less than before.

Dinar. A unit of currency used in some European countries (including Bosnia, Macedonia and Serbia) and in many Arabic countries: Algeria, Bahrain, Iraq, Jordan, Kuwait, Libya, Tunisia, South Yemen and Sudan.

Direct. To manage or organize something.

Direct action. A strike or go-slow by a workforce.

Direct business. Insurance business transacted between an insurance company and the person taking out the insurance (without going through a broker).

Direct cost. A cost which can be directly related to the making of a product, i.e. its production cost.

Direct debit. A system where a customer allows a company to charge costs to his or her bank account automatically and where the amount charged can be increased or decreased with the agreement of the customer.

Direction. 1. The process of organizing or managing. 2. Instructions showing how to use something.

Directive. An order or command to someone to do something.

Direct mail. The practice of selling a product by sending publicity material to possible buyers through the post.

Direct-mail advertising. Advertising by sending leaflets to people through the post.

Direct mailing. The sending of publicity material by post to possible buyers.

Director. 1. A senior employee appointed by the shareholders to help run a company, who is usually in charge of one or other of its main functions, e.g. sales or human relations, and usually, but not always, a member of the board of directors. 2. The person who is in charge of a project, an official institute or other organization.

Note: Directors are elected by shareholders at the AGM, though they are usually chosen by the chairman or chief executive. A board will consist of a chairman (who may be non-executive), a chief executive or managing director and a series of specialist directors in charge of various activities of the company (such as a finance director, production director or sales director). The company secretary will attend board meetings, but need not be a director. Apart from the executive directors, who are in fact employees of the company, there may be several non-executive directors, appointed either for their expertise and contacts, or as representatives of important shareholders such as banks.

Directorate. Group of directors.

Directors' report. The annual report from the board of directors to the shareholders.

Directory. 1. A reference book containing information on companies and their products. 2. A list of people or businesses with information about their addresses and telephone numbers.

Direct selling. The work of selling a product direct to the customer without going through a shop.

Direct share ownership. The ownership of shares by private individuals, buying or selling through brokers, and not via holdings in unit trusts.

Direct tax. A tax (such as income tax) paid directly to the government.

Direct taxation. A tax, such as income tax which is paid direct to the government.

Dirty float. A process of floating a currency, where the government intervenes to regulate the exchange rate.

Disbursement. The payment of money.

Discharge. 1. A payment of debt. 2. While carrying out her duties as director.

Discharged bankrupt. A person who has been released from being bankrupt because his or her debts have been paid.

Disciplinary procedure. A way of warning a worker officially that he or she is breaking rules or is working badly.

Disclaimer. A legal refusal to accept responsibility.

Disclosure. The act of telling something that was previously unknown to other people or secret.

Disclosure of shareholding. The act of making public the fact that someone owns shares in a company.

Discount. 1. The percentage by which the seller reduces the full price for the buyer. 2. The amount by which something is sold for less than its value.

Discountable. Which can be discounted.

Discount broker. A broker who charges a lower commission than other brokers.

Discounted cash flow. The calculation of the forecast return on capital investment by discounting future cash flows from the investment, usually at a rate equivalent to the company's minimum required rate of return. Abbr. DCF.

Note: Discounting is necessary because it is generally accepted that money held today is worth more than money to be received in the future. The effect of discounting is to reduce future income or expenses to their 'present value'. Once discounted, future cash flows can be compared directly with the initial cost of a capital investment which is already stated in present value terms. If the present value of income is greater than the present value of costs, the investment can be said to be worthwhile.

Discounted value. The difference between the face value of a share and its lower market price.

Discounter. A person or company that discounts bills or invoices, or sells goods at a discount.

Discount market. A market for borrowing and lending money, through Treasury bills, certificates of deposit, etc.

Discount points. Extra payments made to a lender to produce a reduction in the interest rate on a mortgage.

Discount price. The full price less a discount.

Discount rate. The percentage taken when a bank buys bills.

Discount store. A shop which specializes in cheap goods bought at a high discount.

Discrepancy. A situation where figures are not correct.

Discrete compounding. A system where interest is calculated at certain times, such as the end of a month or year, and then added to the principal.

Discretionary account. A client's account with a stockbroker, where the broker invests and sells at his own discretion without the client needing to give him specific instructions.

Discretionary client. A client whose funds are managed on a discretionary basis.

Discretionary funds. Funds managed on a discretionary basis.

Diseconomies of scale. A situation where increased production leads to a higher production cost per unit or average production cost.

Note: After having increased production using the existing workforce and machinery, giving economies of scale, the company finds that in order to increase production further it has to employ more workers and buy more machinery, leading to an increase in unit cost.

Disenfranchise. To take away someone's right to vote.

Disequilibrium. An imbalance in the economy when supply does not equal demand or a country's balance of payments is in deficit.

Dishonoured cheque. A cheque which the bank will not pay because there is not enough money in the account to pay it.

Disinflation. The process of reducing inflation in the economy by increasing tax and reducing the level of money supply.

Disinvest. 1. To reduce investment by not replacing capital assets when they wear out. 2. To reduce investment by selling shares.

Disinvestment. 1. A reduction in capital assets by not replacing them when they wear out. 2. A process of reducing investments by selling shares.

Disk. A round flat object, used to store information in computers.

Dismissal procedures. The correct way to dismiss someone, following the rules in the contract of employment.

Dispatch note. A note saying that goods have been sent.

Disposable personal income. The income left after tax and national insurance have been deducted (also called 'take-home' pay).

Disqualification. The act of making someone disqualified to do something.

Disqualify. To make a person unqualified to do something, such as to be a director of a company.

Dissolution. The ending (of a partnership).

Dissolve. To bring to an end.

Distress. The act of taking someone's goods to pay for debts.

Distressed companies. Companies which may go into liquidation, and whose shares are seen as a speculative buy.

Distress sale. A sale of goods at low prices to pay a company's debts.

Distress securities fund. A type of fund which invests in companies where there may be a major problems.

Distributable profits. Profits which can be distributed to shareholders as dividends if the directors decide to do so.

Distribute. 1. To share out dividends. 2. To send out goods from a manufacturer's warehouse to retail shops.

Distributed profits. Profits passed to shareholders in the form of dividends.

Distribution. The act of sending goods from the manufacturer to the wholesaler and then to retailers.

Distribution channel. The route by which a product or service reaches a customer after it leaves the producer or supplier.

Note: A distribution channel usually consists of a chain of intermediaries, for example wholesalers and retailers that is designed to move goods from the point of production to the point of consumption in the most efficient way.

Distribution network. A series of points or small warehouses from which goods are sent all over a country.

Distribution of income. Payment of dividends to shareholders.

Distributive trades. All businesses involved in the distribution of goods.

Distributor. A company which sells goods for another company which makes them.

Distributorship. The position of being a distributor for a company.

Diversification. The process of adding another quite different type of business to a firm's existing trade.

Diversify. 1. To add new types of business to existing ones. 2. To invest in different types of shares or savings so as to spread the risk of loss.

Divestiture. A sale of an asset.

Dividend. A percentage of profits paid to shareholders.

Note: The dividend is calculated as the proportion of profits a company can pay to its shareholders after tax has been paid, always keeping some of the profit back to reinvest in the company's products or activities. Large companies usually pay dividends twice a year, once after the half-year results have been declared (called the 'interim dividend') and gain when the final results are published.

Dividend cover. The ratio of profits to dividends paid to shareholders.

Dividend forecast. A forecast of the amount of an expected dividend.

Dividend payout. Money paid as dividends to shareholders.

Dividend per share. An amount of money paid as dividend for each share held.

Dividend yield. A dividend expressed as a percentage of the current market price of a share.

Divisional headquarters. The main office of a division of a company.

Dock dues. A payment which a ship makes to the harbour authorities for the right to use the harbour.

Document. A paper, especially an official paper, with written information on it.

Documentary. In the form of documents.

Documentary credit. A credit document used in export trade, when a bank issues a letter of credit against shipping documents.

Documentary proof. A proof in the form of a document.

Documentation. All the documents referring to something.

Document image processing. A system for scanning documents, such as cheques, and storing the information in a retrieval system.

Documents against acceptance. 1. An arrangement whereby buyers receive documents for the goods on their acceptance of a bill of exchange. 2. A note to a bank to instruct it that documents attached to a draft should be given to the drawee when the draft is accepted.

Dollar. A unit of currency used in the US and other countries, such as Australia, Bahamas, Barbados, Bermuda, Brunei, Canada, Fiji, Hong Kong, Jamaica, New Zealand, Singapore and Zimbabwe.

Domestic. To the home market or the market of the country where the business is situated.

Domestic consumption. Use in the home country.

Domestic demand deflator. A figure used to remove inflation from the calculations for domestic demand.

Domestic interest rates. Interest rates payable in a local currency on deposits placed in that country.

Domestic market. The market in the country where a company is based.

Domestic production. The production of goods for use in the home country.

Domestic sales. Sales in the home country.

Donor. A person who gives, especially someone who gives money.

Door-to-door salesman. A man who goes from one house to the next, asking people to buy something.

Double. Twice as large or two times the size.

Double-entry bookkeeping. A system of bookkeeping where both debit and credit entries are recorded in the accounts at the same time (e.g., when a sale is credited to the sales account the purchaser's debt is debited to the debtors account).

Double option. An option to buy or sell at a certain price in the future (a combination of call and put options).

Double taxation. The act of taxing the same income twice.

Down. Preposition in a lower position or to a lower position.

Downgrade. To reduce the forecast for a share.

Down market. A stock market which is falling or is at its lowest level.

Down payment. A part of a total payment made in advance.

Downside factor or Downside potential. The possibility of making a loss in an investment.

Downside risk. A risk that an investment will fall in value.

Downswing. A downward movement of share prices.

Downtick. A price of stock sold which is lower than the price of the previous sale.

Down time. 1. The time when a machine is not working or not available because it is broken or being mended. 2. Time when a worker cannot work because machines have broken down or because components are not available.

Down trend. Trend a falling trend in prices.

Downturn. The movement towards lower prices, sales or profits.

Draft. 1. An order for money to be paid by a bank. 2. A first rough plan or document which has not been finished.

Drafting. An act of preparing the draft of a document.

Drain. A gradual loss of money flowing away.

Draw. 1. To take money away. 2. To write a cheque.

Drawback. 1. Something which is not convenient or which is likely to cause problems. 2. A rebate on customs duty for imported goods when these are then used in producing exports.

Draw down. To draw money which is available under a credit agreement.

Drawee. The person or bank asked to make a payment by a drawer.

Drawer. The person who writes a cheque or a bill asking a drawee to pay money to a payee.

Drawing account. A current account, or any account from which the customer may take money when he or she wants.

Drift. Gradual movement without any control to move gradually in a particular direction.

Drop. A fall.

Drop ship. To deliver a large order direct to a customer.

Drop shipment. The delivery of a large order from the manufacturer direct to a customer's shop or warehouse without going through an agent or wholesaler.

Dual control. A system where two people have to sign a cheque, or validate a transaction, or have keys to a safe, etc.

Dual listing. The listing of a share on two stock exchanges.

Dual pricing. The fact of giving different prices to the same product depending on the market in which it is sold.

Due. 1. Owed. 2. Correct and appropriate in the situation.

Due diligence. 1. An examination of the accounts of a company before it is taken over to see if there are any problems which have not been disclosed. 2. The duty of an official such as a bank manager not to act in an irresponsible way.

Dues. Orders taken but not supplied until new stock arrives.

Dull market. A market where little business is done.

Dumping. The act of getting rid of excess goods cheaply in an overseas market.

Duplicate. A copy.

Duplication. The act of doing something that is already being done in the same way by somebody else, copying.

Dutiable goods. Goods on which a customs duty has to be paid.

Duty. 1. A tax which has to be paid. 2. Work which has to be done.

Duty-free. Sold with no duty to be paid.

Duty-free shop. A shop at an airport or on a ship where goods can be bought without paying duty.

Duty-paid goods. Goods where the duty has been paid.

E

E. & O.E. Abbr. Errors and omissions excepted.

Early. Before the usual time.

Early closing day. A weekday, usually Wednesday or Thursday, when some shops close in the afternoon.

Early withdrawal. The act of withdrawing money from a deposit account before the due date.

Early withdrawal penalty. A penalty which a depositor pays for withdrawing money early from an account.

Earmark. 1. To reserve for a special purpose. 2. To link a tax to a particular service, such as earmarking road taxes for the upkeep of roads.

Earn. 1. To be paid money for working. 2. To produce interest or dividends.

Earned income. Income from wages, salaries, pensions, fees, rental income, etc. (as opposed to 'unearned' income from investments).

Earnest. Money paid as an initial payment by a buyer to a seller, to show commitment to the contract of sale.

Earning capacity. The amount of money someone should be able to earn.

Earning potential. 1. The amount of money which someone should be able to earn. 2. The amount of dividend which a share is capable of earning.

Earning power. The amount of money someone should be able to earn.

Earnings. 1. Salary, wages, dividends or interest received. 2. Money which is earned in interest or dividend. 3. The profit made by a company.

Earnings cap. The upper limit on the amount of salary that can be taken into account when calculating pensions.

Earnings credit. An allowance which reduces bank charges on checking accounts.

Earnings drift. A situation where an increase in pay is greater than that of officially negotiated rates. Also called salary drift, wage drift.

Earnings growth. An increase in profit per share.

Earnings number. Profits expressed as a percentage.

Earnings performance. A way in which shares earn dividends.

Earnings per share. The money earned in dividends per share, shown as a percentage of the market price of one share. Abbr. EPS.

Earnings projection. A forecast of earnings per share.

Earnings-related contributions. Contributions to social security which rise as the worker's earnings rise.

Earnings-related pension. A pension which is linked to the size of a person's salary.

Earnings season. The time of year when major companies declare their results for the previous period.

Earnings yield. The money earned in dividends per share as a percentage of the current market price of the share.

Easy. 1. Not difficult. 2. To a market where few people are buying, so prices are lower than they were before.

Easy money. 1. Money which can be earned with no difficulty. 2. A loan available on easy repayment terms.

Easy money policy. A government policy of expanding the economy by making money more easily available (through lower interest rates and easy access to credit).

Easy terms. Financial terms which are not difficult to accept.

e-business. A general term that refers to any type of business activity on the Internet, including marketing, branding and research.

e-cash. Same as digital cash.

e-cheque. Same as electronic cheque.

e-commerce. A general term that is normally used to refer to the process of buying and selling goods over the Internet.

Econometrics. The study of the statistics of economics, using computers to analyze these statistics and make forecasts using mathematical models.

Economic. 1. Which provides enough money to make a profit. 2. To the financial state of a country.

Economical. Which saves money or materials or which is cheap.

Economic crisis Or Economic depression. A situation where a country is in financial collapse.

Economic cycle. A period during which trade expands, then slows down and then expands again.

Economic development. The expansion of the commercial and financial situation.

Economic forecaster. A person who says how he thinks a country's economy will perform in the future.

Economic growth. The rate at which a country's national income grows.

Economic indicator. Various statistics, e.g. for the unemployment rate or overseas trade, which show how the economy is going to perform in the short or long term.

Economic model. A computerized plan of a country's economic system, used for forecasting economic trends.

Economic planning. The process of planning the future financial state of the country for the government.

Economics. The study of the production, distribution, selling and use of goods and services plural the study of financial structures to show how a product or service is cost and what returns it produces.

Economic sanctions. Restrictions on trade with a country in order to influence its political situation or in order to make its government change its policy.

Economic slowdown. A general reduction in a country's economic activity.

Economic stagnation. A lack of expansion in the economy.

Economic value added. The difference between a company's profit and the cost of its capital. A company does not have simply to make a profit from its business-it has to make enough profit to cover the cost of its capital, including equity invested by shareholders. Abbr. EVA.

Economies of scale. A situation in which a product is made more profitable by manufacturing it in larger quantities so that each unit costs less to make.

Economist. A person who specializes in the study of economics.

Economy. 1. An action which is intended to stop money or materials from being wasted, or the quality of being careful not to waste money or materials. 2. The financial state of a country, or the way in which a country makes and uses its money.

Economy class. A lower-quality, less expensive way of travelling.

Economy drive. A vigorous effort to save money or materials.

Economy size. A large size or large packet which is cheaper than normal.

ECU. Abbr. European Currency Unit.

EDI. Abbr. Electronic Data Interchange.

EDP. Abbr. Electronic Data Processing.

EEA. Abbr. European Economic Area.

Effect. 1. A result. 2. Operation.

Effective control. A situation where someone owns a large number of shares in a company, but less than 50%, and so in effect controls the company because no other single shareholder can outvote him or her.

Effective date. The date on which a rule or contract starts to be applied, or on which a transaction takes place.

Effective demand. The actual demand for a product which can be paid for.

Effective exchange rate. A rate of exchange for a currency calculated against a basket of currencies.

Effectiveness. The quality of working successfully or producing results.

Effective price. A share price which has been adjusted to allow for a rights issue.

Effective rate. A real interest rate on a loan or deposit. (i.e. the APR)

Effective yield. An actual yield shown as a percentage of the price paid after adjustments have been made.

Efficiency. The ability to work well or to produce the right result or the right work quickly.

Efficient. Able to work well or to produce the right result quickly.

Efficient-market theory. A theory that the prices operating in a certain market reflect all known information about the market and therefore make it impossible for abnormal profits to be made.

EFT. Abbr. Electronic Funds Transfer.

EFTA. Abbr. European Free Trade Association.

EFTPOS. Abbr. Electronic funds transfer at a point of sale.

EGM. Abbr. Extraordinary General Meeting.

EIS. Abbr. Enterprise Investment Scheme.

Elastic. Which can expand or contract easily because of small changes in price.

Elasticity. The ability to change easily in response to a change in circumstances.

Elasticity of supply and demand. Changes in supply and demand of an item depending on its market price.

Elect. To choose someone by a vote.

Election. The act of electing someone.

Electronic. To computers and electronics.

Electronic banking. The use of computers to carry out banking transactions, such as withdrawals through cash dispensers or transfer of funds at point of sale.

Electronic business. Same as e-business.

Electronic cash. Same as digital cash.

Electronic cheque. An electronic cheque, which a person writes and sends via a computer and the Internet.

Electronic commerce. Same as e-commerce.

Electronic data interchange. A standard format used when business documents such as invoices and purchase orders are exchanged over electronic networks such as the Internet. Abbr. EDI.

Electronic funds transfer. A system for transferring money from one account to another electronically (as when using a smart card). Abbr. EFT.

Electronic purse. Same as digital wallet.

Element. A basic part or the smallest unit into which something can be divided.

Eligibility. The fact of being eligible.

Eligibility date. The date at which someone becomes eligible for benefits.

Eligible liabilities. Liabilities which go into the calculation of a bank's reserves.

Eliminate. To remove.

e-mail. 1. a system of sending messages from one computer terminal to another, using a modem and telephone lines. 2. A message sent electronically.

Embargo. A government order which stops a type of trade, such as exports to or other commercial activity with another country.

Embezzle. To use illegally money which is not yours, or which you are looking after for someone.

Emergency. A dangerous situation where decisions have to be taken quickly.

Emerging growth fund. Growth fund that invests in emerging markets.

e-money. Same as digital money.

Note: This normally refers to either credit card payments or virtual tokens or a virtual credit card or a micro payment.

Employed. 1. In regular paid work. 2. To money used profitably plural people who are working.

Employee. A person employed by another.

Employee buyout. A purchase of a company by its employees.

Employee share scheme. A plan which allows employees to obtain shares in the company for which they work (though tax may be payable if the shares are sold to employees at a price which is lower than the current market price). Abbr. ESOP.

Employer. A person or company that has regular workers and pays them.

Employer's contribution. Money paid by an employer towards an employee's pension.

Employers' liability insurance. Insurance to cover accidents which may happen at work, and for which the company may be responsible.

Employment tribunal. A government body responsible for dealing with disputes between employees and employers.

Empower. To give someone the power to do something.

Encashment. An act of exchanging for cash.

Encryption. A conversion of plain text to a secure coded form by means of a cipher system.

Encumbrance. A liability, such as a mortgage or charge, which is attached usually to a property or land.

End. The final point or last part.

Endorsee. A person whose name is written on a bill or cheque as having the right to cash it.

Endorsement. 1. The act of endorsing. 2. A signature on a document which endorses it. 3. A note on an insurance policy which adds conditions to the policy.

Endowment. The act of giving money to provide a regular income.

Endowment assurance Or Endowment insurance. An insurance policy where a sum of money is paid to the insured person on a certain date or to his heirs if he dies before that date.

Endowment mortgage. A mortgage backed by an endowment policy.

Note: The borrower pays interest on the mortgage in the usual way, but does not repay the capital. Instead, he or she takes out an endowment assurance (a life insurance) policy, which is intended to cover the total capital sum borrowed. When the assurance matures, the capital is in theory paid off, though this depends on the performance of the investments made by the company providing the endowment assurance and the actual yield of the policy may be less or more than the sum required. A mortgage where the borrower repays both interest and capital is called a 'repayment mortgage'.

End product. A manufactured product resulting from a production process.

End user. A person who actually uses a product.

Energy shares. Shares in companies which provide energy.

Enforcement. The act of making sure that something is obeyed.

Engagement. An agreement to do something.

Entail. A legal condition which passes ownership of a property only to certain persons.

Enter into. To begin.

Enterprise. 1. A system of carrying on a business. 2. A business.

Enterprise zone. An area of the country where businesses are encouraged to develop by offering special conditions such as easy planning permission for buildings or a reduction in the business rate.

Entertain. To offer such things as meals, hotel accommodation and theatre tickets for the comfort and enjoyment of business visitors.

Entertainment. The practice of offering meals or other recreation to business visitors.

Entertainment allowance. Money which managers are allowed by their company to spend on meals with visitors.

Entertainment expenses. Money spent on giving meals to business visitors.

Entitle. To give the right to someone to have something.

Entitlement. A person's right to something.

Entrepreneur. A person who directs a company and takes commercial risks.

Entry. 1. An item of written information put in an accounts ledger. 2. An act of going in or the place where you can go in.

Entry charge. Money which you have to pay before you go in.

EPS. Abbr. Earnings per share.

Equilibrium. The state of balance in the economy where supply equals demand or a country's balance of payments is neither in deficit nor in excess.

Equities. Ordinary shares.

Equity. 1. The ordinary shares in a company. 2. The value of a company which is the property of its shareholders (the company's assets less its liabilities, not including the ordinary share capital). 3. The value of an asset, such as a house, less any mortgage on it.

Note: 'Equity' (also called 'capital' or 'shareholders' equity' or 'shareholders' capital' or 'shareholders' funds') is the current net value of the company including the nominal value of the shares in issue. After several years a company would expect to increase its net worth above the value of the starting capital. 'Equity capital' on the other hand is only the nominal value of the shares in issue.

Equity accounting. A method of accounting which puts part of the profits of a subsidiary into the parent company's books.

Equity capital. The nominal value of the shares owned by the ordinary shareholders of a company.

Note: Preference shares are not equity capital. If the company were wound up, none of the equity capital would be distributed to preference shareholders.

Equity earnings. Profits after tax, which are available for distribution to shareholders in the form of dividends, or which can be retained in the company for future development.

Equity finance. Finance for a company in the form of ordinary shares paid for by shareholders.

Equity fund. A fund which is invested in equities, not in government securities or other funds.

Equity gearing. The ratio between a company's borrowings at interest and its ordinary share capital.

Equity growth fund. A fund invested in equities, aiming to provide capital growth.

Equity release. The act of remortgaging a property on which there is currently no mortgage, in order to use it as security for new borrowing.

Equity risk premium. An extra return on equities over the return on bonds, because of the risk involved in investing in equities.

Equivalence. The condition of having the same value or of being the same.

ERM. Abbr. Exchange rate mechanism.

Error rate. The number of mistakes per thousand entries or per page.

Errors and omissions excepted. Words written on an invoice to show that the company has no responsibility for mistakes in the invoice. Abbr. E. & O.E.

Escalation. A steady increase.

Escalator clause. A clause in a contract allowing for regular price increases because of increased costs, or regular wage increases because of the increased cost of living.

Escape clause. A clause in a contract which allows one of the parties to avoid carrying out the terms of the contract under certain conditions.

Escrow. An agreement between two parties that something should be held by a third party until certain conditions are fulfilled.

ESOP. Abbr. Employee share ownership plan and Employee Stock Option Plan.

Establish. To set up or to open.

Establishment. 1. A commercial business. 2. The number of people working in a company.

Establishment charges. The cost of people and property in a company's accounts.

Estimate. 1. A calculation of the probable cost, size or time of something. 2. A calculation by a contractor or seller of a service of how much something is likely to cost, given to a client in advance of an order.

Estimated. Calculated approximately.

Ethical. Morally right.

Ethical criteria. Standards used to judge if something is morally right or not.

Ethical fund. A fund which invests in companies which follow certain moral standards, e.g. companies which do not manufacture weapons, or which do not trade with certain countries or which only use environmentally acceptable sources of raw materials.

Ethical index. An index of shares in companies which follow certain moral standards.

Ethical investment. An investment in companies which follow certain moral standards.

Ethical screening. Checking companies against certain moral standards, and removing those which do not conform.

Euro. A unit of currency adopted as legal tender in several European countries from January 1st, 1999.

Note: The countries which are joined together in the European Monetary Union and adopted the euro as their common currency in 1999 are: Austria, Belgium, Finland, France, Germany, Ireland, Italy, Luxembourg, the Netherlands, Portugal, and Spain. The conversion of these currencies to the euro was fixed on 1st January 1999.

Eurocurrency. Any currency used for trade within Europe but outside its country of origin, the euro-dollar being the most important.

Evaluate. To calculate a value for something.

Evaluation. The calculation of value.

Ex-all. To a share price where the share is sold without the dividend, rights issue, or any other current issue. Abbr. xa.

Exceed. To be more than.

Except. Preposition, conjunction not including.

Exceptional. Different or not usual.

Exceptional items. 1. Items which arise from normal trading but which are unusual because of their size or nature; such items are shown separately in a note to the company's accounts but not on the face of the P & L account unless they are profits or losses on the sale or termination of an operation, or costs of a fundamental reorganization or restructuring which have a material effect on the nature and focus of the reporting entity's operations, or profits or losses on the disposal of fixed assets. 2. Items in a balance sheet which do not appear there each year and which are included in the accounts before the pre-tax profit is calculated (as opposed to extraordinary items, which are calculated after the pre-tax profit).

Excess. (an amount) which is more than what is allowed.

Excess capacity. Spare capacity which is not being used.

Excessive. Too large.

Excess profit. Profit which is higher than what is thought to be normal.

Exchange. 1. The act of giving one thing for another. 2. A market for shares, commodities, futures, etc. 3. To change money of one country for money of another.

Exchange control. The control by a government of the way in which its currency may be exchanged for foreign currencies.

Exchange controls. Government restrictions on changing the local currency into foreign currency.

Exchange dealer. A person who buys and sells foreign currency.

Exchange dealings. The buying and selling of foreign currency.

Exchange of contracts. The point in the sale of property when the buyer and the seller both sign the contract of sale, which then becomes binding.

Exchange premium. An extra cost above the normal rate for buying a foreign currency.

Exchange rate. 1. A rate at which one currency is exchanged for another. Also called rate of exchange. 2. A figure that expresses how much a unit of one country's currency is worth in terms of the currency of another country.

Exchange rate mechanism. A method of stabilizing exchange rates within the European Monetary System, where currencies could only move up or down within a narrow band (usually 2.25% either way, but for certain currencies widened to 6%) without involving a realignment of all the currencies in the system. Abbr. ERM.

Excise duty. A tax on goods such as alcohol and petrol which are produced in the country.

Exclude. To keep out, or not to include.

Exclusion. 1. The act of not including something. 2. An item reported on the tax return but on which no tax is payable.

Exclusion clause. A clause in an insurance policy or warranty which says which items or events are not covered.

Exclusive. 1. Limited to one person or group. 2. Not including.

Execution. 1. The carrying out of a commercial order or contract. 2. The carrying out of a legal order or contract.

Executive. Which puts decisions into action a person in a business who takes decisions, a manager or director.

Executive committee. A committee which runs a society or a club.

Executive director. A director who works full-time in the company (as opposed to a 'non-executive director').

Exempt. Not forced to do something, especially not forced to obey a particular law or rule, or not forced to pay something.

Exemption. The act of exempting something from a contract or from a tax.

Exercise. 1. A use of something. 2. A financial year.

Exercise date. A date when an option can be put into effect.

Exercise price. A price at which an option will be put into effect.

Expand. To get bigger, or make something bigger.

Expansion. An increase in size.

Expense. Money spent.

Expense account. An allowance of money which a business pays for an employee to spend on travelling and entertaining clients in connection with that business.

Expiration. The act of coming to an end.

Expiry date. 1. A date when something will end. 2. The last date on which a credit card can be used.

Export. The practice or business of sending goods to foreign countries to be sold.

Export duty. A tax paid on goods sent out of a country for sale.

Export licence. A government permit allowing something to be exported.

Exposure. The amount of risk which a lender or investor runs.

Note: Exposure can be the amount of money lent to a customer (a bank's exposure to a foreign country) or the amount of money which an investor may lose if his investments collapse (his or her exposure in the stock market).

Express money transfer. A foreign currency payment to an individual or organization delivered electronically to a bank.

Extend. 1. To offer something. 2. To make something longer.

Extended credit. 1. Credit allowing the borrower a very long time to pay. 2. An extra long credit used by commercial banks borrowing from the Bank of India.

Extension. A longer time allowed for something than was originally agreed.

External. 1. Outside a country 2. Outside a company.

External audit. 1. An audit carried out by an independent auditor (who is not employed by the company). 2. An evaluation of the effectiveness of a company's public relations carried out by an outside agency.

External auditor. An independent person who audits the company's accounts.

External debt. Money which a company has borrowed from outside sources (such as a bank) as opposed to money raised from shareholders.

External growth. Growth by buying other companies, rather than by expanding existing sales or products.

External trade. Trade with foreign countries.

Extraordinary General Meeting. A special meeting of shareholders to discuss an important matter (such as a change in the company's articles of association) which cannot wait until the next AGM. Abbr. EGM.

Extraordinary items. Formerly, large items of income or expenditure which did not arise from normal trading and which did not occur every year (they were shown separately in the P&L account, after taxation).

F

Face value. The value written on a coin, banknote or share certificate.

Facility. 1. Something that allows something to be done something easily. 2. The total amount of credit which a lender will allow a borrower.

Facility fee. A charge made to a borrower by a bank for arranging credit facilities.

Factor. 1. Something which is important, or which is taken into account when making a decision. 2. A person or company which is responsible for collecting debts for companies, by buying debts at a discount on their face value. 3. A person who sells for a business or another person and earns a commission.

Note: A factor collects a company's debts when due, and pays the creditor in advance part of the sum to be collected, so 'buying' the debt.

Factor in. To add a factor when making calculations.

Factoring. The business of buying debts from a firm at a discount and then getting the debtors to pay.

Factoring charges. The cost of selling debts to a factor for a commission.

Factors of production. The three things needed to produce a product (land, labour and capital).

Factory gate price. The actual cost of manufacturing goods before any mark-up is added to give profit.

Note: The factory gate price includes direct costs such as labour, raw materials and energy, and indirect costs such as interest on loans, plant maintenance or rent.

Factory price. A price not including transport from the maker's factory.

Fail. 1. Not to do something which you were trying to do. 2. To be unsuccessful.

Failure. Not doing something which you promised to do.

Fair copy. A document which is written or typed with no changes or mistakes.

Fair deal. An arrangement where both parties are treated equally.

Fair dealing. The legal buying and selling of shares.

Fair price. A good price for both buyer and seller.

Fair trade. An international business system where countries agree not to charge import duties on some items imported from their trading partners.

Fair trading. 1. A way of doing business which is reasonable and does not harm the consumer. 2. A legal trade in shares or the legal buying and selling of shares.

Fair value. A price paid by a buyer who knows the value of what he is buying to a seller who also knows the value of what he is selling (i.e. neither is cheating the other).

Fair wear and tear. Acceptable damage caused by normal use.

Fall. 1. A sudden reduction or loss of value. 2. To happen or to take place.

Fall away. To become less.

Fall back. To become lower or cheaper after rising in price.

Fall back on. To have to use something kept for emergencies.

Fall behind. To be late in doing something.

Fallen angel. A share that was once in favour, but whose attraction has slipped and whose share price is on the way down.

Falling. Which is becoming smaller or dropping in price.

Fall off. To become lower, cheaper or less.

Fallout. A bad result or collapse.

False. Not true or not correct.

False market. A market in shares caused by persons or companies conspiring to buy or sell and so influence the share price to their advantage.

False pretences. Doing or saying something to cheat someone.

Falsification. The act of making false entries in accounts.

Falsify. To change something to make it wrong.

FAQ. An item on a menu which gives answers to questions which people often ask about the website, service or product. Full form frequently asked question.

Favourable. Which gives an advantage

Favourable balance of trade Or Favourable trade balance. A situation where a country's exports are larger than its imports.

Fax. A system for sending the exact copy of a document via telephone lines.

Note: Banks will not accept fax messages as binding instructions (as for example, a faxed order for money to be transferred from one account to another).

FD. Abbr. Financial director.

FDI. Abbr. Foreign direct investment.

Feasibility report. A document which says if it is worth undertaking something.

Federal Reserve Bank. Any one of the twelve regional banks in the USA which are owned by the state and directed by the Federal Reserve Board. Abbr. FRB.

Federal Reserve Board. A government organization which runs the central banks in the US. Abbr. FRB.

Federation. A group of societies, companies or organizations which have a central organization which represents them and looks after their common interests.

Fee. 1. Money paid for work carried out by a professional person (such as an accountant, a doctor or a lawyer). 2. Money paid for something.

Few. 1. Not many. 2. Some.

Fiat money. Coins or notes which are not worth much as paper or metal, but are said by the government to have a value and are recognized as legal tender.

Fictitious assets. Assets which do not really exist, but are entered as assets to balance the accounts.

Fiduciary. (a person) in a position of trust.

Fiduciary deposits. Bank deposits which are managed for the depositor by the bank.

FIFO. Abbr. First in first out.

Figure. 1. A number, or a cost written in numbers. 2. To calculate something.

File. 1. A cardboard holder for documents, which can fit in the drawer of a filing cabinet. 2. Documents kept for reference. 3. A section of data on a computer (such as payroll, address list or customer accounts).

File copy. A copy of a document which is kept for reference in an office.

Filing system. A way of putting documents in order for easy reference.

Fill. To carry out a client's instructions to buy or sell.

Final. Last, coming at the end of a period.

Final date for payment. Last date by which payment should be made.

Final demand. The last reminder from a supplier, after which they will sue for payment.

Final discharge. The last payment of what is left of a debt.

Final dividend. A dividend paid at the end of a year's trading, which has to be approved by the shareholders at an AGM.

Finalize. To agree final details.

Final product. A manufactured product, made at the end of a production process.

Finance. 1. Money used by a company, provided by the shareholders or by loans. 2. Money (used by a club, local authority, etc.).

Finance charge. 1. The cost of borrowing money. 2. An additional charge made to a customer who asks for extended credit.

Finance company Or Finance corporation. A company, usually part of a commercial bank, which provides money for hire-purchase.

Finance house deposits. Amounts of money deposited by banks with finance houses and used by them to provide hire-purchase loans to clients.

Finance market. A place where large sums of money can be lent or borrowed.

Finance Ministry. A government department dealing with a country's finance.

Financial. Concerning money.

Financial adviser. A person or company which gives advice on financial problems for a fee.

Financial assistance. Help in the form of money.

Financial centre. A town or part of a town where the main banks and financial institutions are located.

Financial correspondent. A journalist who writes articles on money matters for a newspaper.

Financial futures Or financial futures contract. A contract for the purchase of gilt-edged securities for delivery at a date in the future.

Financial futures market. The market in gilt-edged securities for delivery at a date in the future.

Financial institution. A bank, investment trust or insurance company whose work involves lending or investing large sums of money.

Financial instrument. 1. A document showing that money has been lent or borrowed, invested or passed from one account to another (such as a bill of exchange, share certificate, certificate of deposit or an IOU). 2. Any form of investment in the stock market or in other financial markets, such as shares, government stocks, certificates of deposit or bills of exchange.

Financial intermediary. An institution which takes deposits or loans from individuals and lends money to clients.

Financial position. The state of a person's or company's bank balance in terms of assets and debts.

Financial report. A document which gives the financial position of a company or of a club, etc.

Financial resources. The supply of money for something.

Financial review. An examination of an organization's finances.

Financial risk. The possibility of losing money.

Financial Services Authority. A government agency set up to regulate all financial services, such as banks, stockbrokers, unit trusts, pension companies, professional bodies, stock exchanges, etc., including the ombudsmen for these services. Abbr. FSA.

Financial statement. A document which shows the financial situation of a company.

Financial supermarket. A company which offers a range of financial services (e.g. a bank offering loans, mortgages, pensions and insurance as well as the normal personal banking services).

Financial year. The twelve month period for a firm's accounts (not necessarily the same as a calendar year).

Financier. A person who lends large amounts of money to companies or who buys shares in companies as an investment.

Financing. The act of providing money for a project.

Finder's fee. 1. A fee paid to a person who finds a client for another (e.g., someone who introduces a client to a stock broking firm). 2. A fee paid to a person who arranges a loan for someone, finds a property for someone to buy, etc.

Fine. Money paid because of something wrong which has been done.

Fine-tune. To make small adjustments to a plan or the economy so that it works better.

Fine-tuning. The act of making of small adjustments in areas such as interest rates, tax bands or the money supply, to improve a nation's economy.

Finish. An end of a day's trading on the Stock Exchange.

Finished goods. Manufactured goods which are ready to be sold.

Fire insurance. Insurance against damage by fire.

Fire sale. 1. A sale of fire-damaged goods. 2. A sale of anything at a very low price.

Firm. 1. A company, business or partnership. 2. Which cannot be changed. 3. Not dropping

Note: Strictly speaking, a 'firm' is a partnership or other trading organization, which is not a limited company. In practice, it is better to use the term for unincorporated businesses such as 'a firm of accountants' or 'a firm of stockbrokers'.

Firmness. The fact of being steady at a certain price, or likely to rise.

Firm order. 1. A confirmed order, which the purchaser cannot withdraw. 2. An order to a broker to sell or buy on a certain date.

Firm price. A price which will not change.

Firm sale. A sale which does not allow the purchaser to return the goods.

Firm up. To agree on the final details of something.

First in first out. 1. A redundancy policy, where the people who have been working longest are the first to be made redundant. 2. An accounting policy where it is assumed that stocks in hand were purchased last, and that stocks sold during the period were purchased first. Abbr. FIFO.

First option. Allowing someone to be the first to have the possibility of deciding something.

First quarter. The period of three months from January to the end of March.

Fiscal. Referring to tax or to government revenues.

Fiscal drag. 1. The effect of inflation on a government's tax revenues. As inflation increases so do prices and wages, and tax revenues rise proportionately; even if inflation is low, increased earnings will give the government increased revenues anyway. 2. The negative effect of higher personal taxation on an individual's work performance.

Fiscal measures. Tax changes made by a government to improve the working of the economy.

Fiscal policy. The policy of a government regarding taxation and revenues.

Fiscal year. A twelve-month period on which taxes are calculated.

Five-Year Plan. Proposals for running a country's economy over a five-year period.

Fixation. The act of stating a price on an options market.

Fixed. Unable to be changed or removed.

Fixed assets. Property or machinery which a company owns and uses, but which the company does not buy or sell as part of its regular trade, including the company's investments in shares of other companies.

Fixed capital. Capital in the form of buildings and machinery.

Fixed costs. Business costs which do not change with the quantity of the product made.

Fixed deposit. A deposit which pays a stated interest over a set period.

Fixed exchange rate. A rate of exchange of one currency against another which cannot fluctuate, and can only be changed by devaluation or revaluation.

Fixed expenses. Expenses which do not vary with different levels of production, e.g. rent, secretaries' salaries and insurance.

Fixed income. Income which does not change from year to year (as from an annuity).

Fixed-income derivatives. Derivatives which pay a fixed interest at stated dates in the future.

Fixed-interest. Which has an interest rate which does not vary.

Fixed-interest investments. Investments producing an interest which does not change.

Fixed-interest securities. Securities (such as government bonds) which produce an interest which does not change.

Fixed-price. Which has a price which cannot be changed.

Fixed-price agreement. An agreement where a company provides a service or a product at a price which stays the same for the whole period of the agreement.

Fixed-price offer for sale. An offer to purchase shares in a new company for a price which has been fixed at flotation (as opposed to tendering).

Fixed rate. A rate, e.g. an exchange rate, which does not change.

Fixed rate loan. A loan on which the rate of interest stays the same for the duration of the loan.

Fixed scale of charges. A rate of charging which does not change.

Fixed-term. Lasting for a fixed number of years.

Fixed-term product. A financial product, such as a bond, which runs for a fixed number of years.

Fixed yield. A percentage return which does not change.

Fixing. 1. Arranging. 2. A regular meeting to set a price.

Flag. A term used by chartists to refer to a period when prices consolidate a previous advance or fall.

Flat. 1. Referring to market prices which do not fall or rise, because of low demand. 2. Not changing in response to different conditions a set of rooms for one family in a building with other sets of similar rooms.

Flat rate. A charge which always stays the same.

Flat yield. An interest rate as a percentage of the price paid for fixed-interest stock.

Flexibility. The ability to be easily changed.

Flexible. Which can be altered or changed.

Flexible mortgage. A mortgage that gives the borrower the freedom to change the amount and frequency of his or her mortgage payments.

Flexible working hours Or flexible work. A system where employees can start or stop work at different hours of the morning or evening provided that they work a certain number of hours per day or week.

Flight to quality. A tendency of investors to buy safe blue-chip securities when the economic outlook is uncertain.

Flip side. The negative factors (in a proposal).

Float. 1. Cash taken from a central supply and used for running expenses. 2. The process of starting a new company by selling shares in it on the Stock Exchange. 3. The process of allowing a currency to settle at its own exchange rate, without any government intervention.

Floating. The act of starting a new company by selling shares in it on the stock exchange.

Floating charge. A charge linked to any of the company's assets of a certain type, but not to any specific item.

Floating rate. 1. Same as variable rate. 2. An exchange rate for a currency which can vary according to market demand, and is not fixed by the government.

Floor. 1. The part of the room which you walk on. 2. A bottom level of something (such as the lowest exchange rate which a government will accept for its currency or the lower limit imposed on an interest rate).

Floor broker. A stockbroker who is a member of a brokerage house.

Floor limit. A highest sale through a credit card that a retailer can accept without having to get authorization from the bank that issued the card.

Floor price. A lowest price, a price which cannot go any lower.

Floor trader. An independent trader on a stock exchange, who buys and sells on his or her own account.

Flop. A failure, or something which has not been successful.

Flotation. The act of starting a new company by selling shares in it.

Flow. 1. A movement. 2. Cash income is not coming in fast enough to pay for the expenditure going out.

Flow chart Or Flow diagram. A chart which shows the arrangement of work processes in a series.

Fluctuate. To move up and down.

Folio. A page with a number, especially two facing pages in an account book which have the same number to put a number on a page.

Forbes 500. A list of the largest US corporations, published each year in Forbes magazine.

Forbid. To tell someone not to do something, or to say that something must not be done.

Force. 1. Strength. 2. A group of people to make someone do something.

Force down. To make something such as prices become lower.

Forced sale. A sale which takes place because a court orders it or because it is the only way to avoid a financial crisis.

Force up. To make something become higher.

Forecast. A description or calculation of what will probably happen in the future.

Forecast dividend. A dividend which a company expects to pay at the end of the current year. Also called prospective dividend.

Forecasting. The process of calculating what will probably happen in the future.

Foreclose. To acquire a property because the owner cannot repay money which he or she has borrowed (using the property as security).

Foreign banks. Banks from other countries which have branches in a country.

Foreign currency. Money of another country.

Foreign currency reserves. A country's reserves held in currencies of other countries. Also called foreign exchange reserves, international reserves.

Foreign direct investment. An investment in a developing country by foreign companies or governments. Abbr. FDI.

Foreign exchange. 1. The business of exchanging the money of one country for that of another. 2. Foreign currencies.

Foreign exchange broker Or Foreign exchange dealer. A person who deals on the foreign exchange market.

Foreign exchange dealing. The business of buying and selling foreign currencies.

Foreign exchange desk. A section of a bank which deals with foreign exchange transactions.

Foreign exchange market. 1. A market where people buy and sell foreign currencies. 2. Dealings in foreign currencies.

Foreign exchange reserves. Foreign money held by a government to support its own currency and pay its debts.

Foreign exchange transaction. A purchase or sale of foreign currency.

Foreign exchange transfer. The sending of money from one country to another.

Foreign investments. Money invested in other countries.

Forex. Same as foreign exchange.

Form. 1. Words correctly laid out for a legal document 2. An official printed paper with blank spaces which have to be filled in with information.

Formal documents. Documents giving full details of a takeover bid.

Formality. Something which has to be done to obey the law.

Form letter. A letter which can be sent without any change to several correspondents (such as a letter chasing payment).

Formula investing. A method of investing according to a set plan.

Forward. In advance or to be paid at a later date.

Forward buying. The act of buying shares, currency or commodities at today's price for delivery at a later date.

Forward contract. A one-off agreement to buy foreign currency or shares or commodities for delivery at a later date at a specific price.

Forward cover. An arrangement to cover the risks on a forward contract.

Forward dealing. The activity of buying or selling commodities forward.

Forward delivery. A delivery at some date in the future which has been agreed between the buyer and seller.

Forwarding. The act of arranging shipping and customs documents.

Forward integration. A process of expansion in which a company becomes its own distributor or takes over a company in the same line of business as itself.

Forward margin. The difference between the current (or spot) price and the forward price.

Forward market. A market for purchasing foreign currency, oil or commodities for delivery at a later date.

Forward sales. The sales of shares, commodities or foreign exchange for delivery at a later date.

Forward trading. The activity of buying or selling commodities forward.

Founder. A person who starts a company.

Fourth quarter. A period of three months from 1st October to the end of the year.

Fraction. A very small amount.

Fractional certificate. A certificate for part of a share.

Fractional reserve. A reserve held by a bank which is a small proportion of its total deposits.

Fragile. Which can be easily broken.

Fragility. The fact of being weak or likely to collapse.

Franchise. A licence to trade using a brand name and paying a royalty for it.

Franchising. The act of selling a licence to trade as a franchise.

Franchising operation. An operation involving selling licences to trade as a franchise.

Fraud. An act of making money by making people believe something which is not true.

Free. 1. Not costing any money. 2. With no restrictions.

Free capital. An amount of a company's capital in shares which are available for trading on a stock exchange.

Free collective bargaining. Negotiations between management and trade unions about wage increases and working conditions.

Free competition. The fact of being free to compete without government interference.

Free market. A market in which there is no government control of supply and demand, and the rights of individuals and organizations to physical and intellectual property are upheld.

Free market economy. A system where the government does not interfere in business activity in any way.

Free on board. Including in the price all the seller's costs until the goods are on the ship for transportation. Abbreviation f.o.b.

Free online sessions. The number of times a customer can access his online bank account without paying a charge.

Free period. The period of grace allowed to credit card holders before payment for credit card purchases is demanded.

Free port. A port where there are no customs duties to be paid.

Free reserves. The part of a bank's reserves which are above the statutory level and so can be used for various purposes as the bank wishes.

Free sample. A sample given free to advertise a product.

Free trade. A system where goods can go from one country to another without any restrictions.

Free trial. An opportunity to test a machine or product with no payment involved.

Freight. The cost of transporting goods by air, sea or land.

Freight charges. Money charged for transporting goods.

Freight forwarder. A person or company that arranges shipping and customs documents for several shipments from different companies, putting them together to form one large shipment.

Fringe benefit. An extra item given by a company to workers in addition to a salary, e.g. company cars or private health insurance.

FRN. Abbr. Floating rate note.

Front. A business or person used to hide an illegal trade.

Front-end. Referring to the start of an investment or insurance.

Front-end fee. An initial loading of the management charges into the first premium paid for an insurance.

Front-end loaded. Referring to an insurance or investment scheme where most of the management charges are incurred in the first year of the investment or insurance, and are not spread out over the whole period.

Front office. The front-line staff and support staff in a financial institution.

Frozen. Not allowed to be changed or used.

Frozen account. A bank account where the money cannot be moved or used because of a court order.

Frozen assets. A company's assets which by law cannot be sold because someone has a claim against them.

Frozen credits. Credits in an account which cannot be moved.

Fulfill. To complete something in a satisfactory way.

Full. 1. Complete, including everything. 2. Completely.

Full costs. All the costs of manufacturing a product, including both fixed and variable costs.

Full cover. Insurance cover against all risks.

Full employment. A situation where all the people who can work have jobs.

Full price. A price with no discount.

Full rate. The full charge, with no reductions.

Full-scale. Complete or very thorough.

Full-service banking. Banking that offers a whole range of services (including mortgages, loans, pensions, etc.)

Full-service broker. A broker who manages portfolios for clients, and gives advice on shares and financial questions in general (as opposed to an execution-only broker or discount broker).

Fully diluted earnings per share Or Fully

diluted EPS. Earnings per share calculated over the whole number of shares assuming that convertible shares have been converted to ordinary shares.

Fully diluted shares. Total number of shares which includes convertible shares, stock options, etc.

Fully-paid shares. Shares for which the full face value has been paid.

Fully paid-up capital. All money paid for the issued capital shares.

Function key. A key switch that has been assigned a particular task or sequence of instructions.

Fund. 1. Money set aside for a special purpose. 2. Money invested in an investment trust as part of a unit trust, or given to a financial adviser to invest on behalf of a client.

Fundamental. Basic or most important.

Fundamental issues. Matters relating to a company's profits or assets.

Fundamental research Or fundamental analysis. An examination of the basic factors which affect a market.

Fundamentals. The basic realities of a stock market or of a company (such as its assets, profitability and dividends).

Funding. 1. Money for spending. 2. The act of changing a short-term debt into a long-term loan.

Fund management. The business of dealing with the investment of sums of money on behalf of clients.

Fund manager. 1. A person who invests money on behalf of clients. 2. A person who manages the investments made by a fund in such a way as to fulfill the fund's stated objectives.

Funds. 1. Money which is available for spending. 2. Government stocks and securities.

Funny money. Strange types of shares or bonds offered by companies or their brokers, which are not the usual forms of loan stock.

Future. To time to come or to something which has not yet happened.

Futures. Shares, currency or commodities that are bought or sold for now for delivery at a later date.

Futures contract. A contract for the purchase of commodities for delivery at a date in the future.

Note: A futures contract is a contract to purchase; if investors are bullish, they will buy a contract, but if they feel the market will go down, they will sell one.

Futures exchange. A commodity market which only deals in futures.

G

GAAP. Abbr. Generally Accepted Accounting Principles.

GAB. Abbr. General Arrangements to Borrow

Gain. 1. An increase, or the act of becoming larger. 2. An increase in profit, price or value.

Galloping inflation. Very rapid inflation which is almost impossible to reduce.

Gamma shares Or Gamma securities. Shares of companies which are not frequently traded on the London Stock Exchange, but which are listed.

Gap in the market. An opportunity to make a product or provide a service which is needed but which no one has sold before.

Gap financing. Arranging extra loans (such as a bridging loan) to cover a purchase not covered by an existing loan.

Garnishee. A person who owes money to a creditor and is ordered by a court to pay that money to a creditor of the creditor, and not to the creditor himself.

Garnishee order. A court order, making a garnishee pay money not to the debtor, but to a third party.

GATT. Abbr. General Agreement on Tariffs and Trade.

GDP. Abbr. Gross domestic product.

Gearing. The act of borrowing money at fixed interest which is then used to produce more money than the interest paid.

Note: High gearing (when a company is said to be 'highly geared') indicates that the level of borrowings is high when compared to its ordinary share capital. A lowly-geared company has borrowings which are relatively low. High gearing has the effect of increasing a company's profitability when the company's trading is expanding. If the trading pattern slows down, then the high interest charges associated with gearing will increase the rate of slowdown.

GEB. Abbr. Guaranteed Equity Bond.

General. 1. Ordinary or not special. 2. Dealing with everything or with everybody.

General Agreement on Tariffs and Trade. An international agreement to try to reduce restrictions in trade between countries (replaced in 1998 by the World Trade Organization). Abbr. GATT.

World Trade Organization General Arrangements to Borrow. An agreement between members of the G10 group of countries, by which members make funds available to the IMF to cover loans which it makes. Abbr. GAB.

General audit. A process of examining all the books and accounts of a company.

General average. A process by which the cost of lost goods is shared by all parties to an insurance (in cases where some goods have been lost in an attempt to save the rest of the cargo).

General expenses. All kinds of minor expenses, the money spent on the day-to-day costs of running a business.

General fund. A unit trust with investments in a variety of stocks.

General insurance. Insurance covering all kinds of risk, e.g. theft, loss or damage, but excluding life insurance.

General ledger. A book which records a company's income and expenditure in general.

General manager. A manager in charge of the administration of a company.

General meeting. Meeting of all the shareholders of a company or of all the members of a society.

General office. The main administrative office of a company.

General partner. A partner in a partnership whose responsibility for its debts is not limited.

General partnership. A partnership where the liability of each partner is not limited.

General undertaking. An undertaking signed by the directors of a company applying for a stock exchange listing, promising to work within the regulations of the stock exchange.

Gentleman's agreement. All agreement between two parties who trust each other.

Get back. To receive something which you had before.

Get out. 1. To produce something. 2. To sell an investment (informal).

Get out of. To stop trading in (a product or an area).

Gift coupon Or Gift token. A card that can be used to buy specified goods up to the value printed on it, often issued by chain stores. The person receiving the voucher is able to redeem it in any store in the chain.

Global. To the whole world.

Global economy. The economy of the whole world.

Globalization. The process of making something international or worldwide, especially the process of expanding business interests, operations and strategies to countries all over the world.

Note: Globalization is due to technological developments that make global communications possible, political developments such as the fall of communism and developments in transportation that make travelling faster and more frequent. It can benefit companies by opening up new markets, giving access to new raw materials and investment opportunities and enabling them to take advantage of lower operating costs in other countries.

GNP. Abbr. Gross national product.

Go back on. Not to carry out something after you have promised to do it.

Go-go fund. A fund which aims to give very high returns because it is invested in speculative stocks.

Going concern. A company that is actively trading (and making a profit).

Going concern value. The value of a corporation as it continues trading (in effect, the goodwill) as opposed to its breakup value.

Going price. The usual or current price, the price which is being charged now.

Going rate. The usual or current rate of payment.

Go into. To examine something carefully.

Gold. A very valuable yellow metal.

Note: Gold is the traditional hedge against investment uncertainties. People buy gold in the form of coins or bars, because they think it will maintain its value when other investments such as government bonds, foreign currency, property, etc., may not be so safe. Gold is relatively portable, and small quantities can be taken from country to country if an emergency occurs. This view, which is prevalent when the political situation is uncertain, has not been borne out in recent years, and gold has not maintained its value for some time.

Gold card. A credit card issued to important customers (i.e. those with a certain level of income), which gives certain privileges, such as a higher spending limit than ordinary credit cards.

Gold-collar worker. An employee who earns a very high salary and bonuses.

Golden handcuffs. A contractual arrangement to make sure that a valued member of staff stays in their job, by which they are offered special financial advantages if they stay and heavy penalties if they leave.

Golden hello. A cash inducement paid to someone to encourage them to change jobs and move to another company.

Golden umbrella. A special contract for a director of a company, which gives him advantageous financial terms if he has to resign when the company is taken over.

Golden share. A share in a privatized company which is retained by the government and carries special privileges (such as the right to veto foreign takeover bids).

Gold point. An amount by which a currency which is linked to gold can vary in price.

Gold reserves. The country's store of gold kept to pay international debts.

Gold standard. An arrangement that links the value of a currency to the value of a quantity of gold.

Go liquid. To convert as many assets as possible into cash.

Go long. To buy securities as a long-term investment.

Goods. Items which can be moved and are for sale.

Goodwill. 1. Good feeling towards someone. 2. The good reputation of a business, which can be calculated as part of a company's asset value, though separate from its tangible asset value.

Note: Goodwill can include such things as the trading reputation, the patents, the trade names used and the value of a 'good site' and is very difficult to establish accurately. It is an intangible asset, and so is not shown as an asset in a company's accounts, unless it figures as part of the purchase price paid when acquiring another company.

Go private. To become a private company again, by concentrating all its shares in the hands of one or a few shareholders and removing its stock exchange listing.

Go public. To become a public company by placing some of its shares for sale on the stock market so that anyone can buy them.

Go short. To sell shares now which you have contracted to purchase at a later date, on the assumption that the market will fall further.

Governance. The philosophy of ruling, whether a country or a company.

Government. An organization which administers a country.

Government economic indicators. Statistics which show how the country's economy is going to perform in the short or long term.

Government organization. An official body run by the government.

Government-sponsored. Encouraged by the government and backed.

Government support. A financial help given by the government.

GPM. Abbr. Graduated payment mortgage.

Grace period. The time given to a debtor to repay a loan, to pay the amount purchased using a credit card, or to pay an insurance premium.

Gradual. Slow and steady.

Graduated income tax. A tax which rises in steps (each level of income is taxed at a higher percentage).

Graduated payment mortgage. A mortgage where the monthly payments gradually rise over the lifetime of the mortgage. Abbr. GPM.

Graduated pension scheme. A pension scheme where the benefit is calculated as a percentage of the salary of each person in the scheme.

Grand total. The final total made by adding several subtotals.

Grant. Money given by the government to help pay for something.

Grantee. A person who receives a grant.

Graph. A diagram which shows the relationship between two sets of quantities or values, each of which is represented on an axis.

Gratuity. A tip, money given to someone who has helped you.

Graveyard. A market where prices are low and no one is buying because investors prefer to remain liquid (informal).

Green chips. Small companies with potential for growth.

Greenmail. The practice of making a profit by buying a large number of shares in a company, threatening to take the company over, and then selling the shares back to the company at a higher price.

Grey market. An unofficial market run by dealers, where new issues of shares are bought and sold before they officially become available for trading on the stock exchange (even before the share allocations are known).

Gross borrowings. The total of all monies borrowed by a company (such as overdrafts, long-term loans, etc.) but without deducting cash in bank accounts and on deposit.

Gross dividend per share. The dividend per share paid before tax is deducted.

Gross domestic product. The annual value of goods sold and services paid for inside a country. Abbr. GDP.

Gross earnings. Total earnings before tax and other deductions.

Gross income. Salary before tax is deducted.

Gross income yield. The yield of an investment before tax is deducted.

Gross margin. The percentage difference between the received price and the unit manufacturing cost or purchase price of goods for resale.

Gross national product. The annual value of goods and services in a country including income from other countries. Abbr. GNP.

Gross negligence. The act of showing very serious neglect of duty towards other people.

Gross premium. The total premium paid by a policyholder before any tax relief or discount is taken into account.

Gross profit. Profit calculated as sales income less the cost of the goods sold, i.e. without deducting any other expenses.

Gross receipts. The total amount of money received before expenses are deducted.

Gross salary. Salary before tax is deducted.

Gross sales. Money received from sales before deductions for goods returned, special discounts, etc.

Gross turnover. The total turnover including VAT and discounts.

Gross yield. A profit from investments before tax is deducted.

Group. 1. Several things or people together. 2. Several companies linked together in the same organization.

Group balance sheet. A consolidated balance sheet, the balance sheets of subsidiary companies grouped together into the balance sheet of the parent company.

Group health insurance. A health insurance for a group of people under a single policy, issued to their employer or to an association.

Group income protection insurance. Insurance for a group of people which gives them a replacement income when they are sick or incapacitated.

Group of Ten. The major world economic powers working within the framework of the IMF: Belgium, Canada, France, Germany, Italy, Japan, Netherlands, Sweden, the United Kingdom and the United States. There are in fact now eleven members, since Switzerland has joined the original ten. Abbr.G10.

Group results. The results of a group of companies taken together.

Grow. To become larger.

Growth. 1. The fact of becoming larger or increasing. 2. The second stage in a product life cycle, following the launch, when demand for the product increases rapidly.

Growth-and-income fund. A fund which aims to provide both capital growth and income.

Growth company. Company whose share price is expected to rise in value.

Growth fund. A fund which aims at providing capital growth rather than income.

Growth index. An index showing how something has grown.

Growth industry. An industry that is expanding or has the potential to expand faster than other industries.

Growth market. A market where sales are increasing rapidly.

Growth number. Growth expressed as a percentage.

Growth prospects. Potential for growth in a share.

Growth rate. The speed at which something grows.

GST. Abbr. Goods and Services Tax.

Guarantee. 1. A legal document in which the producer agrees to compensate the buyer if the product is faulty or becomes faulty before a specific date after purchase. 2. A promise that someone will pay another person's debts. 3. Something given as a security.

Guaranteed Income Bond. A bond which guarantees a certain rate of interest over a certain period of time. Abbr. GIB.

Guaranteed wage. A wage which a company promises will not fall below a specific figure.

Guarantor. A person who promises to pay someone's debts.

Guardian. A person appointed by law to act on behalf of someone (such as a child) who cannot act on his or her own behalf.

Guess. A calculation made without any real information.

H

Haggle. To discuss prices and terms and try to reduce them.

Haircut. 1. The difference between the market value of a security and the amount lent to the owner using the security as collateral. 2. An estimate of possible loss in investments.

Half. One of two equal parts into which something is divided.

Half-life. The number of years needed to repay half the capital borrowed on mortgage.

Half-price sale. A sale of items at half the usual price.

Half-year. Six months of an accounting period.

Hammering. 1. A beating or severe losses. 2. (on the London Stock Exchange) The removal of a member firm because it has failed. 3. The massive selling of stock on a stock market.

Handle. The whole number of a share price quoted.

Handling charge. Money to be paid for packing, invoicing and dealing with goods which are being shipped.

Handout. Money paid to help someone in difficulties.

Hard. 1. Strong, not weak. 2. Difficult. 3. Solid. 4. After weeks of difficult discussions.

Hard bargain. A bargain with difficult terms.

Hard cash. Money in notes and coins, as opposed to cheques or credit cards.

Hard copy. A printout of a text which is on a computer.

Hard currency. The currency of a country which has a strong economy, and which can be changed into other currencies easily. Also called scarce currency.

Harden. To become more fixed or more inflexible.

Hardening. 1. (of a market) slowly moving upwards. 2. (of prices) becoming settled at a higher level.

Hard landing. A change in economic strategy to counteract inflation which has serious results for the population (high unemployment, rising interest rates, etc.).

Hard market. A market which is strong and not likely to fall.

Hardness of the market. The state of the market when it is strong and not likely to fall.

Hard sell. To make great efforts to persuade people to buy a product.

Harmonization. A standardization, making things the same in several countries.

Harmonize. To make things such as tax rates or VAT rates the same in several countries.

Harmonized. Which has been made standard in several countries.

Harmonized European index. A method of calculating inflation which is standard throughout the EU.

Head. The most important person.

Head and shoulders. A term used by chartists showing a share price which rises to a peak, then falls slightly, then rises to a much higher peak, then falls sharply and rises to a lower peak before falling again, looking similar to a person's head and shoulders when shown on a graph.

Head buyer. The most important buyer in a store.

Headhunt. To look for managers and offer them jobs in other companies.

Head of department. A person in charge of a department.

Head office. An office building where the board of directors works and meets.

Headquarters. The main office, where the board of directors meets and works. Abbr. HQ.

Heads of agreement. 1. A draft agreement with not all the details complete. 2. The most important parts of a commercial agreement.

Health. 1. Being fit and well, not ill. 2. To report that a company is trading profitably.

Health insurance. Insurance which pays the cost of treatment for illness, especially when travelling abroad.

Health warning. A warning message printed on advertisements for investments, stating that the value of investments can fall as well as rise.

Healthy balance sheet. The balance sheet which shows a good profit.

Heavy. 1. Large or in large quantities. 2. To a share which has such a high price that small investors are reluctant to buy it (in which case the company may decide to split the shares so as to make them more attractive. 3.Having too many investments in the same type of share.

Heavy industry. An industry which deals in heavy raw materials such as coal or makes large products such as ships or engines.

Heavy market. A stock market where prices are falling.

Hectic. Wild, very active.

Hedge. A protection against a possible loss (which involves taking an action which is the opposite of an action taken earlier).

Hedge fund. A partnership open to a small number of rich investors, which invests in equities, currency futures and derivatives and may produce high returns but carries a very high risk.

Note: Originally, hedge funds were funds planned to protect equity investments against possible falls on the stock market. Nowadays the term is applied to funds which take speculative positions in financial futures or equities, and are usually highly-geared: in other words, they do nothing to 'hedge' their holdings.

Hedging. The act of buying investments at a fixed price for delivery later, so as to protect oneself against possible loss.

Hemline theory. The theory that movements of the stock market reflect the current fashionable length of women's skirts (the shorter the skirt, the more bullish the market).

Herewith. Together with this letter.

Hidden asset. An asset which is valued much less in the company's accounts than its true market value.

Hidden reserves. 1. Reserves which are not easy to identify in the company's balance sheet (reserves which are illegally kept hidden are called 'secret reserves'). 2. Illegal reserves which are not declared in the company's balance sheet.

High. 1. Large, not low. 2. The person who offers the most money at an auction.

High finance. The lending, investing and borrowing of very large sums of money organized by financiers.

High flier. 1. A person who is very successful or who is likely to rise to a very important position. 2. A share whose market price is rising rapidly.

High gearing. A situation where a company has a high level of borrowing compared to its share price.

High-income. Which gives a large income.

Highly-geared company. Company which has a high proportion of its funds from fixed-interest borrowings.

Highly-paid. Earning a large salary.

Highly-placed. Occupying an important post.

High pressure. A strong insistence that somebody should do something.

High-risk. Which involves more risk than normal.

High-risk investment. An investment which carries a higher risk than other investments.

High security area. A special part of a bank with strong doors where cash can be kept safely.

High-tech companies. The companies in advanced technological fields, such as computers, telecommunications or scientific research.

High yield. A dividend yield which is higher than is normal for the type of company.

Hike. An increase.

Hire. 1. An arrangement whereby customers pay money to be able to use a car, boat or piece of equipment owned by someone else for a time. 2. To work freelance.

Note: An agreement to hire a piece of equipment, etc., involves two parties: the hirer and the owner. The equipment remains the property of the owner while the hirer is using it. Under a hire-purchase agreement, the equipment remains the property of the owner until the hirer has complied with the terms of the agreement (i.e. until he or she has paid all monies due).

Hire and fire. To employ new staff and dismiss existing staff very frequently.

Hire purchase. A system of buying something by paying a sum regularly each month.

Hire purchase agreement. A contract to pay for something by installments.

Hire-purchase company. A company which provides money for hire purchase.

Hiring. The act of employing new staff.

Historical. Which goes back over a period of time.

Note: By tradition, a company's accounts are usually prepared on the historical cost principle, i.e. that assets are cost at their purchase price. With inflation, such assets are undervalued, and current-cost accounting or replacement- cost accounting may be preferred.

Historical cost accounting. The preparation of accounts on the basis of historical cost, with assets valued at their original cost of purchase.

Historical cost depreciation. Depreciation based on the original cost of the asset.

Historical trading range. The difference between the highest and lowest price for a share or bond over a period of time.

Historical cost. The actual cost of purchasing something which was bought some time ago.

Hit. 1. To reach something. 2. To hurt or to damage someone or something.

Hive off. To split off part of a large company to form a smaller subsidiary, giving shares in this to its existing shareholders.

Hoard. 1. To buy and store goods in case of need. 2. To keep cash instead of investing it.

Hoarder. A person who buys and stores goods in case of need.

Hoarding. The buying of large quantities of goods to keep in case of need.

Hold. 1. The action of keeping something. 2. To make something happen. 3. Not to sell.

Hold back. To wait, not to do something at the present time.

Holdback. A part of a loan to a property developer which is not paid until the development is almost finished.

Hold down. 1. To keep at a low level. 2. To manage to do a difficult job.

Holder. 1. A person who owns or keeps something. 2. A thing which keeps something, which protects something.

Holder in due course. A person who holds a negotiable instrument, such as a bill of exchange, in good faith, without knowing of any other claim against it.

Holder of record. The person who is registered as the owner of shares in a company.

Holding. A group of shares owned.

Holding company. 1. A company which owns more than 50% of the shares in another company. 2. A company which exists only or mainly to own shares in subsidiary companies.

Hold out for. To wait and ask for something.

Hold to. Not to allow something or someone to change.

Hold up. 1. To stay at a high level. 2. To delay something.

Hologram. A three-dimensional picture which is used on credit cards as a means of preventing forgery.

Home banking. A system of banking using a personal computer in your own home to carry out various financial transactions (such as paying invoices or checking your bank account).

Home equity credit. A loan made to a homeowner against the security of the equity in his or her property (i.e. the value of the property now less the amount outstanding on any mortgage).

Home income plan. A method of releasing equity from an un mortgaged property so that a homeowner has income or cash without actually leaving the property.

Home loan. A loan by a bank or building society to help someone buy a house.

Home market. The market in the country where the selling company is based.

Home trade. Trade in the country where a company is based.

Honorary. Not paid a salary for the work done for an organization.

Horizontal integration. The process of joining similar companies or taking over a company in the same line of business as yourself.

Horizontal spread. The buying and selling of two options at the same price but with different maturity dates.

Horse trading. Hard bargaining which ends with someone giving something in return for a concession from the other side.

Hostile takeover bid. A takeover where the board of the company do not recommend it to the shareholders and try to fight it.

Hot money. Money which is moved from country to country to get the best returns.

Hot stock. A stock (usually in a new issue) which rises rapidly on the Stock Exchange because of great demand.

Hourly wage. The amount of money paid for an hour's work.

House insurance. Insuring a house and its contents against damage.

Human resources department. The section of the company which deals with its staff.

Hurdle rate. 1. The rate of growth in a portfolio required to repay the final fixed redemption price of zero dividend preference shares. 2. A minimum rate of return needed by a bank to fund a loan, the rate below which a loan is not profitable for the bank.

Hyperinflation. Inflation which is at such a high percentage rate that it is almost impossible to reduce.

Hypothecation. 1. An arrangement in which property such as securities is used as collateral for a loan, but without transferring legal ownership to the lender (as opposed to a mortgage, where the lender holds the title to the property). 2. An action of earmarking money derived from certain sources for certain related expenditure, as when investing taxes from private cars or petrol sales solely on public transport.

I

IBRD. Abbr. International Bank for Reconstruction and Development (the World Bank)

Idle capital. Capital which is not being used productively.

IFC. Abbr. International Finance Corporation.

Illegal. Not legal or against the law.

Illiquid. To an asset which is not easy to change into cash.

ILO. Abbr. International Labour Organization.

IMF. Abbr. International Monetary Fund.

IMM. Abbr. International Monetary Market.

IMMA. Abbr. Insured money market account.

Immovable property. Houses and other buildings on land.

Immunization. Arrangements to protect the income from a portfolio of investments against any risk in a volatile stock market.

Impact. A shock or strong effect.

Impaired. Not certain, not perfect.

Impaired credit. A situation where a person becomes less creditworthy than before.

Implementation. The process of putting something into action.

Import. To bring goods from abroad into a country for sale.

Importation. The act of importing.

Import ban. An order forbidding imports.

Import duty. A tax on goods imported into a country.

Import-export. (Referring to) business which deals with both bringing foreign goods into a country and sending locally made goods abroad.

Import licence or Import permit. An official document which allows goods to be imported.

Import quota. A fixed quantity of a particular type of goods which the government allows to be imported.

Import restrictions. Actions taken by a government to reduce the level of imports (by imposing quotas, duties, etc.)

Import surcharge. The extra duty charged on imported goods, to try to stop them from being imported and to encourage local manufacture.

Impose. To give orders for something, e.g. a tax or a ban, which other people have to pay or obey.

Impound. To take something away and keep it until a tax is paid.

Imprinter. A hand-operated machine for printing the details of a customer's credit card on a sales voucher.

Improve. To make something better, or to become better.

Improved offer. An offer which is larger or has better terms than the previous offer.

Improvement. 1. The process of getting better. 2. Something which is better.

Impulse. A sudden decision.

Impulse buyer. A person who buys something on impulse, not because he or she intended to buy it.

Impulse buying. The practice of buying items which you have just seen, not because you had planned to buy them.

Impulse purchase. Something bought as soon as it is seen.

Imputation system. A system of taxation of dividends, where the company pays advance corporation tax on the dividends it pays to its shareholders, and the shareholders pay no tax on the dividends received, assuming that they pay tax at the standard rate (the ACT is shown as a tax credit which is imputed to the shareholder).

Impute. To pass the responsibility for something to someone else.

Imputed value. A value which is given to figures, for which an accurate value cannot be calculated.

IMRO. Abbreviation Investment Management

Regulatory Organization. Inactive account A bank account which is not used (i.e. no deposits or withdrawals are made) over a period of time.

Inactive market. Stock market with few buyers or sellers.

Incentive. Something which encourages a customer to buy, or employees to work better.

Incentive bonus or Incentive payment. An extra payment offered to workers to make them work better.

Incentive scheme. A plan to encourage better work by paying higher commission or bonuses.

Incidental. Which is not important, but connected with something else.

Incidental expenses. Small amounts of money spent at various times in addition to larger amounts.

Include. To count something along with other things.

Inclusive. Counts something in with other things.

Inclusive charge or Inclusive sum. A charge which includes all items or costs.

Income. 1. Money which a person receives as salary or dividends the groups of people who earn low or high salaries considered for tax purposes. 2. Money which an organization receives as gifts or from investments.

Income fund. A fund which aims at providing a high income rather than capital growth.

Income gearing. The ratio of the interest a company pays on its borrowing shown as a percentage of its pretax profits (before the interest is paid).

Income shares. Shares in an investment trust which receive income from the investments, but do not benefit from the rise in capital value of the investments.

Incomes policy. The government's ideas on how incomes should be controlled,

Income statement. A statement of company expenditure and sales which shows whether the company has made a profit or loss.

Income support. A government benefit paid to low-income earners who are working less than 16 hours per week, provided they can show that they are actively looking for jobs. Abbr. IS.

Income tax. 1.The tax on a person's income (both earned and unearned). 2. The tax on the profits of a corporation.

Income tax form. A form to be completed which declares all income to the tax office.

Income tax return. A form used for reporting how much income you have earned and working out how much tax you have to pay on it. Also called declaration of income.

Income units. Units in a unit trust, from which the investor receives dividends in the form of income.

Income yield. An actual percentage yield of government stocks, the fixed interest being shown as a percentage of the market price.

Incoming. To someone who has recently been elected or appointed.

Inconvertible. To currency which cannot be easily converted into other currencies.

Incorporate. 1. To bring something in to form part of main group. 2. To form a registered company.

Increase. 1. An act of becoming larger. 2. A higher salary.

Increment. A regular automatic increase in salary.

Incremental cost. The cost of making extra units above the number already planned (this may then include further fixed costs).

Incremental increase. An increase in salary according to an agreed annual increment.

Incremental scale. A salary scale with regular annual salary increases.

Incur. To make yourself liable to something.

Indebted. Owing money to someone.

Indemnification. Payment for damage.

Indemnity. 1. A guarantee of payment after a loss. 2. Compensation paid after a loss.

Indent. 1. An order placed by an importer for goods from overseas. 2. A line of typing which starts several spaces from the left-hand margin.

Indenture. A formal agreement showing the terms of a bond issue.

Independent. Not under the control or authority of anyone else.

Independent authenticator. A company that has the authority (from the government or the internet controlling body) to issue certificates of authentication when they are sure that a company is who it claims to be.

Independent company. A company which is not controlled by another company.

Independent financial adviser. A person who gives impartial advice on financial matters, who is not connected with any financial institution. Abbr. IFA.

Independent trader or Independent shop. A shop which is owned by an individual proprietor, not by a chain.

Index. 1. A list of items classified into groups or put in alphabetical order. 2. A regular statistical report which shows rises and falls in prices, values or levels. 3. A figure based on the current market price of certain shares on a stock exchange.

Index arbitrage. Buying or selling a basket of stocks against an index option or future.

Indexation. The linking of something to an index.

Indexation of wage increases. The linking of wage increases to the percentage rise in the cost of living.

Index card. A card used to make a card index.

Indexed portfolio. A portfolio of shares in all the companies which form the basis of a stock exchange index.

Index fund. An investment fund consisting of shares in all the companies which are used to calculate a Stock Exchange index.

Index-linked. Which rises automatically by the percentage increase in the cost of living.

Index number. 1. A number of something in an index. 2. A number showing the percentage rise of something over a period.

Index tracker. An investor or fund manager who tracks an index.

Index-tracking. Which tracks an index.

Indicate. To show something.

Indicator. Something which indicates.

Indirect costs or Indirect expenses. Costs which are not directly related to the making of a product (such as cleaning, rent or administration).

Indirect labour costs. The cost of paying employees not directly involved in making a product such as cleaners or canteen staff. Such costs cannot be allocated to a cost centre.

Indirect tax. A tax (such as VAT) paid to someone who then pays it to the government.

Indirect taxation. Taxes (such as sales tax) which are not paid direct to the government.

Inducement. Something which helps to persuade someone to do something.

Industrial. To manufacturing work.

Industrial accident. An accident which takes place at work.

Industrial arbitration tribunal. A court which decides in industrial disputes.

Industrial bank. A finance house which lends to business customers.

Industrial capacity. The amount of work which can be done in a factory or several factories.

Industrial centre. A large town with many industries.

Industrial court. A court which can decide in industrial disputes if both parties agree to ask it to judge between them.

Industrial debenture. A debenture raised by an industrial company.

Industrial development. The planning and building of new industries in special areas.

Industrial espionage. The practice of trying to find out the secrets of a competitor's work or products, usually by illegal means.

Industrial expansion. The growth of industries in a country or a region.

Industrialization. The process of change by which an economy becomes based on industrial production rather than on agriculture.

Industrialize. To set up industries in a country which had none before.

Industrial loan. A loan raised by an industrial company.

Industrial processes. The various stages involved in manufacturing products in factories.

Industrial relations. Relations between management and employees.

Industrial training. The training of new employees to work in an industry.

Industrial tribunal. A court which can decide in disputes about employment.

Industry. 1. All factories, companies or processes involved in the manufacturing of products. 2. A group of companies making the same type of product or offering the same type of service.

Ineligible bill. A bill of exchange which cannot be discounted by a central bank.

Inflate. To increase prices without any reason.

Inflation. A greater increase in the supply of money or credit than in the production of goods and services, resulting in higher prices and a fall in the purchasing power of money.

Inflation accounting. An accounting system, where inflation is taken into account when calculating the value of assets and the preparation of accounts.

Inflationary. Which tends to increase inflation.

Inflation-proof. To a pension, etc. which is index-linked, so that its value is preserved in times of inflation.

Inflation-proof pension. A pension which will rise to keep pace with inflation.

Inflation rate. A figure, in the form of a percentage, which shows the amount by which inflation has increased over a period of time, usually a year. Also called rate of inflation.

Note: The inflation rate in the India is calculated on a series of figures, including prices of consumer items: petrol, gas and electricity, interest rates, etc. This gives the 'underlying' inflation rate which can be compared to that of other countries. The calculation can also include mortgage interest and local taxes which give the 'headline' inflation figure. This is higher than in other countries because of these extra items. Inflation affects businesses, in that as their costs rise, so their profits may fall and it is necessary to take this into account when pricing products.

Inflation target. An inflation rate which the government aims to reach at some date in the future.

Inflow. The act of coming in or being brought in.

Influx. An inflow, especially one where people or things come in large quantities.

Information office. An office which gives information to tourists or visitors.

Information officer. 1. A person whose job is to give information about a company, an organization or a government department to the public. 2.

A person whose job is to give information to other departments in the same organization.

Infringe. To break a law or a right.

Infringement of patent. An act of illegally using, making or selling an invention which is patented, without the permission of the patent holder.

Inherit. To get something from a person who has died.

Initial. First or starting.

Initial capital. Capital which is used to start a business.

Initial public offering. The process of offering new shares in a corporation for sale to the public as a way of launching the corporation on the stock exchange. Abbr.IPO.

Initial sales. The first sales of a new product.

Initial yield. An expected yield on a new unit trust.

Initiative. The decision to start something.

Injunction. A court order telling someone not to do something.

Inland. Inside a country.

Inland freight charges. Charges for carrying goods from one part of the country to another.

Input tax. VAT which is paid by a company on goods or services bought.

Inquiry office. An office which members of the public can go to have their questions answered.

Inside. Ad in, especially in a company's office or building.

Inside information. Information which is passed from people working in a company to people outside (and which can be valuable to investors in the company).

Insider buying Or insider dealing. The illegal buying or selling of shares by staff of a company or other persons who have secret information about the company's plans.

Insider trader. A person who carries out insider dealing, i.e. illegal buying or selling of shares by staff of a company or other persons who have secret information about the company's plans.

Insolvency. The fact of not being able to pay debts.

Insolvent. Adjective not able to pay debts.

Note: A company is insolvent when its liabilities are higher than its assets; if this happens it must cease trading.

Inspect. To examine in detail.

Inspection. The close examination of something.

Inspection stamp. A stamp placed on something to show it has been inspected.

Instability. The state of being unstable or moving up and down.

Install. 1. To set up a piece of machinery or equipment, e.g. a new computer system, so that it can be used. 2. To configure a new computer program to the existing system requirements.

Installment sales Or Installment buying. A system of buying something by paying a sum regularly each month.

Note: The India term is hire purchase.

Installment. A part of a payment which is paid regularly until the total amount is paid.

Installment credit. An arrangement by which a purchaser pays for goods bought in installments over a period of time.

Instant. Immediately available.

Instant access account. A deposit account which pays interest and from which you can withdraw money immediately without penalty.

Institutional buying. Buying or selling shares by financial institutions.

Institutional buyout. A takeover of a company by a financial institution, which backs a group of managers who will run it. Abbr. IBO.

Institutional investor. 1. A financial institution which invests money in securities. 2. An organization (such as a pension fund or insurance company) with large sums of money to invest.

Instruction. An order which tells what should be done or how something is to be used.

Instrument. 1. A tool or piece of equipment. 2. A legal document.

Insurable. Which can be insured.

Insurable interest. The value of the thing insured which is attributed to the person who is taking out the insurance.

Insurance. An agreement that in return for regular payments (called 'premiums'), a company will pay compensation for loss, damage, injury or death.

Insurance agent Or Insurance broker. A person who arranges insurance for clients.

Insurance claim. A request to an insurance company to pay compensation for damage or loss.

Insurance company. A company whose business is insurance.

Insurance contract. An agreement by an insurance company to insure.

Insurance cover. Protection guaranteed by an insurance policy.

Insurance policy. A document which shows the conditions of an insurance contract.

Insurance premium. An annual payment made by a person or a company to an insurance company.

Insure. To have a contract with a company whereby, if regular small payments are made, the company will pay compensation for loss, damage, injury or death.

Insured account. An account with a bank which is insured by the customer's insurance.

Insured money market account. A high-yield account, in which the investor has to deposit a certain minimum sum, which is insured by the provider against capital loss. Abbr. IMMA.

Insurer. A company which insures.

Intangible. Which cannot be touched.

Intangible assets. Assets which have a value, but which cannot be seen, e.g. goodwill, or a patent or a trademark.

Integrate. To link things together to form one whole group.

Integration. The act of bringing several businesses together under a central control.

Inter-company dealings. The dealings between two companies in the same group.

Inter-company comparisons. The comparing the results of one company with those of another in the same product area.

Inter-bank loan. A loan from one bank to another.

Inter-bank market. A market where banks lend to or borrow from each other.

Inter-dealer broker. A broker who acts as an intermediary between dealers in government securities.

Interest. 1. Payment made by a borrower for the use of money, calculated as a percentage of the capital borrowed. 2. Money paid as income on investments or loans. 3. A part of the ownership of something, e.g. if you invest money in a company you acquire a financial share or interest in it.

Interest-bearing account. A bank account which gives interest.

Interest-bearing deposits. Deposits which produce interest.

Interest charges. Money paid as interest on a loan.

Interest cover. The ability to pay interest payments on a loan.

Interested party. A person or company with a financial interest in a company.

Interest-free credit. A credit or loan where no interest is paid by the borrower.

Interesting. Which attracts attention.

Interest rate. A figure which shows the percentage of the capital sum borrowed or deposited which is to be paid as interest. Also called rate of interest.

Interest rate margin. The difference between the interest a bank pays on deposits and the interest it charges on loans.

Interest rate swap. An agreement between two companies to exchange borrowings (a company with fixed-interest borrowings might swap them for variable interest borrowings of another company).

Interest-sensitive purchases. Purchases (such as houses or items bought on hire-purchase) which are influenced by interest rates.

Interest yield. A yield on a fixed-interest investment.

Interface. A point where two groups of people come into contact.

Interim. Made, measured or happening in the middle of a period, such as the financial year, and before the final result for the period is available a statement of interim profits or dividends.

Interim dividend. A dividend paid at the end of a half-year.

Interim payment. A payment of part of a dividend.

Interim report Or Interim statement. A report given at the end of a half-year.

Intermediary. A person who is the link between people or organizations who do not agree or who are negotiating.

Intermediate term. A period of one or two years.

Intermediation. The arrangement of finance or insurance by an intermediary.

Internal. 1. Inside a company. 2. Inside a country or a region.

Internal audit. An audit carried out by a department inside the company.

Internal audit department. A department of a company which examines the internal accounting controls of that company.

Internal auditor. A member of staff who audits a company's accounts.

Internal control. A system set up by the management of a company to monitor and control the company's activities.

Internal growth. The development of a company by growing its existing business with its own finances, as opposed to acquiring other businesses. Also called organic growth.

Internal market. As one single market, with no tariff barriers between its member states.

Internal rate of return. An average annual yield of an investment, where the interest earned over a period of time is the same as the original cost of the investment. Abbr. IRR.

Internal revenue service. A government department which deals with tax. Abbr. IRS.

Internal trade. Trade between various parts of a country.

International. Working between countries.

International Bank for Reconstruction and Development. The official name of the World Bank. Abbr. IBRD.

International Commodities Clearing House. A clearing house which deals in settlements of futures contracts in commodities and financial futures. Abbr. ICCH.

International Finance Corporation. A subsidiary of the World Bank which makes loans to private companies. Abbr. IFC.

International Labour Organization. A section of the United Nations which tries to improve working conditions and workers' pay in member countries. Abbr. ILO.

International law. Laws referring to the way countries deal with each other.

International Monetary Fund. A type of bank which is part of the United Nations and helps member states in financial difficulties, gives financial advice to members and encourages world trade. Abbr. IMF.

International Monetary Market. A part of the Chicago Mercantile Exchange dealing in financial futures. Abbr. IMM.

International monetary system. Methods of controlling and exchanging currencies between countries.

International money markets. Markets, such as the Euro market, the international market for lending or borrowing in Eurocurrencies.

International money order. A money order in a foreign currency which is payable to someone living in a foreign country.

International Petroleum Exchange. A London commodity exchange dealing in crude oil and natural gas futures. Abbr. IPE.

International trade. Trade between different countries.

Internet. The global, public network of computers and telephone links that houses websites, allows email to be sent and is accessed with the aid of a modem.

Internet bank. A bank that allows it customers to have credit in an account on the internet, and use it to pay for purchases made on the internet.

Intervene. To try to make a change in a situation in which you have not been involved before.

Intervention. The act of becoming involved in a situation in order to change it.

Intervention mechanism. A method used by central banks in maintaining exchange rate parities (such as buying or selling foreign currency).

Intervention price. A price at which the EU will buy farm produce which farmers cannot sell, in order to keep prices high.

Intraday liquidity. Availability of cash in the banking system.

Intrinsic value. A value which exists as part of something, such as the value of an option (for a call option, it is the difference between the current price and the higher striking price).

Introduce. To make someone get to know somebody or something.

Introduction. 1. A letter making someone get to know another person. 2. The act of bringing an established company to the stock exchange (i.e. getting permission for the shares to be traded on the stock exchange, used when a company is formed by a demerger from an existing larger company, and no new shares are being offered for sale).

Introductory offer. A special price offered on a new product to attract customers.

Invalid. Not valid or not legal.

Invalidate. To make something invalid.

Invalidation. The act of making invalid.

Inventory. 1. Especially all the stock or goods in a warehouse or shop. 2. A list of the contents of a building such as a house for sale or an office for rent.

Inventory control. A system of checking that there is not too much stock in a warehouse, but just enough to meet requirements.

Inventory financing. The use of money from working capital to purchase stock for resale.

Inventory turnover. The total value of stock sold during a year, divided by the value of the goods remaining in stock.

Invest. 1. To put money into shares, bonds, a building society, etc., hoping that it will produce interest and increase in value. 2. To spend money on something which you believe will be useful.

Investigation. An examination to find out what is wrong.

Investment. 1. The placing of money so that it will produce interest and increase in value. 2. A share, bond or piece of property bought in the hope that it will produce more money than was used to buy it.

Investment adviser. A person who advises people on what investments to make.

Investment environment. The general economic situation in which an investment is made.

Investment fund. A fund that invests in start-up companies or other new projects.

Investment grant. A government grant to a company to help it to invest in new machinery.

Investment income. Income (such as interest and dividends) from investments.

Investment trust. A company whose shares can be bought on the stock exchange and whose business is to make money by buying and selling stocks and shares.

Investor. A person who invests money.

Investor protection. Legislation to protect small investors from unscrupulous investment brokers and advisers.

Invisible assets. Assets which have a value but which cannot be seen, e.g. goodwill or patents.

Invisible earnings. Foreign currency earned by a country by providing services, receiving interests or dividends, but not by selling goods.

Invisible exports. Services (such as banking, insurance or tourism) which do not involve selling a product and which are provided to foreign customers and paid for in foreign currency.

Invisible imports. Services (such as banking, insurance or tourism) which do not involve selling a product and which are provided by foreign companies and paid for in local currency.

Invisibles. Invisible imports and exports.

Invisible trade. Trade involving invisible imports and exports.

Invitation. An act of asking someone to do something.

Invoice. A note asking for payment for goods or services supplied.

Invoice clerk. An office worker who deals with invoices.

Invoice discounting. A method of obtaining early payment of invoices by selling them at a discount to a company which will receive payment of the invoices when they are paid. (The debtor is not informed of this arrangement, as opposed to factoring, where the debtor is informed.).

Invoice price. The price as given on an invoice, including any discount and VAT.

Invoicing. The work of sending invoices.

Invoicing department. The department in a company which deals with preparing and sending invoices.

Involuntary. Not done willingly or deliberately.

Inward bill. A bill of lading for goods arriving in a country.

Inward investment. Investment from outside a country, as when a foreign company decides to set up a new factory there.

Inward mission. A visit to your home country by a group of foreign businesspeople.

IOU. 'I owe you'; a signed document promising that you will pay back money borrowed.

Irrecoverable. Which cannot be recovered.

Irrecoverable debt. A debt which will never be paid.

Irredeemable. Which cannot be redeemed.

Irredeemable bond. A government bond which has no date of maturity and which therefore provides interest but can never be redeemed at full value.

Irregular. Not correct or not done in the correct way.

Irregularities. Things which are not done in the correct way and which are possibly illegal.

Irrevocable. Which cannot be changed.

Irrevocable acceptance. Acceptance which cannot be withdrawn.

Irrevocable letter of credit. A letter of credit which cannot be cancelled or changed, except if agreed between the two parties involved.

IS. Abbr. Income support.

ISA. Abbr. Individual savings account.

Issuance. An action of issuing new shares or new bonds.

Issue. An act of giving out new shares.

Issued capital. An amount of capital which is given out as shares to shareholders.

Issued price or Issue price. The price of shares in a new company when they are offered for sale for the first time.

Issuer. A financial institution that issues credit and debit cards and maintains the systems for billing and payment.

Issuing. Which organizes an issue of shares.

IT. Abbr. Information technology.

Item. 1. Something for sale. 2. A piece of information. 3. A point on a list.

Itemized account. A detailed record of money paid or owed.

Itemized invoice. An invoice which lists each item separately.

Itemized statement. A bank statement where each transaction is recorded in detail.

J

J curve. A line on a graph shaped like a letter 'J', with an initial short fall, followed by a longer rise (used to describe the effect of a falling exchange rate on a country's balance of trade).

Job. 1. An order being worked on. 2. Regular paid work.

Job analysis. A detailed examination and report on the duties involved in a job.

Jobber. 1. (Stock) jobber formerly on the London Stock Exchange, a person who bought and sold shares from other traders. 2. A wholesaler.

Jobbing(stock). Formerly on the London Stock Exchange, the business of buying and selling shares from other traders.

Job classification. The process of describing jobs listed in various groups.

Job creation scheme. A government-backed scheme to make work for the unemployed.

Job cuts. Reductions in the number of jobs.

Job description. A description of what a job consists of and what skills are needed for it.

Job evaluation. The process of examining different jobs within an organization to see what skills and qualifications are needed to carry them out.

Jobless. People with no jobs, the unemployed.

Job lot. 1. A group of miscellaneous items sold together. 2. A small parcel of shares traded on a stock exchange.

Job opportunities. New jobs which are available.

Job performance. The degree to which a job is done well or badly.

Job satisfaction. An employee's feeling that he or she is happy at work and pleased with the work he or she does.

Job security. 1. The likelihood that an employee will keep his or her job for a long time or until retirement. 2. A worker's feeling that he has a right to keep his job, or that he will never be made redundant.

Job specification. A very detailed description of what is involved in a job.

Job title. The name given to the person who does a particular job.

Joint. 1. Carried out or produced together with others. 2. One of two or more people who work together or who are linked.

Joint account. A bank or building society account shared by two people.

Joint-life annuity. An annuity which continues to pay an amount to a spouse after the main beneficiary dies.

Jointly. Ad together with one or more other people.

Joint management. Management done by two or more people.

Joint ownership. The owning of a property by several owners.

Joint-stock bank. A bank which is a public company quoted on the stock exchange.

Joint-stock company. Formerly, a public company whose shares were owned by very many people (now called a Public Limited Company or Plc).

Joint venture. A situation where two or more companies join together for one specific large business project.

Journal. A book with the account of sales and purchases made each day.

Judge. A person who decides in a legal case.

Judgment. A legal decision or official decision of a court.

Judgment debtor. A debtor who has been ordered by a court to pay a debt.

Judgment lien. A court order putting a lien on the property of a judgment debtor.

Judicial. Referring to the law.

Judicial processes. The ways in which the law works.

Judicial review. 1. The examination of a case a second time by a higher court because a lower court has acted wrongly. 2. The examination of administrative decisions by a court.

Jump. A sudden rise.

Junior. Less important than something else.

Junior capital. Capital in the form of shareholders' equity, which is repaid only after secured loans (called 'senior capital') have been paid if the firm goes into liquidation.

Junior mortgage. A second mortgage.

Junior partner. A person who has a small part of the shares in a partnership.

Junior security. A security which is repaid after other securities.

Junior staff. People in less important positions in a company.

Junk bond. A high-interest bond raised as a debenture on the security of a company which is the subject of a takeover bid.

Junk mail. Unsolicited advertising material sent through the post and usually thrown away immediately by the people who receive it.

K

Keen. 1. Eager or active. 2. Prices which are kept low so as to be competitive.

Keep. 1. To do what is necessary for something. 2. To hold items for sale or for information. 3. To hold things at a certain level.

Keep back. To hold on to something which you could give to someone.

Keep up. To hold at a certain high level.

Key. The part of a computer or typewriter which you press with your fingers or valuable persons.

Key holding. An important block of shares owned by a single investor, which is large enough to influence the decisions of the board of directors.

Key money. A premium paid when taking over the keys of a flat or office which you are renting.

Key-person insurance. An insurance policy taken out to cover the costs of replacing an employee who is particularly important to an organization if he or she dies or is ill for a long time.

Key rate. An interest rate which gives the basic rate on which other rates are calculated.

Kickback. An illegal commission paid to someone, especially a government official, who helps in a business deal.

Kicker. A special inducement to buy a bond (such as making it convertible to shares at a preferential rate) (informal).

Kite flier. A person who tries to impress people by putting forward a proposal.

Knockdown price. A very low price.

Knock off. To reduce a price by a particular amount.

Knock-on effect. The effect which an action will have on other situations.

L

Labor union. An organization which represents employees who are its members in discussions about wages and conditions of work with management. It is also called as trade union.

Labour. 1. Heavy work charge for both the materials used in a job and also the hours of work involved. 2. Workers, the workforce.

Labour costs. The cost of the workers employed to make a product (not including materials or overheads).

Labour dispute. A conflict or disagreement between employer and employees or between the groups who represent them.

Labour force. All the workers in a company or in an area.

Labour-intensive industry. An industry which needs large numbers of workers and where labour costs are high in relation to turnover.

Labour laws. Laws concerning the employment of workers.

Labour market. The number of people who are available for work.

Labour relations. Relations between management and employees.

Lack. The fact of not having enough.

Ladder. 1. A series of different levels through which an employee may progress. 2. An investment portfolio consisting of bonds with a series of maturity dates from very short-dated to long-dated.

Laddering. 1. The action of repeatedly buying shares in a newly launched corporation so as to force up the price, then selling the whole investment at a profit. 2. The action of making a series of investments which mature at different times, cashing each one at maturity and then reinvesting the proceeds.

Lading. The work of putting goods on a ship.

Lagging indicator. An indicator (such as the gross national product) which shows a change in economic trends later than other indicators.

Laissez-faire economy. An economy where the government does not interfere because it believes it is right to let the economy run itself.

Lame duck. A company which is in financial difficulties.

Land. 1. To put goods or passengers onto land after a voyage by sea or by air. 2. To come down to earth after a flight.

Landed costs. The costs of goods which have been delivered to a port, unloaded and passed through customs.

Landing charges. Payments for putting goods on land and paying customs duties.

Landing order. A permit which allows goods to be unloaded into a bonded warehouse without paying customs duty.

Land registration. A system of registering land and its owners.

Lapse. A period of time which has passed to stop being valid, or to stop being active.

Lapsed option. An option which has not been taken up, and now has expired.

Lapsed policy. An insurance policy which has been terminated because premiums have not been paid.

Last in first out. 1. A redundancy policy using the principle that the people who have been most recently appointed are the first to be made redundant. 2. An accounting method where stock is valued at the price of the earliest purchases (it is assumed that the most recently purchased stock is sold first). Abbr. LIFO.

Last quarter. A period of three months at the end of the financial year.

Launch. To put a company on the stock exchange for the first time.

Launder. To pass illegal profits, money from selling drugs, money which has not been taxed, etc.,

Law. A rule governing some aspect of human activity made and enforced by the state.

Law of diminishing returns. A general rule that as more factors of production such as land, labour and capital are added to the existing factors, so the amount they produce is proportionately smaller.

Law of supply and demand. A general rule that the amount of a product which is available is related to the needs of potential customers.

Lawsuit. A case brought to a court.

Lay off. 1. To dismiss employees for a time (until more work is available). 2. To dismiss employees permanently.

Lay out. To spend money.

LBO. Abbr. Leveraged buyout.

LC. Abbr. Letter of credit.

LCE. Abbr. London Commodity Exchange.

LDC. Abbr. 1. Least Developed Country. 2. Less developed country.

LDT. Abbr. Licensed deposit-taker.

Lead. 1. Information which may lead to a sale. 2. A prospective purchaser who is the main decision-maker when buying a product or service adjective most important, in the front.

Lead bank. The main bank in a loan syndicate.

Leader. 1. A product which sells best. 2. An important share, a share which is often bought or sold on the stock exchange.

Leading. 1. Most important. 2. Which comes first.

Leading indicator. An indicator (such as manufacturing order books) which shows a change in economic trends earlier than other indicators.

Lead manager. A person who organizes a syndicate of underwriters for a new issue of securities.

Lead time. 1. The time between deciding to place an order and receiving the product. 2. The time between the start of a task and its completion.

Lead underwriter. An underwriting firm which organizes the underwriting of a share issue.

Learning curve. 1. A process of learning something that starts slowly and then becomes faster. 2. A line on a graph which shows the relationship between experience in doing something and competence at carrying it out. 3. A diagram or graph that represents the way in which people gain knowledge or experience over time. 4. The decrease in the effort required to produce each single item when the total number of items produced is doubled.

Note: A steep learning curve represents a situation where people learn a great deal in a short time; a shallow curve represents a slower learning process. The curve eventually levels out, representing the time when the knowledge gained is being consolidated.

Lease. 1. A written contract for letting or renting a building, a piece of land or a piece of equipment for a period against payment of a fee. 2. To use an office, land or machinery for a time and pay a fee.

Lease back. To sell a property or machinery to a company and then take it back on a lease.

Lease-back. An arrangement where property is sold and then taken back on a lease.

Leasehold. (The fact of) possessing property on a lease, for a fixed time.

Leaseholder. A person who holds a property on a lease.

Leasing. Which leases or which is using equipment under a lease.

Least developed country. A country in the Third World which is not economically advanced, especially one of those which borrowed heavily from commercial banks in the 1970s and 1980s to finance their industrial development, and so created an international debt crisis. Abbr. LDC.

Ledger. A book in which accounts are written.

Ledger balance. Same as current balance.

Legacy. A piece of property given by someone to someone else in a will.

Legal. 1. According to the law or allowed by the law. 2. Referring to the law.

Legal adviser. A person who advises clients about the law.

Legal charge. A legal document held by the Land Registry showing who has a claim on a property.

Legal claim. A statement that someone owns something legally.

Legal charges Or legal expenses. Money spent on fees to lawyers.

Legal currency. Money which is legally used in a country.

Legal department. A section of a company dealing with legal matters.

Legal expert. A person who knows a lot about the law.

Legalization. The act of making something legal.

Legal list. A list of blue-chip securities in which banks and financial institutions are allowed to invest by the state in which they are based.

Legal personality. Existence in a form that enables something to be affected by the law.

Legal proceedings. Legal action or a lawsuit.

Legal section. A department in a company dealing with legal matters.

Legal tender. Coins or notes which can be legally used to pay a debt.

Legatee. A person who receives property from someone who has died.

Lend. To allow someone to use something for a period.

Lender. A person who lends money.

Lending. An act of letting someone use money for a time.

Lending limit. A restriction on the amount of money a bank can lend.

Lending margin. An agreed spread for lending.

Length of service. The number of years someone has worked.

Less. Smaller than, of a smaller size or of a smaller value.

Lessee. A person who has a lease or who pays money for a property he leases.

Let. To allow the use of a house, an office or a farm to someone for the payment of rent.

Let-out clause. A clause which allows someone to avoid doing something in a contract.

Letter of acknowledgement. A letter which says that something has been received.

Letter of advice. 1. A letter to a customer giving details of goods ordered and shipped but not yet delivered. 2. A letter from one bank to another, advising that a transaction has taken place.

Letter of application. A letter in which someone applies for a job.

Letter of appointment. A letter in which someone is appointed to a job.

Letter of comfort. A letter supporting someone who is trying to get a loan.

Letter of credit. A document issued by a bank on behalf of a customer authorizing payment to a supplier when the conditions specified in the document are met. Abbr. LC.

Letter of indemnity. A letter promising payment as compensation for a loss.

Letter of intent. A letter which states what a company intends to do if something happens.

Letter of reference. A letter in which an employer recommends someone for a new job.

Letter of renunciation. A form sent with new shares, which allows the person who has been allotted the shares to refuse to accept them and so sell them to someone else.

Letters of administration. A letter given by a court to allow someone to deal with the estate of a person who has died.

Letters patent. The official term for a patent.

Letting agency. An agency which deals in property to let.

Level. The position of something compared to others.

Leverage. 1. A ratio of capital borrowed by a company at a fixed rate of interest to the company's total capital. 2. The act of borrowing money at fixed interest which is then used to produce more money than the interest paid.

Note: High leverage (or high gearing) has the effect of increasing a company's profitability when trading is expanding; if the company's trading slows down, the effect of high fixed-interest charges is to increase the rate of slowdown.

Leveraged. Using borrowings for finance.

Leveraged buyout Or Leveraged takeover. An act of buying all the shares in a company by borrowing money against the security of the shares to be bought. Abbr. LBO.

Leveraged stock. Stock bought with borrowed money.

Levy. Money which is demanded and collected by the government.

Liabilities. The debts of a business, including dividends owed to shareholders.

Liability. 1. A legal responsibility for damage, loss or harm. 2. Responsibility for a payment (such as the repayment of a loan).

Liable. Legally responsible for.

License. 1. An official document which allows someone to do something. 2. To give someone official permission to do something for a fee, e.g. when a company allows another company to manufacture its products abroad.

Licensed deposit-taker or Licensed institution. A deposit taking institution, such as a building society, bank or friendly society, which is licensed to receive money on deposit from private individuals and to pay interest on it. Abbr. LDT.

Licensee. A person who has a license, especially a license to sell alcohol or to manufacture something.

Lien. The legal right to hold someone's goods and keep them until a debt has been paid.

Life of a contract. The remaining period of a futures contract before it expires.

Life assurance. Insurance which pays a sum of money when someone dies, or at a certain date if they are still alive.

Life assurance Company. A company providing life assurance, but usually also provides other services such as investment advice.

Life assured. The person whose life has been covered by a life assurance policy.

Lifeboat operation. Actions taken to rescue of a company (especially of a bank) which is in difficulties.

Life expectancy. The number of years a person is likely to live.

Life interest. A situation where someone benefits from a property as long as he or she is alive.

Lifestyle. The way of living of a particular section of society.

Lifestyle audit. A study of a person's living standards to see if it is consistent with his reported income.

LIFFE. Abbr. London International Financial Futures and Options Exchange.

LIFO. Abbr. Last in first out.

Light. 1. Not heavy, not very busy or active. 2. Not having enough of a certain type of share in a portfolio.

Lighten. To sell shareholdings if a portfolio is too 'heavy' in a certain type of share.

Light industry. An industry making small products such as clothes, books or calculators.

Limit. The point at which something ends or the point where you can go no further.

Limit 'down'. Upper or lower limits to share price movements which are regulated by some stock exchanges to stop something from going beyond a specific point, to restrict the number or amount of something.

Limitation. The act of allowing only a specific quantity of something.

Limited company. A company where each shareholder is responsible for repaying the company's debts only to the face value of the shares he or she owns. Abbr. Ltd. Also called limited liability company.

Limited liability. A situation where someone's liability for debt is limited by law.

Limited market. A market which can take only a specific quantity of goods.

Limited partnership. A registered business where the liability of the partners is limited to the amount of capital they have each provided to the business and where the partners may not take part in the running of the business.

Limit order. An order to a broker to sell if a security falls to a certain price.

Line chart. A chart or graph using lines to indicate values.

Line of credit. 1. The amount of money made available to a customer by a bank as an overdraft. 2. The borrowing limit on a credit card.

Line of shares. A large block of shares sold as one deal on the stock exchange.

Link. To join or to attach to something else.

Liquid assets. Cash, or investments which can be quickly converted into cash.

Liquidation. 1. Payment of a debt. 2. The winding up or closing of a company and selling of its assets.

Liquidator. A person named to supervise the closing of a company which is in liquidation.

Liquidity. Cash, or the fact of having cash or assets which can be changed into cash.

Liquidity ratio. A ratio of liquid assets (that is, current assets less stocks, but including debtors) to current liabilities, giving an indication of a company's solvency. Also called acid test ratio, quick ratio.

Liquid market. A market in a security where there are enough shares available to allow sales to take place without distorting the price (the opposite is a 'thin' market).

List. 1. Several items written one after the other. 2. A catalogue.

Listed company. A company whose shares can be bought or sold on the stock exchange.

Listed securities. Shares which can be bought or sold on the stock exchange, shares which appear on the official stock exchange list.

Listing Agreement. A document which a company signs when being listed on the stock exchange, in which it promises to abide by stock exchange regulations.

Listing details or Listing particulars. 1. Details of a company which are published when the company applies for a stock exchange listing. 2. Details of the institutions which are backing an issue.

Listing requirements. The conditions which must be met by a corporation before its stock can be listed on the Bombay Stock Exchange.

List price. The price for something as given in a catalogue.

Load. An amount of goods which are transported in a particular vehicle or aircraft Insurance to add extra charges to a price.

Load factor. A number of seats in a bus, plane or train which are occupied by passengers who have paid the full fare.

Load fund. A fund sold through a broker, with a high initial management charge or commission.

Loan. Money which has been lent.

Loan capital. A part of a company's capital which is a loan to be repaid at a later date.

Loan committee. A committee which examines applications for special loans, such as higher loans than normally allowed by a bank.

Loan participation. An arrangement whereby several banks come together as a group to share a very large loan to one single customer.

Loan portfolio. All the loans which a financial institution has made and which are still outstanding.

Loan shark. A person who lends money at a very high interest rate.

Loan stock. Stock issued by a company at a fixed rate of interest, as a means of raising a loan.

Loan to value. The amount of a mortgage expressed as a percentage of the value of the property. Abbr. LTV.

Local authority bond. A fixed-interest bond, repayable at a certain date, used by a local authority in order to raise a loan and similar to a Treasury bond.

Local authority deposits. Money deposited with a local authority to earn interest for the depositor.

Lock into or Lock in. To be fixed to a certain interest rate or exchange rate.

Lock up. To have capital invested in such a way that it cannot be used for other investments.

London Bullion Market. An international market dealing in gold and silver bullion and gold coins.

London Commodity Exchange. A London exchange dealing in commodities such as cotton, coffee, cocoa, etc., but not in metals. Abbr. LCE.

London Stock Exchange. The main British Stock Exchange where securities are bought and sold. Abbr. LSE

London Traded Options Market. A market where options are traded. Abbr. LTOM.

Long. For a large period of time.

Long credit. Credit terms which allow the borrower a long time to pay.

Long-dated bill. A bill which is payable in more than three months' time.

Long lease. A lease which runs for fifty years or more.

Long position. A situation where an investor sells long (i.e. sells forward shares which he owns).

Long-range. For a long period of time in the future.

Long-tail business. Insurance business where a claim only arises some years after the insurance contract was taken out.

Long-term. Over a long period of time.

Long-term loan. A loan to be repaid many years later.

Long-term borrowings. Borrowings which do not have to be repaid for some years.

Long-term security. A security which will mature in more than fifteen years' time.

Lose. 1. Not to have something any more. 2. To have less money. 3. To drop to a lower price.

Loss. 1. The state or process of not having something any more. 2. Damage to property or destruction of property, which is then subject to an insurance claim.

Loss-leader. An article which is sold at a loss to attract customers.

Loss relief. An amount of tax not to be paid on one year's profit to offset a loss in the previous year.

Lot. 1. A group of items sold together at an auction. 2. A group of shares which are sold.

Low. Not high or not much.

Lower. Smaller or less high.

Lowering. The act of making smaller or less expensive.

Low gearing. The fact of not having much borrowing in proportion to your capital.

Low yield. A yield on the share price which is low for the sector, suggesting that investors anticipate that the company will grow fast, and have pushed up the share price in expectation of growth.

Loyalty. The state of being faithful to someone or something.

Loyalty bonus. A special privilege given to shareholders who keep their shares for a certain period of time (used especially to attract investors to privatization issues).

LSE. Abbr. London Stock Exchange.

Ltd. Abbr. Limited company.

LTOM. Abbr. London Traded Options Market.

LTV. Abbr. Loan to value.

Lull. A quiet period.

Lump sum. Money paid in one single amount, not in several small sums.

Luncheon voucher. A ticket given by an employer to an employee in addition to their wages, which can be exchanged for food in a restaurant.

Luxury goods Or Luxury items. Expensive items which are not basic necessities.

Luxury tax. An extra tax levied on luxury goods.

M

M. Abbr. Million.

Machine-readable code. A set of signs or letters (such as a bar code or post code) which can be read by computers.

Macro. Very large, covering a wide area.

Macroeconomics. A study of the economics of a whole area, a whole industry, a whole group of the population or a whole country, in order to help in economic planning.

Macro funds. Large hedge funds which bet on whole economies.

Macro hedge fund. A hedge fund which invests in whole regions.

Magazine. A special type of newspaper, usually published only weekly or monthly, often with a glossy cover and often devoted to a particular subject.

Magnetic character reading or Magnetic ink character recognition. A system that recognizes characters by sensing magnetic ink (used on cheques). Abbr. MCR or MICR.

Magnetic ink. A special ink with magnetic particles in it, used for printing cheques.

Magnetic strip or Magnetic stripe. A black strip on credit cards and cash point cards, on which personal information about the account is recorded.

Mail. 1. A system of sending letters and parcels from one place to another. 2. Same as email.

Mail box. 1. One of several boxes where incoming mail is put in a large building. 2. A box where letters which are being sent are put to be collected. 3. An area of a computer memory where emails are stored.

Mailing list. A list of names and addresses of people who might be interested in a product, or a list of names and addresses of members of a society.

Mailing piece. A leaflet suitable for sending by direct mail.

Mail order. A system of buying and selling from a catalogue, placing orders and sending goods by mail.

Mail-order business. A company which sells its products by mail.

Mail-order catalogue. A catalogue from which a customer can order items to be sent by mail.

Mail-order selling. A method of selling in which orders are taken and products are delivered by mail.

Mail shot. 1. Leaflets sent by post to possible customers. 2. A single mailing of direct-mail advertising literature.

Maintain. 1. To keep something going or working. 2. To keep something working at the same level.

Maintenance. 1. The process of keeping things going or working. 2. The process of keeping a machine in good working order.

Maintenance contract. A contract by which a company keeps a piece of equipment in good working order.

Maintenance fee. A fee charged for keeping an account or a contract going.

Major. Important.

Major shareholder. A shareholder with a large number of shares.

Majority. More than half of a group.

Majority shareholder. A person who owns more than half the shares in a company.

Majority shareholding. A group of shares which are more than half the total.

Majority vote or Majority decision. A decision which represents the wishes of the largest group as shown by a vote.

Make. 1. To do an action. 2. To earn money. 3. To increase in value. 4. To have more money after a deal.

Make out. To write something.

Make over. To transfer property legally.

Maker. A person who signs a promissory note in which he or she promises to pay money.

Make up. To complete the accounts.

Make up for. To compensate for something.

Mal administration. Incompetent administration.

Malfeasance. An unlawful act.

Manage. 1. To direct or to be in charge of something. 2. To look after rented property for the owner.

Manageable. Which can be dealt with.

Managed derivatives fund. A fund which uses mainly futures and options instead of investing in the underlying securities.

Managed float. A process of floating of a currency where the exchange rate is controlled by the central bank. Also called dirty float.

Managed fund. A unit trust fund which is invested in specialist funds within the group and can be switched from one specialized investment area to another.

Managed unit trust. Same as managed fund.

Management. 1. The process of directing or running a business. 2. A group of managers or directors. 3. The process of running a fund or investment portfolio for a client.

Management accountant. An accountant who prepares financial information for managers so that they can take decisions.

Management accounts. Financial information prepared for a manager so that decisions can be made, including monthly or quarterly financial statements, often in great detail, with analysis of actual performance against the budget.

Management buy in. The purchase of a subsidiary company by a group of outside directors. Abbr. MBI.

Management buyout. The takeover of a company by a group of employees, usually senior managers and directors. Abbr. MBO.

Management by objectives (MBO). A way of managing a business by planning work for the managers to do and testing if it is completed correctly and on time.

Management consultant. A person who gives advice on how to manage a business.

Management course. A training course for managers.

Management team. All the managers who work in a particular company.

Management trainee. A young member of staff who is being trained to be a manager.

Management training. The process of training staff to be managers, by making them study problems and work out solutions.

Manager. 1. The head of a department in a company. 2. The person in charge of a branch or shop.

Managerial. Referring to managers.

Manager ship. The job of being a manager.

Managing director. The director who is in charge of a whole company. Abbr. MD.

Managing underwriter. An underwriting firm which organizes the underwriting of a share issue.

M&A. Abbr. Mergers and acquisitions.

Mandate. An order which allows something to take place.

Mandatory. Which everyone must obey.

Mandatory meeting. A meeting which all staff have to attend.

Mandatory bid. An offer to purchase the shares of a company which has to be made when a shareholder acquires 30% of that company's shares.

Manpower forecasting. The process of calculating how many employees will be needed in the future, and how many will actually be available.

Manpower planning. The process of planning to obtain the right number of employees in each job.

Manufactured goods. Items which are made by machine.

Margin. 1. The difference between the money received when selling a product and the money paid for it. 2. Extra space or time allowed. 3. The difference between interest paid to depositors and interest charged to borrowers (by a bank, building society, etc.) 4. A deposit paid when purchasing a futures contract.

Marginal. 1. Hardly worth the money paid. 2. Not very profitable.

Marginal cost. The cost of making a single extra unit above the number already planned.

Marginal land. Land which is almost not worth farming.

Marginal pricing. 1. The practice of basing the selling price of a product on its variable costs of production plus a margin, but excluding fixed costs. 2. The practice of making the selling price the same as the cost of a single extra unit above the number already planned.

Marginal purchase. Something which a buyer feels is only just worth buying.

Marginal rate of tax or Marginal rate of taxation. The percentage of tax which a taxpayer pays at the top rate.

Marginal revenue. The income from selling a single extra unit above the number already sold.

Margin call. A request for a purchaser of a futures contract or an option to pay more margin, since the fall in the price of the securities or commodity has removed the value of the original margin deposited.

Margin of error. The number of mistakes which can be accepted in a document or in a calculation.

Margin of safety. The units produced (or sales of such units) which are above the breakeven point.

Marine underwriter. A person or company that insures ships and their cargoes.

Marital status. The condition of being married or not.

Maritime law. Laws referring to ships, ports, etc.

Maritime lawyer. A lawyer who specializes in legal matters concerning ships and cargoes.

Mark. 1. A sign put on an item to show something. 2. A former unit of currency in Germany.

Mark down. To make the price of something lower.

Mark-down. 1. A reduction of the price of something to less than its usual price. 2. The percentage amount by which a price has been lowered.

Market. 1. An area where a product might be sold or the group of people who might buy a product. 2. A place where money or commodities are traded. 3. To buy shares on the stock exchange, not privately. 4. A place where shares are bought and sold. 5. To make products which appeal to a wealthy section of the market or to a wider, less wealthy section of the market to sell a product, or to present and promote a product in a way which will help to sell it.

Marketability. The fact of being able to be sold easily.

Marketable securities. Stocks, shares, CDs etc., which can be bought or sold on a stock market.

Market analysis. The detailed examination and report of a market.

Market analyst. A person who studies the stock market in general.

Market cycle. A period during which a market expands, then slows down and then expands again.

Market economist. A person who specializes in the study of financial structures and the return on investments in the stock market.

Market forces. The influences on the sales of a product which bring about a change in prices.

Market forecast. A forecast of prices on the stock market.

Marketing. The business of presenting and promoting goods or services in such a way as to make customers want to buy them.

Marketing agreement. A contract by which one company will market another company's products.

Marketing department. The section of a company dealing with marketing and sales.

Marketing manager. A person in charge of a marketing department.

Market leader. 1. A product which sells most in a market. 2. The company with the largest market share.

Market maker. A person who buys or sells shares on the stock market and offers to do so in a certain list of securities (a market maker operates a book, listing the securities he or she is willing to buy or sell, and makes his or her money by charging a commission on each transaction).

Market neutral funds. Hedge funds not related to general market movements, but which try to find opportunities to arbitrage temporary slight changes in the relative values of particular financial assets.

Market operator. A person who trades on a stock market or financial market.

Market opportunity. The possibility of going into a market for the first time.

Market optimism. A feeling that the stock market will rise.

Market order. An order to a broker to buy or sell at the current price.

Market polarization. A situation where a market is concentrated round a few suppliers or traders.

Market price. 1. The price at which a product can be sold. 2. The price at which a share stands in a stock market.

Market professionals. People who work in a stock market, as brokers, analysts, etc.

Market purchases. Purchases of shares in a company on the normal stock market (by a company planning a takeover bid).

Market rate. The normal price in the market.

Market research. The process of examining the possible sales of a product and the possible customers for it before it is put on the market.

Market sentiment. A general feeling among investors or financial analysts on a stock market.

Market share. The percentage of a total market which the sales of a company's product cover.

Market strategist. A person who plans how to buy and sell on the stock market.

Market trends. Gradual changes taking place in a market.

Market value. The value of an asset, a share, a product or a company if sold today.

Market value added. The difference between a company's market value and the amount of its invested capital. Abbr. MVA.

Market value adjuster. A method of calculating the loss in market value of a bond or insurance when it is being surrendered. Abbr. MVA.

Market watcher. A person who follows stock market trends closely.

Mark up. 1. To increase the price of something. 2. The difference between the cost of a product or service and its selling price.

Mass production. The manufacture of large quantities of identical products.

MasterCard. An international credit organization, backed by a group of banks.

Matched bargains. Sales and purchases of shares which are conducted at the same time, where the buyers and sellers come together to agree on the price (as opposed to the 'quotation' system, where the market makers make the selling prices for shares).

Maturity. 1. The third stage in a product life cycle when a product is well established in the market though no longer enjoying increasing sales, after which sooner or later it will start to decline. 2. The time at which something becomes due for payment or repayment.

Maturity date. A date when a government stock, an assurance policy or a debenture will become due for payment. Also called date of maturity.

Maturity yield. A calculation of the yield on a fixed-interest investment, assuming it is bought at a certain price and held to maturity.

Maximization. The process of making something as large as possible.

Maximize. To make something as large as possible.

Maximum. The largest possible number, price or quantity.

Mean. Min adjective average.

Mean price. The average price of a share in a day's trading.

Means test. An inquiry into how much money someone earns to see if they are eligible for state benefits.

Measure. 1. A way of calculating size or quantity. 2. A type of action.

Measurement. A way of judging something.

Measurement of profitability. A way of calculating how profitable something is.

Median. The middle number in a list of numbers.

Medical insurance. Insurance which pays the cost of medical treatment, especially when someone is travelling abroad.

Medium. Middle or average.

Medium-term. Referring to a point between short term and long term.

Medium-term bond. A bond which matures within five to fifteen years.

Meet. 1. To be satisfactory for something. 2. To pay for something.

Meeting. An event at which a group of people come together in order to discuss matters of common interest to them.

Mega-cap. A share with the very highest capitalization and growth.

Membership. All the members of a group.

Memorandum and articles of association or Memorandum of association. The legal documents which set up a limited company and give details of its name, aims, authorized share capital, conduct of meetings, appointment of directors and registered office.

Mentor. A person who is respected and trusted by a less experienced employee and offers special guidance and support to them.

Mercantile law. Laws relating to business.

Mercantile agent. A person who sells on behalf of a business or another person and earns a commission.

Mercantile marine. All the commercial ships of a country.

Merchant. A company, shop or other business which accepts a certain type of credit card for purchases.

Merchant bank. 1. A bank which arranges loans to companies, deals in international finance, buys and sells shares and launches new companies on the stock exchange, but does not provide normal banking services to the general public. 2. A bank which operates a credit card system (accepting payment on credit cards from retailers or 'merchants')

Merchant banker. A person who has a high position in a merchant bank.

Merchant number. A number of the merchant, printed at the top of the report slip when depositing credit card payments.

Merger. The joining together of two or more companies.

Merger accounting. A way of presenting the accounts of a newly acquired company within the group accounts, so as to show it in the best possible light.

Merit increase. An increase in pay given to an employee because his or her work is good.

Merit rating. The process of judging how well an employee works, so that payment can be according to merit.

Method. A way of doing something.

Micro-cap. A share in a company with very small capitalization.

Microeconomics. The study of the economics of people or single companies.

Micro-payments. A technology developed to allow visitors to spend very small amounts of money (normally for information) on an Internet site.

Middle-income. People with average incomes, not very high or very low.

Middle management. Department managers in a company, who carry out the policy set by the directors and organize the work of a group of employees.

Middle price. A price between the buying and selling price (usually shown in indices).

Middle rate. An exchange rate between the buy and sell rates for a foreign currency.

Millionaire. A person who has more than one million pounds or dollars.

Mini budget. An interim statement about financial plans from a finance minister.

Minimum. The smallest possible quantity, price or number.

Minimum dividend. The smallest dividend which is legal and accepted by the shareholders.

Minimum balance. The smallest amount of money which must be kept in an account to qualify for the services provided.

Minimum reserves. The smallest amount of reserves which a commercial bank must hold with a central bank.

Minimum wage. The lowest hourly wage which a company can legally pay its employees.

Minor. Less important.

Minority. 1. A number or quantity which is less than half of the total. 2. A section of the population from a specific racial group, which does not make up the majority of the population.

Minority shareholder. A person who owns a group of shares but less than half of the shares in a company.

Minority shareholding. A group of shares which are less than half the total.

Minus factor. An unfavorable factor.

Mirror fund. An investment trust where the manager also runs a unit trust with the same objectives.

Misappropriate. To use illegally money which is not yours, but with which you have been trusted.

Misappropriation. The illegal use of money by someone who is not the owner but who has been trusted to look after it.

Miscalculate. To calculate wrongly, or to make a mistake in calculating something.

Misfeasance. The offence of doing something in an improper way.

Mismanage. To manage something badly.

Mismanagement. Bad management.

Misrepresent. To report facts or what someone says wrongly.

Misrepresentation. 1. The act of making a wrong statement in order to persuade someone to enter into a contract such as one for buying a product or service. 2. The act of wrongly reporting facts.

Mixed. 1. Made up of different sorts or of different types of things together. 2. Neither good nor bad.

Mixed economy. A system which contains both nationalized industries and private enterprise.

MMC. Abbr. Monopolies and Mergers Commission

Mobilize. To bring things or people together and prepare them for action, especially to fight.

Mode. A way of doing something.

Mode of payment. The way in which payment is made, e.g. cash or cheque.

Model. 1. A small copy of something made to show what it will look like when finished. 2. A style or type of product. 3. A person whose job is to wear new clothes to show them to possible buyers. 4. Something which can be copied. 5. A description in the form of mathematical data adjective which is a perfect example to be copied.

Model risk. The possibility that a computer model used when investing may have a flaw which makes it function badly in extreme market conditions.

Modified accounts. Less detailed annual accounts which can be deposited with the Registrar of Companies by small or medium-sized companies.

Momentum. A movement upwards of share prices, suggesting that prices will continue to rise.

Momentum investor. An investor who buys shares which seem to be moving upwards.

Monetarism. A theory that the amount of money in the economy affects the level of prices, so that inflation can be controlled by regulating money supply.

Monetary. Referring to money or currency.

Monetary control. Control of the money supply.

Monetary policy. The government's policy relating to finance, e.g. bank interest rates, taxes, government expenditure and borrowing.

Monetary standard. The fixing of a fixed exchange rate for a currency.

Monetary unit. A main item of currency of a country (a dollar, pound, yen, etc.)

Money. 1. Coins and notes used for buying and selling. 2. Referring to an option to buy at a lower price or to sell at a higher price.

Money-back guarantee or Money-back offer. A guarantee that money will be paid back to customers who are not satisfied with their purchases.

Money-back option. An option that guarantees to return the premium if the option is not taken up.

Money broker. A dealer operating in the inter bank and foreign exchange markets.

Money laundering. The act of passing illegal money into the normal banking system.

Moneylender. A person who lends money at interest.

Money lying idle. Money which is not being used to produce interest, which is not invested in business.

Money management. Same as fund management.

Money market. 1. A place where large sums of money are lent or borrowed. 2. A market for buying and selling short-term loans or financial instruments such as Treasury bills and CDs, which can be easily converted to cash.

Money market fund. An investment fund, which only invests in money market instruments.

Money market instruments. Short-term investments, such as CDs, which can be easily turned into cash and are traded on the money markets.

Money order. A document which can be bought as a way of sending money through the post.

Money purchase scheme. Any pension scheme to which members make contributions which determine the final pension (as opposed to a 'final salary scheme' where the pension is a percentage of the final salary earned).

Money rates. Rates of interest for borrowers or lenders.

Money-spinner. An item which sells very well or which is very profitable.

Money supply. The amount of money which exists in a country.

Note: Money supply is believed by some to be at the centre of control of a country's economy. If money supply is tight (i.e. the government restricts the issue of new notes and reduces the possibility of lending) the amount of money available in the economy is reduced and thus may reduce spending.

Monitor. A screen on a computer.

Monopoly. A situation where one person or company is the only supplier of a particular product or service.

Month end. The end of a calendar month, when accounts have to be drawn up.

Monthly. Happening every month or which is received every month.

Monthly statement. A statement sent to a customer at the end of each month, itemizing transactions which have taken place in his or her account ad every month.

Monthly sales report. A report made every month showing the number of items sold or the amount of money a company has received for selling stock.

Moratorium. A temporary stop to repayments of interest on loans or capital owed.

Mortality and expense risk charge. An extra charge to pay on some annuities to guarantee that if the policyholder dies his heirs will receive a benefit, and also that the insurance company will be compensated for an annuitant who lives longer than he or she should according to the mortality tables. Also called M&E fee.

Mortality rate. The number of deaths occurring during a particular period, shown as a percentage of the total population.

Mortgage. Money lent on the security of a house or other property owned by the borrower, usually in order to enable the borrower to buy the property.

Mortgage payments. Money paid each month as interest on a mortgage, plus repayment of a small part of the capital borrowed.

Mortgage arrears. Mortgage payments which are due but have not been paid.

Mortgage-backed securities. Shares which are backed by the security of a mortgage.

Mortgage bank. A bank which lends money to purchasers of properties, on the security of the property.

Mortgage bond. A certificate showing that a mortgage exists and that property is security for it.

Mortgage broker. A person who arranges mortgages, by putting a borrower in touch with a possible lender.

Mortgage debenture. A debenture where the lender can be repaid by selling the company's property.

Mortgagee. A person or company which lends money for someone to buy a property.

Mortgage portfolio. All the mortgages made by a bank or building societies which have not been paid off.

Mortgage refinancing. The act of arranging to increase a mortgage on a property so as to pay for improvements to the property.

Mounting. Increasing.

Movement. An act of changing position or going up or down.

Movement of capital. Same as capital flow.

Moving average. An average of share prices on a stock market, where the calculation is made over a period which moves forward regularly.

Note: The commonest are 100-day or 200-day averages, or 10- or 40-week moving averages. The average is calculated as the average figure for the whole period, and moves forward one day or week at a time. These averages are often used by chartists.

Multilateral. Between several organizations or countries.

Multilateral netting. A method of putting together sums from various sources into one currency (used by groups of banks trading in several currencies at the same time).

Multi-manager fund. A hedge fund which uses a wide portfolio of fund managers to produce a balanced exposure for relatively small investors.

Multimillionaire. A person who owns property or investments worth several million pounds or dollars.

Multinational. A company which has branches or subsidiary companies in several countries. Also called transnational.

Multiple applications. Several applications for a new issue of shares, made by the same person, but under different names (in some share issues, people making multiple applications may be prosecuted).

Multiple ownership. A situation where something is owned by several parties jointly.

Multiplier. A number which multiplies another, or a factor which tends to multiply something (as the effect of new expenditure on total income and reserves).

Multiply. 1. To calculate the sum of various numbers added together a certain number of times. 2. To grow or to increase.

Mutual fund. An organization which takes money from small investors and invests it in stocks and shares for them, the investment being in the form of shares in the fund.

Mutual insurance company. A company which belongs to insurance policy holders. Also called mutual company.

Mutual savings bank. A savings bank which is owned by the customers who have deposits with it.

MVA. Abbr. 1. Market value added. 2. Market value adjuster.

N

Narrow market. A market in a share where very few shares are available for sale, and where the price can vary sharply.

NASDAQ. A system which provides quotations via computer for the US electronic trading market, mainly in high-tech stocks, and also for some large corporations listed on the NYSE, and publishes an index of stock price movements. Full form National Association of Securities.

National currency. The official currency of a country, which is legal tender in that country.

National debt. Money borrowed by a government.

National income. The value of income from the sales of goods and services in a country.

Nationalization. The taking over of private industry by the state.

Nationalize. To put a privately-owned industry under state ownership and control.

Nationalized industry. An industry which was privately owned, but is now owned by the state.

Nationality declaration. A declaration on some share application forms that the applicant is of a certain nationality.

NAV. Abbr. Net asset value.

Negative carry. A deal where the cost of finance is more than the return on the capital used.

Negative cash flow. A situation where more money is going out of a company than is coming in.

Negative equity. A situation where a house bought with a mortgage becomes less valuable than the money borrowed to buy it (because of falling house prices).

Negative yield curve. A situation where the yield on a long-term investment is less than that on a short-term investment.

Neglected business. A company which has not been actively run by its owners and could therefore do better.

Negligence. 1. A lack of proper care or failure to carry out a duty (with the result that a person or property is harmed). 2. The act of not doing a job properly when one is capable of doing it.

Negotiable. 1. Which can be transferred from one person to another or exchanged for cash. 2. Which can be discussed so that an agreement is reached.

Negotiated commission. A commission agreed with an advertising agency before work starts, and which may be different from standard commissions.

Negotiation. The discussion of terms and conditions in order to reach an agreement.

Negotiator. 1. A person who discusses a problem with the aim of achieving agreement between different people or groups of people. 2. A person who works in an estate agency.

Net. 1. Referring to a price, weight, pay, etc., after all deductions have been made. 2. Payment has to be the full price, with no discount allowed to make a true profit.

Net asset value per share. The value of a company calculated by dividing the shareholders' funds by the number of shares issued.

Net borrowings. A company's borrowings, less any cash the company is holding in its bank accounts.

Net cash flow. The difference between the money coming in and the money going out.

Net change on the day. The difference between the opening price of a share at the beginning of a day's trading and the closing price at the end.

Net current assets. The current assets of a company (cash and stocks) less any liabilities. Also called net working capital.

Net dividend per share. The dividend per share after deduction of personal income tax.

Net earnings. The total earnings of a business after tax and other deductions.

Net income. A person's income which is left after taking away tax and other deductions.

Net interest margin. The difference between what a bank receives in interest on loans and what it pays out in interest on deposits.

Net loss. An actual loss, after deducting overheads.

Net margin. The percentage difference between received price and all costs, including overheads.

Net price. The price of goods or services which cannot be reduced by a discount.

Net profit. The amount by which income from sales is larger than all expenditure. Also called profit after tax.

Net receipts. Receipts after deducting commission, tax, discounts, etc.

Net return. A return on an investment after tax has been paid.

Net salary. The salary which is left after deducting tax and national insurance contributions.

Net sales. The total amount of sales less damaged or returned items and discounts to retailers.

Net weight. The weight of goods after deducting the packing material and container.

Net working capital. Same as net current assets.

Net worth. The value of all the property of a person or company after taking away what the person or company owes.

Net yield. The profit from investments after deduction of tax.

New issue. An issue of new shares to raise finance for a company.

New issue market. A market where companies can raise finance by issuing new shares, or by a flotation.

New issue sale. A sale of a new issue of shares.

News agency. An office which distributes news to newspapers and television stations.

Niche. A special place in a market, occupied by one company (a 'niche company').

Niche Company. Company specializing in a particular type of product or service, which occupies a market niche.

Nil return. A report showing no sales, income, tax, etc.

Nominal. (of a payment) very small.

Nominal capital. The total of the face value of all the shares which a company is authorized to issue.

Nominal interest rate. An interest rate expressed as a percentage of the face value of a bond, not on its market value.

Nominal ledger. A book which records a company's transactions in the various accounts.

Nominal value. Same as face value.

Nominate. To suggest someone for a job.

Nomination. The act of nominating someone for a position.

Nominee. A person who is nominated, especially someone who is appointed to deal with financial matters on your behalf.

Nominee account. An account held on behalf of someone.

Non-acceptance. A situation in which the person who is to pay a bill of exchange does not accept it.

Non cash items. Cheques, drafts and similar items which are not in the form of cash.

Nondeductible. Which cannot be deducted from income tax.

Non-durable goods. Goods which are used up soon after they have been bought, e.g. food or newspapers.

Non-executive director. A director who attends board meetings and gives advice, but does not work full-time for the company. Also called outside director.

Note: Non-executive directors keep an eye on the way the company is run, and in particular make sure that the executive directors are doing their work properly. They may also intervene in disputes between directors, or between shareholders and directors.

Non-interest. A bank's income from fees and charges, as opposed to income from interest.

Non-legal investment. An investment which is not on the legal list, and which a bank cannot invest in.

Non-negotiable instrument. A document which cannot be exchanged for cash, e.g. a crossed cheque.

Non-profit organization. An organization (such as a club) which is not allowed by law to make a profit.

Note: Non-profit organizations include charities, professional associations, trade unions, and religious, arts, community, research, and campaigning bodies.

Non-recurring items. Special items in a set of accounts which appear only once.

Non-refundable. Which will not be refunded.

Non-regulated. Which is not subject to government regulations.

Non-taxable. Which is not subject to tax.

Non-voting shares. Shares which do not allow the shareholder to vote at meetings. (also called 'A' shares)

Note of hand. A document stating that someone promises to pay an amount of money on a certain date.

Notice. 1. A piece of written information. 2. An official warning that a contract is going to end or that terms are going to be changed. 3. The time allowed before something takes place.

NYSE. Abbr. New York Stock Exchange.

O

OAC. Abbr. On approved credit.

O & M. Abbr. Organization and methods.

Objective. Something which you hope to achieve.

Obligation. 1. A duty to do something. 2. A debt.

Occupational. Referring to a job.

Occupational accident. An accident which takes place at work.

Occupational pension. A pension which is paid by the company by which a worker has been employed.

Occupational pension scheme. A pension scheme where the worker gets a pension from a fund set up by the company he or she has worked for, which is related to the salary he or she was earning. Also called company pension scheme.

Occupier. A person who lives in a property.

Odd change. Keep the small change which is left over.

Odd lot. 1. A group of miscellaneous items for sale at an auction. 2. A group of miscellaneous items, such as a small block of shares.

OECD. Abbr. Organization for Economic Co-operation and Development.

OFEX. Private trading facilities for buying and selling shares in companies which are not quoted on the London Stock Exchange.

Off. 1. Taken away from a price. 2. Lower than a previous price.

Off-balance-sheet financing. Financing by leasing equipment instead of buying it, so that it does not appear in the balance sheet as an asset.

Offer. 1. A statement that you are willing to give or do something, especially to pay a specific amount of money to buy something. 2. A statement that you are willing to sell something. 3. A statement that you are willing to employ someone. 4. A statement that a company is prepared to buy another company's shares and take the company over.

Offer document. A formal document where a company offers to buy shares at a certain price as part of a takeover bid.

Offered market. A market where there are more sellers than buyers.

Offered price. A price at which shares are offered for sale by a market maker on the stock exchange (the opposite, i.e. the price at which an investor sells shares, is the 'bid price'; the difference between the two is the 'spread')

Offered rate. A rate of interest at which banks are prepared to lend each other money.

Offer for sale. A situation where a company advertises new shares for sale to the public as a way of launching itself on the stock exchange.

Offer for subscription. A similar to an offer for sale, except there is a minimum level of subscription for the shares, and if this is not reached the offer is withdrawn.

Offering. An action of stating that you are prepared to sell something at a certain price.

Offering circular. A document which gives information about a company whose shares are being sold to the public for the first time.

Offer period. A time during which a takeover bid for a company is open.

Offer price. The price at which investors buy new shares or units in a unit trust (the opposite, i.e. the selling price, is called the 'bid price'; the difference between the two is the 'spread').

Office. 1. A set of rooms where a company works or where business is done. 2. A room where someone works and does business. 3. A government department. 4. A post or position.

Office hours. The time when an office is open.

Office staff. People who work in offices.

Official. From a government department or organization.

Official exchange rate. An exchange rate which is imposed by the government.

Official intervention. An attempt by a government to influence the exchange rate by buying or selling foreign currency.

Official List. A daily publication by the Bombay Stock Exchange of the highest and lowest prices recorded for each share during the trading session.

Official market. The market in shares on the Bombay Stock Exchange (as opposed to the grey market).

Official receiver. A government official who is appointed to run a company which is in financial difficulties, to pay off its debts as far as possible and to close it down.

Offset. To balance one thing against another so that they cancel each other out.

Off-the-job training. Training given to employees away from their place of work.

Oil-exporting country. A country which produces oil and sells it to others.

Oil-importing country. A country which imports oil.

Oil-producing country. A country which produces oil.

Oligopoly. A situation where only a few sellers control the market.

Omission. A thing which has been omitted, or the act of omitting something.

On. 1. Being a member of a group. 2. In a certain way. 3. At a time. 4. Doing something.

One-sided. Which favors one side and not the other in a negotiation.

One-stop banking. A type of banking where a single organization offers a whole range of services (including such things as mortgages, loans and pensions).

One-stop shopping. The practice of taking a range of financial services from a single organization, e.g. from a bank which offers loans, mortgages, pensions and insurance as well as the normal personal banking services.

One-way trade. A situation where one country sells to another, but does not buy anything in return.

Online. Ad linked via a computer directly to another computer, a computer network or, especially, the internet; on the internet.

Online banking. A system by which customers have bank accounts which they can access direct from their home computers, using the internet, and can carry out operations such as checking on their account balance, paying invoices and receiving their salaries electronically.

Online bill paying. A system of paying bills directly from an account using the Internet.

On-the-job training. Training given to employees at their place of work.

On the side. Ad separate from your normal work, and hidden from your employer.

Open. 1. At work, not closed. 2. Ready to accept something. 3. To start a new business.

Open account. An account where the supplier offers the purchaser credit without security.

Open credit. Credit given to good customers without security.

Open-ended. With no fixed limit or with some items not specified.

Open-ended fund. A fund (such as a unit trust) where investors buy units, the money paid being invested in a range of securities (as opposed to a closed fund, such as an investment trust, where the investor buys shares in the trust company, and receives dividends).

Open-ended investment company. A new form of unit trust, in which the investor purchases shares at a single price, as opposed to the offer bid pricing system used by ordinary unit trusts. Abbr. OEIC.

Opening. The act of starting a new business.

Opening balance. A balance at the beginning of an accounting period.

Opening entry. The first entry in an account.

Opening hours. The hours when a shop or business is open.

Opening price. A price at the start of a day's trading.

Opening stock. The stock details at the beginning of an accounting period.

Open market. A market where anyone can buy or sell.

Open market operation. A sale or purchase of government stock by ordinary investors, used by the government as a means of influencing money supply.

Open outcry system. A system of buying and selling used in some exchanges, where the brokers shout prices, offers or orders to each other.

Open ticket. A ticket which can be used on any date.

Operate. To do business, or to run a business or a machine.

Operating. The general running of a business or of a machine.

Operating budget. A forecast of income and expenditure over a period of time.

Operating costs. The costs of the day-to-day activities of a company. Also called operating expenses and running costs.

Operating income or Operating profit. The profit made by a company in its usual business. Also called operating earnings.

Operating loss. A loss made by a company in its usual business.

Operating manual. A book which shows how to work a machine.

Operating system. The main program which operates a computer.

Operation. An activity or a piece of work, or the task of running something.

Operational. To the day-to-day activities of a business or to the way in which something is run.

Operational budget. A forecast of expenditure on running a business.

Operational costs. The costs of running a business.

Operational gearing. A situation where a company has high fixed costs which are funded by borrowings.

Operational planning. The planning of how a business is to be run.

Operational research. A study of a company's way of working to see if it can be made more efficient and profitable.

Operations department. The general administration department of a company.

Operations review. An act of examining the way in which a company or department works to see how it can be made more efficient and profitable.

Operator. 1. A person who runs a business. 2. (on the stock exchange) a person who buys and sells shares hoping to make a quick profit.

Opportunity. A chance to do something successfully.

Opportunity cost. 1. The cost of a business initiative in terms of profits that could have been gained through an alternative plan. 2. The value of another method of investment which could have been used, instead of the one adopted.

Oppose. To try to stop something happening; to vote against something.

Optimism. A state of mind in which you are sure that everything will work out well.

Optimistic. Feeling sure that everything will work out well.

Optimum. Best.

Option. The opportunity to buy or sell something within a fixed period of time at a fixed price.

Optional. Which can be done or not done, taken or not taken, as a person chooses.

Option contract. A right to buy or sell shares at a fixed price.

Option dealing. Buying and selling share options.

Option holder. A person (stock exchange) who holds an option (i.e. who has bought an option).

Option to purchase. An option which gives someone the possibility to buy something within a period of time.

Option to sell. An option which gives someone the possibility to sell something within a period of time.

Option trading. The business of buying and selling share options.

Order. 1. The way in which records such as filing cards or invoices are arranged. 2. An official request for goods to be supplied. 3. A document which allows money to be paid to someone. 4. (stock exchange) an instruction to a broker to buy or sell. 5. Pay money.

Order book. A book which records orders received.

Order cheque. A cheque which is paid to a named person with the words 'or order' after the payee's name, showing that he can endorse it and pass it to someone else if he wishes.

Order-driven system or Order-driven market. A price system on a stock exchange, where prices vary according to the level of orders (as opposed to a 'quote-driven' system).

Order fulfillment. The process of supplying items which have been ordered.

Order processing. The work of dealing with orders.

Ordinary interest. Annual interest calculated on the basis of 360 days (as opposed to 'exact interest' which is calculated on 365 days).

Ordinary resolution. A resolution put before an AGM, usually referring to some general procedural matter, and which requires a simple majority of votes to be accepted.

Ordinary share capital. The capital of a company in the form of money paid for ordinary shares.

Ordinary shares. Normal shares in a company, which have no special benefits or restrictions.

Organization. 1. A way of arranging something so that it works efficiently. 2. A group or institution which is arranged for efficient work.

Organizational chart. A chart showing the hierarchical relationships between employees in a company.

Organization and methods. A process of examining how an office works, and suggesting how it can be made more efficient. Abbr. O & M.

Organization for Economic Co-operation and Development. An organization representing the industrialized countries, aimed at encouraging international trade, wealth and employment in member countries. Abbr. OECD.

Organize. 1. To set up a system for doing something. 2. To arrange something so that it works

Organized labour. Employees who are members of trade unions.

Other people's money. Money that belongs to customers, clients or shareholders, i.e. not to the people who are using it or investing it. Abbr. OPM.

Out. 1. On strike. 2. To be wrong in calculating something, or to be wrongly calculated.

Outbid. To offer a better price than someone else.

Outflow. Capital which is sent out of a country for investment abroad.

Outflows. Money withdrawn from a fund in which it was previously invested.

Outgoings. Money which is paid out.

Outlay. Money spent expenditure.

Outlook. A view of what is going to happen in the future.

Out-of-date cheque. A cheque which has not been cleared because its date is too old, normally more than three months.

Out of pocket. Ad having paid out money personally.

Out-of-pocket expenses. An amount of money paid back to an employee who has spent his or her personal money on company business.

Outperform. To do better than other companies.

Out performance. The fact of doing better than other companies.

Output. The amount which a company, person or machine produces.

Output tax. VAT charged by a company on goods or services sold, and which the company pays to the government.

Outside. 1. Not in a company's office or building. 2. Not during office hours, when the office is not open.

Outside dealer. A person who is not a member of the stock exchange but is allowed to trade.

Outside worker. An employee who does not work in a company's offices.

Outstanding. Not yet paid or completed.

Note: The difference between 'outstanding' and 'overdue'. If a debtor has 30 days credit, then his debts are outstanding until the end of the 30 days, and they only become overdue on the 31st day.

Outstanding cheque. A cheque which has been written and therefore has been entered in the company's ledgers, but which has not been presented for payment and so has not been debited from the company's bank account.

Outturn. An amount produced by a country or company.

Overall. Covering or including everything.

Overall balance of payments. The total of current and long-term balance of payments.

Overcapacity. An unused capacity for producing something

Overcapitalized. To a company with more capital than it needs.

Overdraft. 1. An amount of money which a company or person can withdraw from a bank account, with the bank's permission, despite the fact that the account is empty. 2. A negative amount of money in an account, i.e. a situation where a cheque is more than the money in the account on which it is drawn.

Overdraft facilities. An arrangement with a bank to have an overdraft.

Overdraft limit. A total which is agreed between the bank and a customer as the maximum amount the customer's account may be overdrawn.

Overdraft protection. A system which protects a customer from overdrawing his account, either by switching money automatically from another account, or by offering a line of credit.

Overdraw. To take out more money from a bank account than there is in it.

Overdue. Which has not been paid on time.

Overexposure. The fact of being too exposed to risky loans.

Over funding. A situation where the government borrows more money than it needs for expenditure, by selling too much government stock.

Over geared. To a company which has high borrowings in comparison to its assets.

Overhang. A large quantity of shares or of a commodity or of unsold stock available for sale, which has the effect of depressing the market price.

Overhead budget. A plan of probable overhead costs.

Overheads. The indirect costs of the day-to-day running of a business, i.e. not money spent of producing goods, but money spent on such things as renting or maintaining buildings and machinery.

Overheating. A rise in industrial activity in an economy, leading to a rise in inflation (the economy is then said to be 'overheated').

Overnight money. Money deposited for less than 24 hours.

Overnight repo. A repurchase agreement, where banks sell securities for cash and repurchase them the next day at a higher price (used by central banks as a means of regulating the money markets).

Overpaid. Paid too much.

Overpay. 1. To pay too much to someone or for something. 2. To pay an extra amount to reduce the total capital borrowed on a mortgage.

Overpayment. 1. An act of paying too much. 2. The payment of a lump sum to reduce the capital borrowed on a mortgage.

Overrated. Valued more highly than it should be.

Overseas. Across the sea, or to or in foreign countries.

Overseas division. The section of a company dealing with trade with other countries.

Overseas funds. Investment funds based in other countries.

Overseas markets. Markets in foreign countries.

Oversell. To sell more than you can produce.

Overspending. The act of spending more than is allowed.

Overstock. To have a bigger stock of something than is needed.

Over subscription. A situation where people have subscribed for more shares in a new issue than are being issued.

Over-the-counter. Involving shares which are not listed on the main stock exchange. Abbr. OTC.

Over-the-counter market. A secondary market in shares which are not listed on the main stock exchange.

Overtime. Hours worked in addition to your normal working hours.

Overtime pay. Pay for extra time worked.

Overtrading. A situation where a company increases sales and production too much and too quickly, so that it runs short of cash.

Overvalue. To give a higher value to something or someone than is right.

Owe. To have to pay money.

Own. To have or to possess.

Owner. A person who owns something.

Owners' equity. A value of the shares in a company owned by the owners of the company.

Ownership. The fact of owning something.

P

P.a. Abbr. Per annum.

Package. A group of different items joined together in one deal.

Package deal. An agreement which deals with several different items at the same time.

Paid. 1. For which money has been given. 2. To an amount which has been settled.

Paid assistant. An assistant who receives a salary.

Paid-in capital. Capital in a business which has been provided by its shareholders (usually in the form of payments for shares above their par value).

Paid-up capital or Paid-up share capital. An amount of money paid for the issued capital shares (it does not include called-up capital which has not yet been paid for).

Paid-up shares. Shares which have been completely paid for by the shareholders.

Palmtop. A very small computer which can be held in your hand and which usually has a character recognition screen instead of a keyboard.

PAN. Abbr. Permanent account number.

P&L. Abbr. Profit and loss.

Panel. 1. A flat surface standing upright. 2. A group of people who give advice on a problem.

Panic. A state of being very frightened.

Panic buying. A rush to buy something at any price because stocks may run out.

Paper. 1. A document which can represent money (e.g. a bill of exchange or a promissory note) 2. Shares in the form of share certificates.

Paper gain. Same as paper profit.

Paper loss. A loss made when an asset has fallen in value but has not been sold.

Paper offer. A takeover bid, where the purchasing company offers its shares in exchange for shares in the company being taken over (as opposed to a cash offer).

Paper profit. A profit on an asset which has increased in price but has not been sold. Also called paper gain.

Paperwork. Office work, especially writing memos and filling in forms.

Par. Equal, at the same price. (Shares at par shares whose market price is the same as their face value).

Parallel markets. Money markets, where institutions such as banks, or organizations such as local authorities, can lend or borrow money without having to go through the main money markets.

Parameter. A fixed limit.

Parcel of shares. A group of shares (such as 50 or 100) which are sold as a group.

Parent company. A company which owns more than 50% of the shares of another company.

Parity. The fact of being at an equal level or price with something else.

Part delivery. A delivery that contains only some of the items in an order.

Part exchange. The act of giving an old product as part of the payment for a new one.

Participate. To take part in an activity or enterprise.

Participating preference shares or Stock. Preference shares which get an extra bonus dividend if company profits reach a certain level.

Participation. The act of taking part.

Participation fee. A fee paid to a bank for taking part in underwriting a loan.

Participator. A person who has an interest in a company (e.g. an ordinary or preference shareholder, a creditor or the owner of rights to shares).

Particular average. A situation where part of a shipment is lost or damaged and the insurance costs are borne by the owner of the lost goods and not shared among all the owners of the shipment.

Partly-secured creditors. A creditors whose debts are not fully covered by the value of the security.

Partly-paid capital. A capital which represents partly-paid shares.

Partly-paid up shares. Shares where the shareholders have not paid the full face value.

Partner. A person who works in a business and has an equal share in it with other partners.

Partnership. An unregistered business where two or more people (but not more than twenty) share the risks and profits according to a partnership agreement.

Partnership agreement. A document setting up a partnership, giving the details of the business and the amount each partner is contributing to it. Also called articles of partnership.

Part order. Same as part delivery.

Part-owner. A person who owns something jointly with one or more other people.

Part-ownership. A situation where two or more persons own the same property.

Part payment. The paying of part of a whole payment.

Part shipment. Same as part delivery.

Part-time. Ad not working for the whole working week.

Part-time employment. Work for part of a working week.

Party. A person or organization involved in a legal dispute or legal agreement.

Par value. Same as face value.

Pass. 1. To pay no dividend in a certain year. 2. To approve something. 3. To be successful in an examination or test.

Passbook. A book given by a bank or building society which shows money which you deposit or withdraw from your savings account or building society account.

Passbook account. An account which carries a passbook.

Passive. Not taking any action.

Passive investor. Same as sleeping partner.

Passive stake. A shareholding where the shareholder takes no active part in running the company.

Pass off. To pretend that something is another thing in order to cheat a customer.

Password. A special word which a user has to give when carrying out operations on an account by phone.

Patent. An official document showing that a person has the exclusive right to make and sell an invention.

Patent agent. A person who advises on patents and applies for patents on behalf of clients.

Patented. Which is protected by a patent.

Patent rights. The rights which an inventor holds because of a patent.

Pattern. The general way in which something usually happens.

Pattern of trade. A general way in which trade is carried on.

Pawnbroker. A person who lends money against the security of valuable objects.

Pawn ticket. A receipt given by the pawnbroker for an object left in pawn.

Pay. A salary or wages, money given to someone for regular work.

Payable. Which is due to be paid.

Pay as you earn. A tax system, where income tax is deducted from the salary before it is paid to the worker. Abbr. PAYE.

Pay back. To give money back to someone.

Payback. The act of paying back money which has been borrowed.

Payback clause. A clause in a contract which states the terms for repaying a loan.

Payback period. 1. A period of time over which a loan is to be repaid or an investment is to pay for itself. 2. The length of time it will take to earn back the money invested in a project.

Pay-cheque. A monthly cheque by which an employee is paid.

Pay day. A day on which wages are paid to employees. (usually Friday for employees paid once a week, and during the last week of the month for employees who are paid once a month).

Pay desk. A place in a store where you pay for goods bought.

Pay differentials. The difference in salary between employees in similar types of jobs. Also called salary differentials, wage differentials.

Pay down. To make a deposit.

Payee. A person who receives money from someone, or the person whose name is on a cheque.

Payer. A person who gives money to someone.

Payer bank. A bank which pays a cheque drawn on one of its accounts.

Pay hike. An increase in salary.

Paying. 1. Which makes a profit. 2. Which pays the act of giving money.

Paying agent. A bank which pays dividend or interest to a bondholder.

Paying-in slip. A printed form which is filled in when money is being deposited in a bank.

Payment. 1. The act of giving money in exchange for goods or a service. 2. Money paid.

Payment date. A date when a payment should be or has been made.

Payment gateway. Software that processes online credit-card payments. It gets authorization for the payment from the credit-card company and transfers money into the retailer's bank account.

Pay negotiations or Pay talks. Discussions between management and employees about pay increases.

Pay off. 1. To finish paying money which is owed for something. 2. To terminate somebody's employment and pay all wages that are due.

Payoff. Money paid to finish paying something which is owed, such as money paid to a worker when his or her employment is terminated.

Payoff period. Same as payback period.

Pay out. To give money.

Payout. Money paid to help a company or person in difficulties, a subsidy.

Pay package. The salary and other benefits offered with a job.

Pay packet. An envelope containing the pay slip and the cash pay.

Pay restraint. The process of keeping increases in wages under control.

Pay review. An occasion when an employee's salary is considered and usually increased.

Payroll. 1. The list of people employed and paid by a company. 2. The money paid by a company in salaries.

Payroll clerk. A person employed to administer the payment of employees. Also called wages clerk.

Payroll ledger. A list of staff and their salaries.

Payroll tax. A tax on the people employed by a company.

Pay scale. A table that sets out the range of pay offered for each grade of job in an organization. Also called salary scale, wage scale.

Pay slip Or pay statement. A piece of paper showing the full amount of an employee's pay, and the money deducted as tax, pension and National Insurance contributions.

Pay up. To give money which is owed.

PC. Abbr. Personal computer.

PCB. Abbr. Petty cash book.

PE. Abbr. Price earnings.

Peak. The highest point.

Peak output. The highest output.

Peak year. The year when the largest quantity of products was produced or when sales were highest.

Peddle. To sell goods from door to door or in the street.

Peg. To maintain or fix something at a specific level.

Penalize. To punish or fine someone.

Penalty. 1. A punishment, often a fine, which is imposed if something is not done or is done incorrectly or illegally. 2. Money withheld from an investor if he or she withdraws money from an interest-bearing account early.

Penalty clause. A clause which lists the penalties which will be imposed if the terms of the contract are not fulfilled.

Penalty-free. Without incurring any penalty, without losing any interest on money invested.

Pension. Money paid regularly to someone who no longer works.

Pensionable. Able to receive a pension.

Pensionable age. An age after which someone can stop working and take a pension.

Pensionable service. The period of service used in calculating pension benefits from an occupational pension scheme.

Pension contributions. Money paid by a company or employee into a pension fund.

Pension entitlement. The amount of pension which someone has the right to receive when he or she retires.

Pensioner. A person who receives a pension.

Pension fund. A large sum of money made up of contributions from employees and their employer which provides pensions for retired employees.

Pension funds. Investments managed by pension companies to produce pensions for investors.

Pension plan or Pension scheme. A plan worked out by an insurance company which arranges for employees to pay part of their salary over many years and receive a regular payment when they retire.

PEP. Abbr. Personal equity plan.

Per. 1. Preposition. 2. For each.

PER. Abbr. Price earnings ratio.

Per annum. Ad in a year.

PE ratio. Abbr. Price earnings ratio.

Per capita. Ad for each person and average income of one person.

Per cent. Ad out of each hundred, or for each hundred.

Percentage. An amount shown as part of one hundred.

Percentage discount. A discount calculated at an amount per hundred.

Percentage increase. An increase calculated on the basis of a rate for one hundred.

Perform. To do well or badly.

Performance. 1. The way in which someone or something acts. 2. The way in which a share increases in value.

Performance fund. A fund invested in shares to provide capital growth, but probably with less dividend income than usual.

Performance incentive. An extra payment to reward an employee's performance at work.

Performance-linked bonus. A bonus calculated according to the performance of a worker or group of workers.

Performance rating. A judgment of how well a share or a company has performed.

Performance review. A yearly interview between a manager and each worker to discuss how the worker has worked during the year.

Performance share. A share which is likely to show capital growth, though perhaps not income. These are usually riskier shares than those which provide income.

Per head. Ad for each person.

Period. A length of time.

Periodic. Happening from time to time.

Period of account. The period usually covered by a firm's accounts.

Period of qualification. The time which has to pass before someone qualifies for something.

Perk. An extra item given by a company to employees in addition to their salaries (such as company cars or private health insurance) (informal).

Permanent. Which will last for a long time or for ever.

Permit. An official document which allows someone to do something.

Perpetual inventory. A stock recording and valuation system where each item of stock purchased is added to the total and each item sold is deducted, so that the stock figures are always correct and up-to-date.

Personal. Referring to one person.

Personal allowance. A part of a person's income which is not taxed.

Personal assets. Moveable assets which belong to a person.

Personal banker. A bank employee who looks after a client, and is the one whom the client contacts when there are problems.

Personal computer. A small computer which can be used by one person in the home or office. Abbr. PC.

Personal customer. A private individual who has an account with a bank, as opposed to a business customer.

Personal equity plan. An account held under a Indian government-backed scheme to encourage share-ownership and investment in industry, allowing individual taxpayers to invest a certain amount of money in shares each year, and not pay tax on either the income or the capital gains, provided that the shares are held for a certain period of time. Abbr. PEP.

Note: There are several types of equity PEP: the single company PEP, where only shares in one company are allowed, and the general PEP, where shares in several companies can be held or other types of investment.

Personal identification number. A unique number allocated to the holder of a cash card or credit card, by which he or she can enter an automatic banking system, as for example to withdraw cash from a cash machine or to pay in a store. Abbr. PIN.

Personal income. The income received by an individual person before tax is paid.

Personalized. With the name or initials of a person printed on it.

Personal loan. A loan to a person for household or other personal use, not for business use.

Personal pension plan. A pension plan which applies to one employee only, usually a self-employed person, not to a group. Abbr. PPP.

Personal property. Things which belong to a person.

Personal sector. The part of the investment market which is owned by private investors (as opposed to the corporate or institutional sector).

Personnel department. Same as human resources department.

Petrocurrency. A foreign currency which is earned by exporting oil.

Petroleum industry. An industry which uses petroleum to make other products (e.g. petrol or soap).

Petty cash. A small amount of money kept in an office to pay small debts.

Petty cash book. A book in which petty cash payments are noted. Abbr. PCB.

Phase. A period or part of something which takes place.

Phase in. To bring something in gradually.

Phase out. To remove something gradually.

Physical market. A commodity market where purchasers actually buy the commodities (as opposed to the futures market, where they buy and sell the right to purchase commodities at a future date).

Physical price. A current cash price for a commodity for immediate delivery.

Physical stock check. The task of counting actual items of stock (and then checking this figure against stock records).

PIB. Abbr. Permanent interest- bearing share.

Pick up. 1. To get better or to improve. 2. To fetch something or someone in a vehicle.

Piece rate. A rate of pay calculated as an amount for each product produced or for each piece of work done and not as an amount for each hour worked.

Piecework. Work for which employees are paid in accordance with the number of products produced or pieces of work done and not at an hourly rate.

Pieceworker. A person who is employed at a piece rate.

Place an issue. To find buyers (usually a small number of investors) for all of a new issue of shares.

Placement. 1. The act of finding work for someone. 2. The act of finding buyers for an issue of new shares.

Placing. The act of finding a single buyer or a group of institutional buyers for a large number of shares in a new company or a company that is going public.

Plan. 1. An idea of how something should be done, which has been decided on and organized in advance. 2. An organized way of doing something.

Planned economy. A system where the government plans all business activity, regulates supply, sets production targets and itemizes work to be done. Also called command economy, central planning.

Planning. The process of organizing how something should be done in the future.

PLC. Abbr. Public limited company.

Pledge. An object given to a pawnbroker as security for money borrowed.

Plenary session. A meeting at a conference when all the delegates meet together.

Plug. To block or to stop.

Plummet. To fall sharply.

Point of sale. A place where a product is sold, e.g. a shop. Abbr. POS.

Point-of-sale material. Display material to advertise a product where it is being sold, e.g. posters or dump bins. Abbr. POS material.

Point of sale terminal. An electronic cash terminal at a pay desk which records transactions and stock movements automatically when an item is bought. Abbr. POS terminal.

Poison pill. An action taken by a company to make itself less attractive to a potential takeover bid.

Note: In some cases, the officers of a company will vote themselves extremely high redundancy payments if a takeover is successful; or a company will borrow large amounts of money and give it away to the shareholders as dividends, so that the company has an unacceptably high level of borrowing.

Policy. 1. A course of action or set of principles determining the general way of doing something. 2. A contract for insurance.

Note: Company policy the company's agreed plan of action or the company's way of doing things.

Policyholder. A person who is insured by an insurance company.

Pool. 1. An unused supply. 2. A group of mortgages and other collateral used to back a loan.

Poor. 1. Without much money. 2. Not very good.

Population forecast. A calculation of how many people will be living in a country or in a town at some point in the future.

Portability. The fact of being able to be moved around.

Portfolio. 1. All the shares owned by a single investor. 2. A folder containing a selection of samples.

Portfolio investments. Investments in shares and government stocks (as opposed to investments in property, etc.).

Portfolio management. The buying and selling shares to make profits for a single investor.

Portfolio manager. A person who manages a share portfolio.

Portfolio theory. A basis for managing a portfolio of investments (a mix of safe stocks and more risky ones).

Portfolio value. The value of someone's portfolio of investments.

POS. Abbr. Point of sale.

Position. 1. A situation or state of affairs. 2. The state of a person's current financial holding in a stock.

Positioning. The promotion of a product in a particular area of a market.

Position of trust. A job in which a person is trusted to act correctly and honestly.

Positive carry. A deal where the cost of the finance is less than the return.

Positive cash flow. A situation where more money is coming into a company than is going out.

Positive yield curve. A situation where the yield on a short-term investment is less than that on a long-term investment.

POS material. Abbr. Point-of-sale material.

Possess. To own something.

Post. A system of sending letters and parcels from one place to another.

Post-balance sheet event. Something which happens after the date when the balance sheet is drawn up, and before the time when the balance sheet is officially approved by the directors, which affects a company's financial position.

Postdate. To put a later date on a document.

Posting. The action of entering transactions in accounts.

Potential. Possible.

Pound-cost averaging. The practice of buying securities at different times, but always spending the same amount of money.

Power. 1. Strength or ability. 2. A force or legal right.

Power of appointment. The power of a trustee to dispose of interests in property to another person.

Power of attorney. A legal document which gives someone the right to act on someone's behalf in legal matters.

Practice. A way of doing things, a custom or habit.

Precious metals. Very valuable metals, such as gold and platinum.

Predator. An individual (or company) who spends most of the time looking for companies to purchase cheaply.

Predict. To say that something will happen in the future.

Preference. 1. A thing which someone prefers. 2. A thing which has an advantage over something else.

Preference shareholder. An owner of preference shares.

Preference shares. Shares (often with no voting rights) which receive their dividend before all other shares and are repaid first (at face value) if the company goes into liquidation.

Note: Preference shares, because they have less risk than ordinary shares, normally carry no voting rights.

Preferential creditor or Preferred creditor. A creditor who must be paid first if a company is in liquidation.

Preliminary. Early, happening before anything else.

Pre-market trading. Trading that takes place before a stock exchange officially opens in the morning.

Premium. 1. A regular payment made to an insurance company for the protection provided by an insurance policy. 2. An amount to be paid to a landlord or a tenant for the right to take over a lease. 3. An extra sum of money in addition to a normal charge, wage, price or other amount. 4. A gift, discount or other incentive to encourage someone to buy.

Premium bond. A government bond, part of the national savings scheme, which pays no interest, but gives the owner the chance to win a weekly or monthly prize.

Premium income. Income which an insurance company derives from premiums paid by insured persons.

Premium offer. A free gift offered to attract more customers.

Prepaid. Paid in advance.

Prepay. To pay something in advance.

Prepayment. 1. A payment in advance, or the act of paying in advance. 2. The repayment of the principal of a loan before it is due.

Prepayment penalty. A charge levied on someone who repays a loan (such as a mortgage) before it is due.

Present. 1. Happening now. 2. Being there when something happens.

Presentation. The showing of a document.

Present value. 1. The value something has now. 2. The value now of a specified sum of money to be received in the future, if invested at current interest rates. Abbr. PV.

Note: The present value of a future sum of money is found by discounting that future sum, and can be used to decide how much money to invest now at current interest rates in order to receive the sum you want to have in a given number of years' time.

Press recommendation. A share which has been tipped as a good buy in the financial column of a newspaper.

Press release. A sheet giving news about something which is sent to newspapers and TV and radio stations so that they can use the information.

Pressure. Something which forces you to do something.

Pressure group. A group of people who try to influence the government, the local town council or some other organization.

Pretax profit. The amount of profit a company makes before taxes are deducted.

Pretax profit margin. The pretax profit shown as a percentage of turnover in a profit and loss account.

Previous. Which happens earlier or which existed before.

Previous balance. A balance in an account at the end of the accounting period before the current one.

Price. Money which has to be paid to buy something.

Price book ratio. A ratio of the price of a stock to its book value.

Price ceiling. The highest price which can be reached.

Price change. An amount by which the price of a share moves during a day's trading.

Price controls. Legal measures to prevent prices rising too fast.

Price cutting. A sudden lowering of prices.

Price differential. The difference in price between products in a range.

Price earnings ratio. A ratio between the current market price of a share and the earnings per share (the current dividend it produces), calculated by dividing the market price by the earnings per share.

Note: The PE ratio is an indication of the way investors think a company will perform in the future, as a high market price suggests that investors expect earnings to grow and this gives a high PE figure; a low PE figure implies that investors feel that earnings are not likely to rise.

Price ex works. A price not including transport from the maker's factory.

Price fixing. An illegal agreement between companies to charge the same price for competing products.

Price label. A label which shows a price.

Price list. A sheet giving prices of goods for sale.

Price movement. A change in the prices of shares or commodities.

Price range. A series of prices for similar products from different suppliers.

Price-sensitive. To a product for which demand will change significantly if its price is increased or decreased.

Price tag. 1. A label attached to an item being sold that shows its price. 2. The value of a person or thing.

Price war. A competition between companies to get a larger market share by cutting prices. Also called price-cutting war.

Pricing model. A computerized system for calculating a price, based on costs, anticipated margins, etc.

Pricing policy. A company's policy in giving prices to its products.

Primary. 1. Basic. 2. First, most important.

Permanent account number. A series of figures on a credit card, which are the number of the issuing bank and the personal number of the account. Abbr. PAN.

Primary commodities. Farm produce grown in large quantities, such as corn, rice or cotton.

Primary dealer. A market maker dealing in government stocks.

Primary industry. An industry dealing with basic raw materials such as coal, wood or farm produce.

Primary market. A market where new securities or bonds are issued. Also called new issue market.

Primary products. Products which are basic raw materials, e.g. wood, milk or fish.

Prime cost. The cost involved in producing a product, excluding overheads.

Prime time. The most expensive advertising time for TV commercials.

Principal. 1. A person or company that is represented by an agent. 2. A person acting for himself, such as a market maker buying securities on his own account. 3. Money invested or borrowed on which interest is paid.

Principle. A basic point or general rule.

Priority. To have the right to be first.

Privacy. A method of ensuring that a person's personal or credit card payment details cannot be intercepted and read when transferred over the internet.

Private. Belonging to a single person or to individual people, not to a company or the state.

Private banking. A special banking services offered to very rich people.

Private client stockbroker. A stockbroker who deals on behalf of private investors.

Private enterprise. Businesses which are owned privately, not nationalized.

Private income. Income from dividends, interest or rent which is not part of a salary.

Private investor. An ordinary person with money to invest.

Private limited company. 1. A company with a small number of shareholders, whose shares are not traded on the stock exchange. 2. A subsidiary company whose shares are not listed on the stock exchange, while those of its parent company are shortened to Ltd).

Private means. Income from dividends, interest or rent which is not part of someone's salary.

Private ownership. A situation where a company is owned by private shareholders.

Private placing or Private placement. The act of placing a new issue of shares with a group of selected financial institutions.

Private property. Property which belongs to a private person, not to the public.

Private sector. All companies which are owned by private shareholders, not by the state.

Privatization. The process of selling a nationalized industry to private owners.

Privatize. To sell a nationalized industry to private owners.

Probate. Legal acceptance that a document, especially a will, is valid.

Procedure. A way in which something is done.

Proceed. To go on, to continue.

Process. 1. To sort out information to make it easily understood. 2. To deal with something in the usual routine way.

Produce. Products from farms and gardens, especially fruit and vegetables.

Product. 1. Something which is made or manufactured. 2. A manufactured item for sale.

Product advertising. The advertising of a particular named product, not the company which makes it.

Product analysis. An examination of each separate product in a company's range to find out why it sells, who buys it, etc.

Product design. The design of consumer products.

Product development. The process of improving an existing product line to meet the needs of the market.

Product engineer. An engineer in charge of the equipment for making a product.

Production. 1. The act of showing something. 2. The work of making or manufacturing of goods for sale.

Production cost. The cost of making a product.

Product management. The process of directing the making and selling of a product as an independent item.

Product mix. A range of different products which a company has for sale.

Profession. 1. An occupation for which official qualifications are needed and which is often made a lifelong career. 2. A group of specialized workers.

Professional. 1. To one of the professions. (such as a lawyer, doctor or accountant) 2. Doing work for money.

Professional qualification. A document which shows that someone has successfully finished a course of study which allows him or her to work in one of the professions.

Profit. Money gained from a sale which is more than the money spent on making the item sold or on providing the service offered.

Profitability. 1. The ability to make a profit. 2. The amount of profit made as a percentage of costs.

Profit after tax. Same as net profit.

Profit and loss account. The accounts for a company showing expenditure and income over a period of time, usually one calendar year, balanced to show a final profit or loss. Also called P&L account.

Profit centre. A person, unit or department within an organization which is considered separately for the purposes of calculating a profit.

Profit-making. Which makes a profit.

Profit margin. The percentage difference between sales income and the cost of sales.

Profit-sharing. An arrangement where workers get a share of the profits of the company they work for.

Profit squeeze. Strict control of the amount of profits which companies can pay out as dividend.

Profit-taking. The act of selling investments to realize the profit, rather than keeping them.

Performa. An invoice sent to a buyer before the goods are sent, so that payment can be made or so that goods can be sent to a consignee who is not the buyer.

Programme. A set of instructions that tell a computer to carry out specific tasks to write a program for a computer.

Program trading. The practice of buying and selling shares according to instructions given by a computer program (the computer is programmed to buy or sell when certain prices are reached or when a certain volume of sales on the market is reached).

Progressive. Which moves forward in stages.

Progressive taxation. A taxation system where tax levels increase as the income is higher. Also called graduated taxation.

Progress payment. A payment made as a particular stage of a contract is completed.

Prohibitive. With a price so high that you cannot afford to pay it.

Project. 1. A plan. 2. A particular job of work which follows a plan.

Project analysis. The examination of all the costs or problems of a project before work on it is started.

Projection. A forecast of something which will happen in the future.

Project manager. The manager in charge of a project.

Promise. An act of saying that you will do something.

Promissory note. A document stating that someone promises to pay an amount of money on a specific date.

Promote. 1. To give someone a more important job or to move someone to a higher grade. 2. To advertise a product. 3. To organize the setting up of a new company.

Promotion. 1. The fact of being moved up to a more important job. 2. All means of conveying the message about a product or service to potential customers, e.g. publicity, a sales campaign, TV commercials or free gifts. 3. The setting up of a new company.

Promotional budget. A forecast of the cost of promoting a new product.

Prompt. Rapid or done immediately.

Prompt date. A date for delivery, stated on a futures contract.

Proof. Evidence which shows that something is true.

Property. 1. Land and buildings. 2. A building. 3. Things which a person or organization owns.

Property bond. An investment in a fund invested in properties or in property companies.

Proportion. A part of a total.

Prospect. A chance or possibility that something will happen in the future.

Prospective. Which may happen in the future.

Prospective dividend. A dividend which a company expects to pay at the end of the current year.

Prospectus. A document which gives information to attract buyers or customers.

Protect. To defend something against harm.

Protective tariff. A tariff which tries to ban imports to stop them competing with local products.

Protest. 1. A statement or action to show that you do not approve of something. 2. An official document which proves that a bill of exchange has not been paid .

Provide. 1. To give or supply something. 2. To allow for something which may happen in the future. 3. To put money aside in accounts to cover expenditure or loss in the future.

Provision. 1. To see that something is allowed for in the future. 2. A legal condition. 3. An amount of money put aside in accounts for anticipated expenditure where the timing or amount of expenditure is uncertain.

Provisional. Temporary, not final or permanent.

Proxy. 1. A document which gives someone the power to act on behalf of someone else. 2. A person who acts on behalf of someone else.

Proxy form. A form which a shareholders receive with their invitations to attend an AGM, and which they fill in if they want to appoint a proxy to vote for them on a resolution.

Prudent. Careful, not taking any risks.

Pty Ltd. Abbr. Private limited company.

Public expenditure. Money spent by the local or central government.

Public finance. The raising of money by governments (by taxes or borrowing) and the spending of it.

Public funds. Government money available for expenditure.

Public limited company. A company whose shares can be bought on the stock exchange. Abbr. PLC.

Public offering. An offering of new shares in a corporation for sale to the public as a way of launching the corporation on the stock exchange.

Public placement. An act of offering a new issue of shares to certain investing institutions, though not to private investors in general.

Public sector. Nationalized industries and services.

Pull off. To succeed in negotiating a deal (informal).

Pull out. To stop being part of a deal or agreement.

Pump. To put something in by force.

Pump priming. Government investment in new projects which it hopes will benefit the economy.

Purchase. A product or service which has been bought.

Purchase acquisition. Same as acquisition accounting.

Purchase book. A book in which purchases are recorded.

Purchase ledger. A book in which expenditure is noted.

Purchase order. An official order made out by a purchasing department for goods which a company wants to buy.

Purchase price. A price paid for something.

Purchase tax. A tax paid on things which are bought.

Purchasing department. The section of a company which deals with the buying of stock, raw materials, equipment, etc.

Purchasing officer. A person in a company or organization who is responsible for buying stock, raw materials, equipment, etc.

Purchasing power. The quantity of goods which can be bought by a particular group of people or with a particular sum of money.

Put. To place or to fix.

Put down. 1. To make a deposit. 2. To write an item in a ledger or an account book.

Put in. To offer to buy something, usually in writing.

Put option. An option to sell shares at a certain price.

PV. Abbr. Present value.

Pyramiding. 1. The process of building up a major group by acquiring controlling interests in many different companies, each larger than the original company. 2. The illegal practice of using new investors' deposits to pay the interest on the deposits made by existing investors.

Pyramid selling. An illegal way of selling goods or investments to the public, where each selling agent pays for the franchise to sell the product or service, and sells that right on to other agents together with stock, so that in the end the person who makes most money is the original franchiser, and sub-agents or investors may lose all their investments.

Q

Qty. Abbr. Quantity.

Quadruplicate. With the original and three copies.

Qualification. A document or some other formal proof of the fact that someone has successfully completed a specialized course of study or has acquired a skill.

Qualified. 1.Having passed special examinations in a subject. 2. With some reservations or conditions.

Qualified accounts. Accounts which have been noted by the auditors because they contain something with which the auditors do not agree.

Qualify. To be entitled to something.

Qualifying distribution. A payment of a dividend to a shareholder, on which advance corporation tax is paid.

Qualifying period. A time which has to pass before something or someone qualifies for something, e.g. a grant or subsidy.

Qualifying ratio. A calculation of how much mortgage a borrower can afford, by comparing his monthly incoming against his monthly outgoings.

Qualifying service. The period for which an employee must be employed by a company before becoming eligible to join a group pension scheme.

Qualifying shares. The number of shares which you need to earn to get a bonus issue or to be a director of the company, etc.

Quality control. The process of making sure that the quality of a product is good.

Quantifiable. Which can be quantified.

Quantitative. Referring to quantity.

Quantitative funds. Funds which invest according to the instructions given by a computer model.

Quantity. An amount, especially a large amount.

Quantity discount. A discount given to people who buy large quantities.

Quantity purchase. A large quantity of goods bought at one time.

Quarter. 1. One of four equal parts (25%). 2. A period of three months.

Quarterly. Ad happening once every three months.

Queue. 1. A line of people waiting one behind the other. 2. A series of documents (such as orders or application forms) which are dealt with in order.

Quick. Fast, not taking much time.

Quick assets. Cash, or bills which can easily be changed into cash.

Quick ratio. Same as liquidity ratio.

Quiet. Calm, not excited.

Quorum. A minimum number of people who have to be present at a meeting to make it valid.

Quota. A limited amount of something which is allowed to be produced, imported, etc.

Quota system. 1. A system where imports or supplies are regulated by fixed maximum amounts. 2. An arrangement for distribution which allows each distributor only a certain number of items.

Quotation. 1. An estimate of how much something will cost. 2. The company has applied to the stock exchange to have its shares listed.

Quote. 1. To repeat words or a reference number used by someone else. 2. To estimate what a cost or price is likely to be.

Quoted company. A company whose shares can be bought or sold on the stock exchange.

Quote-driven system. A system of working a stock market, where market makers quote a price for a stock (as opposed to an order-driven system).

Quoted shares. Shares which can be bought or sold on the stock exchange.

R

Racket. An illegal deal which makes a lot of money.

Raid. A sudden attack.

Raid alarm. An automatic alarm in a bank which goes off when a robbery is taking place.

Raider. A person or company which buys a stake in another company before making a hostile takeover bid. Also called corporate raider.

Raise. 1. An increase. 2. To increase or to make higher. 3. To obtain money or to organize a loan.

Raised check. A cheque where the amount has been increased by hand illegally.

Rake-off. A person's share of profits from a deal, especially if obtained illegally.

Rally. A rise in price when the trend has been downwards.

Ramp. An act of buying shares in order to force up the price (as when a company buys its own shares illegally during a takeover bid).

R&D. Abbr. Research and development.

Random. Done without making any special selection.

Random check. A check on items taken from a group without any special selection.

Random error. A computer error for which there is no special reason.

Random sample. A sample taken without any selection.

Random walk. 1. A sampling technique which allows for random selection within specific limits set up by a non-random technique. 2. A movement which cannot be predicted (used to describe movements in share prices which cannot be forecast).

Range. A scale of items from a low point to a high one.

Range of prices. The difference between the highest and lowest price for a share or bond over a period of time.

Range forward. A forward currency contract which includes an option to purchase currency futures and so has the effect of limiting potential exchange losses.

Rank. A position in a company or an organization, especially one which shows how important someone is relative to others.

Rate. 1. The money charged for time worked or work completed. 2. An amount of money paid, e.g. as interest or dividend (shown as a percentage). 3. The value of one currency against another. 4. An amount, number or speed compared with something else.

Rate of exchange. Same as exchange rate.

Rate of inflation. The percentage increase in prices over a twelve-month period.

Rate of production. The speed at which items are made. Also called production rate.

Rate of return. The amount of interest or dividend which comes from an investment, shown as a percentage of the money invested.

Rate of sales. The speed at which units are sold.

Rating. 1. The act of giving something a value, or the value given. 2. The valuing of property for local taxes.

Rating agency. An organization which gives a rating to companies or other organizations issuing bonds.

Ratings. The estimated number of people who watch TV programmes.

Ratio. A proportion or quantity of something compared to something else.

Ratio analysis. A method of analyzing the performance of a company by showing the figures in its accounts as ratios and comparing them with those of other companies.

Raw. In the original state or not processed.

Raw data. Data as it is put into a computer, without being analyzed.

Raw materials. Basic materials which have to be treated or processed in some way before they can be used, e.g. wood, iron ore or crude petroleum.

RCPC. Abbr. Regional check processing center.

RD. Abbr. Refer to drawer.

Reaction. A change or action in reply to something said or done.

Readjust. To adjust something again or in a new way, or to change in response to new conditions.

Readjustment. An act of readjusting.

Ready cash. Money which is immediately available for payment.

Ready money. Cash or money which is immediately available.

Real earnings. Income which is available for spending after tax and other contributions have been deducted, corrected for inflation. Also called real income, real wages.

Real estate. Property in the form of land or buildings.

Real interest rate. An interest rate after taking inflation into account.

Realization. The act of making real.

Realization of assets. The act of selling of assets for money.

Realized profit. An actual profit made when something is sold (as opposed to paper profit).

Real money. Cash used for settling debts (as opposed to cheques, drafts, etc.).

Real rate of return. An actual rate of return, calculated after taking inflation into account.

Real return after tax. The return calculated after deducting tax and inflation.

Real time. The time when a computer is working on the processing of data while the event to which the data refers is actually taking place.

Real-time system. A computer system where data is inputted directly into the computer which automatically processes it to produce information which can be used immediately.

Real value. A value of an investment which is kept the same. (e.g. by index-linking).

Reasonable. 1. Sensible, or not annoyed. 2. Moderate or not expensive.

Reassurance. The act of making someone feel less worried.

Reassure. 1. To make someone calm or less worried. 2. To reinsure, to spread the risk of an insurance by asking another insurance company to cover part of it and receive part of the premium.

Rebate. 1. A reduction in the amount of money to be paid. 2. Money returned to someone because they have paid too much.

Rebound. To go back up again quickly.

Recapitalization. A change in the capital structure of a company (as when new shares are issued), especially when undertaken to avoid the company going into liquidation.

Recapitalize. To change the capital structure of a company (as by issuing new shares), especially to avoid the company going into liquidation.

Receipt. 1. A piece of paper showing that money has been paid or that something has been received. 2. The act of receiving something.

Receipt book. A book of blank receipts to be filled in when purchases are made.

Receipts. Money taken in sales.

Receipts and payments basis. A method of preparing the accounts of a business, where receipts and payments are shown at the time when they are made (as opposed to showing debits or credits which are outstanding at the end of the accounting period; also called 'cash basis').

Receivable. Which can be received.

Receiver. A person who receives something.

Receiving. An act of getting something which has been delivered.

Receiving bank. A bank which receives money via electronic transfer.

Receiving order. An order from a court appointing an official receiver to a company.

Recession. A period where there is a decline in trade or in the economy.

Note: There are various ways of deciding if a recession is taking place: the usual one is when the GNP falls for three consecutive quarters.

Reciprocal. Done by one person, company or country to another one, which does the same thing in return.

Reciprocal holdings. A situation where two companies own shares in each other to prevent takeover bids.

Reciprocal trade. Trade between two countries.

Reclamation. The process of recovering money owed by a bank or securities firm to a customer because of an error.

Recognize. To agree that a union can act on behalf of employees in a company.

Recommended retail price. The price at which a manufacturer suggests a product should be sold on the retail market, though this may be reduced by the retailer. Abbr. RRP. Also called administered price, manufacturer's recommended price.

Reconcile. To make two financial accounts or statements agree.

Reconciliation statement. A statement which explains how two accounts can be made to agree.

Record. 1. A report of something which has happened. 2. A success which is better than anything before.

Record book. A book in which minutes of meetings are kept.

Record-breaking. Better or worse than anything which has happened before.

Recorded delivery. A mail service where the letters are signed for by the person receiving them.

Records. Documents which give information.

Recourse. A right of a lender to compel a borrower to repay money borrowed.

Recover. 1. To get back something which has been lost. 2. To get better, to rise.

Recoverable. Which can be got back.

Recoverable amount. The value of an asset, either the price it would fetch if sold, or its value to the company when used (whichever is the larger figure).

Recovery. 1. The act of getting back something which has been lost. 2. A movement upwards of shares or of the economy.

Recovery share. A share which is likely to go up in value because the company's performance is improving.

Recurrent. Which happens again and again.

Recurring payments. Payments, such as mortgage interest or payments on a hire purchase agreement, which are made each month.

Recycle. To use money in a different way (as by investing profits from industry in developing environmental resources).

Redeem. 1. To pay off a loan or a debt. 2. To sell a bond for cash. 3. To exchange a voucher, coupon or stamp for a gift or a reduction in price.

Redeemable preference share. A preference share which must be bought back by the company at a certain date and for a certain price.

Redeemable security. A security which can be redeemed at its face value at a certain date in the future.

Redemption. 1. The repayment of a loan. 2. The repayment of a debt.

Redemption date. A date on which a loan or debt is due to be repaid.

Redemption value. A value of a security when redeemed.

Redemption yield. A yield on a security including interest and its redemption value.

Rediscount. To discount a bill of exchange which has already been discounted by a commercial bank.

Redistribute. To move items, work or money to different areas or people.

Redistribution of risk. The process of spreading the risk of an investment or of an insurance among various insurers.

Redistribution of wealth. The process of sharing wealth among the whole population.

Reduce. 1. To make something smaller or lower. 2. To lower the price of something.

Reducing balance method. A method of depreciating assets, where the asset is depreciated at a constant percentage of it cost each year.

Reduction. An act of making something smaller or less.

Redundancy. The dismissal of a person whose job no longer needs to be done.

Redundancy payment. A payment made to a worker to compensate for losing his or her job.

Redundancy rebate. A payment made to a company to compensate for redundancy payments made.

Redundant. 1. More than is needed, useless. 2. To dismiss an employee who is not needed any more.

Redundant staff. Staff who have lost their jobs because they are not needed any more.

Re-export. The exporting of goods which have been imported.

Ref. Abbr. Reference.

Reference. 1. The process of mentioning or dealing with something. 2. A series of numbers or letters which make it possible to find a document which has been filed. 3. A written report on someone's character or ability.

Refinance. To extend a loan by exchanging it for a new one (normally done when the terms of the new loan are better).

Refinancing of a loan. The act of taking out a new loan to pay back a previous loan.

Refund. Money paid back.

Refundable. Which can be paid back.

Refunding. The process, on the part of a government, of funding a debt again, by issuing new stock to replace stock which is about to mature.

Regional planning. The work of planning the industrial development of a region.

Register. 1. An official list. 2. To write something in an official list. 3. To send a letter by registered post.

Registered company. Company which has been officially set up and registered with the Registrar of Companies.

Registered letter or Registered parcel. A letter or parcel which is noted by the post office before it is sent, so that the sender can claim compensation if it is lost.

Registered security. A security (such as a share in a quoted company) which is registered with Companies House and whose holder is listed in the company's share register.

Register of interests in shares. A list kept by a company of those shareholders who own more than 3% of its shares.

Registration fee. 1. Money paid to have something registered. 2. Money paid to attend a conference.

Registration statement. A document which gives information about a company when it is registered and listed on a stock exchange.

Regression analysis or Regression model. A method of discovering the ratio of one dependent variable and one or more independent variables, so as to give a value to the dependent variable.

Regular. Which happens or comes at the same time each day, each week, each month or each year.

Regular income. An income which comes in every week or month.

Regulate. 1. To adjust something so that it works well or is correct. 2. To change or maintain something by law.

Regulation. 1. A law or rule. 2. The process of making sure that something will work well or correctly.

Regulator. A person whose job it is to see that regulations are followed.

Regulatory powers. Powers to enforce government regulations.

Reimbursement. The act of paying back money.

Reinstatement. The act of giving a borrower back his or her former credit status after he or she has paid off outstanding debts.

Reinsurance. Insurance where a second insurer (the reinsurer) agrees to cover part of the risk insured by the first insurer.

Reinsure. To spread the risk of an insurance, by asking another insurance company to cover part of it and receive part of the premium.

Reinsurer. An insurance company which accepts to insure part of the risk for another insurer.

Reinvest. To invest money again.

Reinvestment. 1. The act of investing money again in the same securities. 2. The act of investing a company's earnings in its own business by using them to create new products for sale.

Rejection. A refusal to accept something, such as a refusal to give a customer credit.

Related company. A company in which another company makes a long-term capital investment in order to gain control or influence.

Relative value funds. Hedge funds not related to general market movements, but which try to find opportunities to arbitrage temporary slight changes in the relative values of particular financial assets.

Release. 1. The act of setting someone free or of making something or someone no longer subject to an obligation or restriction. 2. The act of putting something on the market, or something put on the market.

Release note. A note from a bank to say that a bill of exchange has been paid.

Relevant. Which has to do with what is being discussed or the current situation.

Reminder. A letter to remind a customer that he or she has not paid an invoice.

Remittance. Money which is sent (e.g. to pay back a debt or to pay an invoice).

Remittance advice or Remittance slip. An advice note sent with payment, showing why it is being made (i.e.

quoting the invoice number or a reference number).

Remitting bank. A bank into which a person has deposited a cheque, and which has the duty to collect the money from the account of the writer of the cheque.

Remuneration. Payment for services.

Note: Remuneration can take several forms: e.g. a regular monthly salary cheque, a cheque or cash payment for hours worked or for work completed.

Renegotiate. To negotiate something again.

Renew. To continue something for a further period of time.

Renewal notice. A note sent by an insurance company asking the insured person to renew the insurance.

Renewal premium. A premium to be paid to renew an insurance.

Rent. Money paid to use an office, house or factory for a period of time.

Rental. Money paid to use an office, house, factory, car, piece of equipment, etc., for a period of time.

Rental value. A full value of the rent for a property if it were charged at the current market rate (i.e. calculated between rent reviews).

Rent review. An increase in rents which is carried out during the term of a lease (most leases allow for rents to be reviewed every three or five years).

Renunciation. An act of giving up ownership of shares.

Reorder. A further order for something which has been ordered before.

Reorder interval. A period of time before a new order for a stock item is placed.

Reorder level. A minimum amount of an item which a company holds in stock, such that, when stock falls to this amount, the item must be reordered.

Reorganization. The process of organizing a company in a different way.

Repatriation. The return of foreign investments to the home country of their owner.

Repay. To pay something back, or to pay back money to someone.

Repayable. Which can be paid back.

Repayment. The act of paying money back or money which is paid back.

Repayment mortgage. A mortgage where the borrower pays back both interest and capital over the period of the mortgage (as opposed to an endowment mortgage, where only the interest is repaid, and an insurance is taken out to repay the capital at the end of the term of the mortgage).

Replacement cost accounting. A method of accounting in which assets are valued at the amount it would cost to replace them, rather than at the original cost. Also called current cost accounting.

Replacement cost depreciation. Depreciation based on the actual cost of replacing the asset in the current year.

Replacement price. A price at which the replacement for an asset would have to be bought.

Replacement value. The value of something for insurance purposes if it were to be replaced.

Reply coupon. A form attached to a coupon ad which has to be filled in and returned to the advertiser.

Report. 1. A statement describing what has happened or describing. 2. An official document from a government committee. 3. To publish the results of a company for a period and declare the dividend.

Reporting season. A period when many large companies declare their dividends.

Repossess. To take back an item which someone is buying under a hire-purchase agreement, or a property which someone is buying under a mortgage, because the purchaser cannot continue the payments.

Represent. 1. To work for a company, showing goods or services to possible buyers. 2. To act on behalf of someone.

Representation. 1. The right to sell goods for a company, or a person or organization that sells goods on behalf of a company. 2. The fact of having someone to act on your behalf.

Representative. 1. Which is an example of what all others are like. 2. A company which works for another company, selling their goods. 3. A person who acts on someone's behalf.

Repudiate. To refuse to accept something.

Repurchase. To buy something again, especially something which you have recently bought and then sold.

Repurchase agreement. An agreement, where a bank agrees to buy something and sell it back later (in effect, giving a cash loan to the seller; this is used especially to raise short-term finance).

Require. 1. To ask for or to demand something. 2. To need something.

Requirement. 1. Something which someone wants or needs. 2. Something which is necessary to enable something to be done.

Requisition. An official order for something.

Example: We have requisitioned three trucks to move the stock.

Rerate. To change the rating of a share on the stock exchange (either upwards or downwards).

Resale. The selling of goods which have been bought.

Resale price maintenance. A system in which the price for an item is fixed by the manufacturer and the retailer is not allowed to sell it at a lower price. Abbr. RPM.

Reschedule. To arrange new credit terms for the repayment of a loan.

Rescission. An act of rescinding a contract.

Rescue. The act of saving someone or something from danger.

Rescue operation. An arrangement by a group of people to save a company from collapse.

Research. The process of trying to find out facts or information.

Research and development. 1. Scientific investigation which leads to making new products or improving existing products. 2. Activities that are designed to produce new knowledge and ideas and to develop ways in which these can be commercially exploited by a business. Abbr. R&D.

Note: Research and development activities are often grouped together to form a separate division or department within an organization. Research costs can be divided into (a) applied research, which is the cost of research leading to a specific aim, and (b) basic, or pure, research, which is research carried out without a specific aim in mind: these costs are written off in the year in which they are incurred. Development costs are the costs of making the commercial products based on the research.

Resell. To sell something which has just been bought.

Reseller. Somebody in the marketing chain who buys to sell to somebody else such as wholesalers, distributors, and retailers.

Reserve. Money from profits not paid as dividend but kept back by a company in case it is needed for a special purpose.

Note: The accumulated profits retained by a company usually form its most important reserve.

Reserve currency. A strong currency used in international finance, held by other countries to support their own weaker currencies.

Reserved market. A market in which producers agree not to sell more than a specific amount in order to control competition.

Reserve fund. Profits in a business which have not been paid out as dividend but have been ploughed back into the business.

Reserve price. The lowest price which a seller will accept, e.g. at an auction or when selling securities through a broker.

Reserves. 1. Supplies kept in case of need. 2. Money from profits not paid as dividend, but kept back by a company in case it is needed for a special purpose.

Resist. To fight against something, not to give in to something.

Resolution. A decision to be reached at a meeting.

Note: There are three types or resolution which can be put to an AGM: the 'ordinary resolution', usually referring to some general procedural matter, and which requires a simple majority of votes; and the 'extraordinary resolution' and 'special resolution', such as a resolution to change a company's articles of association in some way, both of which need 75% of the votes before they can be carried.

Resolve. To decide to do something.

Resources. 1. A supply of something. 2. The money available for doing something.

Restitution. 1. The act of giving back property. 2. Compensation or payment for damage or loss.

Restraint of trade. 1. A situation where employees are not allowed to use their knowledge in another company on changing jobs. 2. An attempt by companies to fix prices, create monopolies or reduce competition, which could affect free trade.

Restrict. To limit something or to impose controls on something.

Restrictive covenant. A clause in a contract which prevents someone from doing something.

Restrictive endorsement. An endorsement on a bill of exchange which restricts the use which can be made of it by the person it is endorsed to.

Restrictive trade practices. 1. An arrangement between companies to fix prices or to share the market in order to restrict trade. 2. Ways of working which make people less free (such as trade unions stopping workers from doing certain jobs or companies not allowing customers a free choice of product).

Restructure. To reorganize the financial basis of a company.

Result. 1. A profit or loss account for a company at the end of a trading period. 2. Something which happens because of something else.

Retail. The sale of small quantities of goods to the general public.

Retail dealer. A person who sells to the general public.

Retail deposit. A deposit placed by an individual with a bank.

Retailer. A person who runs a retail business, selling goods direct to the public.

Retail fund. A fund sold direct to private investors.

Retail investor. A private investor, as opposed to institutional investors.

Retail outlet. A shop which sells to the general public.

Retail price. The price at which the retailer sells to the final customer.

Retail price index. An index which shows how prices of consumer goods have increased or decreased over a period of time. Abbr. RPI.

Retail service provider or Retail house. A large stock broking company dealing directly with private retail investors. Abbr. RSP.

Retain. 1. To keep something or someone. 2. To agree with a lawyer that he or she will act for you (and pay him or her a fee in advance).

Retained earnings or Retained income. An amount of profit after tax which a company does not pay out as dividend to the shareholders, but which is kept to be used for the further development of the business.

Retainer. Money paid in advance to someone so that they will work for you, and not for someone else.

Retention. The act of keeping the loyalty of existing customers, as opposed to acquisition, which is the act of acquiring new customers (both can be aims of advertising campaigns).

Retire. 1. To stop work and take a pension. 2. To make an employee stop work and take a pension. 3. To come to the end of an elected term of office.

Retirement. 1. The act of retiring from work. 2. The period when a person is retired.

Retrenchment. A reduction of expenditure or of new plans.

Retroactive. Which takes effect from a time in the past.

Return. 1. A profit or income from money invested. 2. An official statement or form that has to be sent in to the authorities.

Return date. A date by which a company's annual return has to be made to the Registrar of Companies.

Return on capital employed or Return on assets or Return on equity. A profit shown as a percentage of the capital or money invested in a business. Abbr. ROCE, ROA, ROE.

Return on investment. The Investment interest or dividends shown as a percentage of the money invested. Abbr. ROI.

Returns. 1. Profits or income from investment. 2. Unsold goods, especially books, newspapers or magazines, sent back to the supplier.

Revaluation. 1. An act of revaluing. 2. The increasing of the value of a currency.

Revalue. To value something again (usually setting a higher value on it than before).

Revenue. 1. Money received. 2. Money received by a government in tax.

Revenue account. An accounting system which records the revenue and expenditure incurred by a company during its normal business.

Revenue accounts. Accounts of a business which record money received as sales, commission, etc.

Revenue expenditure. Expenditure on purchasing stock (but not on capital items) which is then sold during the current accounting period.

Revenue officer. A person working in the government tax offices.

Revenue reserves. Retained earnings which are shown in the company's balance sheet as part of the shareholders' funds. Also called company reserves reversal.

Reverse bid. A bid made by a company which is the target of a takeover bid for the company which is trying to take it over.

Reverse mortgage. An arrangement where the owner of a property mortgages it to receive a regular income from the mortgage lender (and not vice versa), based on the equity value of the property.

Reverse takeover. A takeover where the company which has been taken over ends up owning the company which has taken it over. The acquiring company's shareholders give up their shares in exchange for shares in the target company.

Reversing entry. An entry in a set of accounts which reverses an entry in the preceding accounts.

Reversion. A return of property to an original owner.

Reversionary. Referring to property which passes to another owner on the death of the present one.

Reversionary annuity. An annuity paid to someone on the death of another person.

Reversionary bonus. An annual bonus on a life assurance policy, declared by the insurer.

Review. A general examination.

Revise. To change something which has been calculated or planned.

Revocable. Which can be revoked.

Revocable trust. A trust which can be changed or revoked.

Revocation. An action of canceling something which has previously been agreed.

Revoke. To cancel something.

Revolving credit. A system where someone can borrow money at any time up to an agreed amount, and continue to borrow while still paying off the original loan. Also called open-ended credit.

RIE. Abbr. Recognized investment exchange.

Rights issue. An arrangement which gives shareholders the right to buy more shares at a lower price.

Ring binder. A file with a stiff cover with rings in it which fit into special holes made in sheets of paper.

Ring fence. 1. To separate valuable assets or profitable businesses from others in a group which are unprofitable and may make the whole group collapse. 2. To identify money from certain sources and only use it in certain areas.

Rise. 1. An increase. 2. An increase in pay.

Rising screen. A panel which moves upwards to protect a cashier in a bank against robbers.

Risk. 1. Possible harm or a chance of danger. 2. A situation where goods shipped or stored are insured by the owner, not by the transport company or the storage. 3. Loss or damage against which you are insured. 4. It is not likely or it is very likely that the insurance company will have to pay out against claims where he is concerned.

Risk-adjusted. Calculated after taking risk into account.

Risk arbitrage. The business of buying shares in companies which are likely to be taken over and so rise in price.

Risk asset ratio. A proportion of a bank's capital which is in risk assets.

Risk assets. Assets of a bank which are in securities or bonds which may fall in value.

Risk-averse. Not wanting to take risks.

Risk-based capital. An internationally approved system of calculating a bank's capital value by assessing the risk attached to its assets.

Risk capital. Same as venture capital.

Risk-free. With no risk involved.

Risk management. The work of managing a company's exposure to risk from its credit terms or exposure to interest rate or exchange rate fluctuations.

Risk premium. An extra payment (increased dividend or higher than usual profits) for taking risks.

Risk-weighted assets. Assets which include off-balance sheet items for insurance purposes.

Rival. A person or company that competes in the same market.

ROA. Abbr. Return on assets.

Robust. Strong, able to survive in difficult circumstances.

ROCE. Abbr. Return on capital employed.

Rocket. To rise fast.

ROE. Abbr. Return on equity.

ROI. Abbr. Return on investment.

Roll. Something which has been turned over and over to wrap round itself.

Rolled-up coupons. Interest coupons on securities, which are not paid out, but added to the capital value of the security.

Rolling account. A system where there are no fixed account days, but stock exchange transactions are paid at a fixed period after each transaction has taken place.

Rolling budget. A budget which moves forward on a regular basis (such as a budget covering a twelve-month period, which moves forward each month or quarter).

Rolling plan. A plan which runs for a period of time and is updated regularly for the same period.

Rollover. An extension of credit or of the period of a loan, though not necessarily on the same terms as previously.

Rollover credit. Credit in the form of a medium-term loan, covered by a series of short-term loans.

Rollover mortgage. A short-term mortgage which is renegotiated with different terms every five years or so.

Roll up. To extend a loan, by adding the interest due to be paid to the capital.

Rough. Approximate, not very accurate.

Rough calculation. A way of working out a mathematical problem approximately, or the approximate result arrived at.

Rough draft. A plan of a document which may have changes made to it before it is complete.

Rough estimate. A very approximate calculation.

Rough out. To make a draft or a general design of something, which may be changed later.

Round down. To decrease a fractional figure to the nearest full figure.

Round-tripping. 1. The practice of borrowing at one rate of interest and lending the same money short-term at a higher rate (used to borrow on overdraft, when short-term deposit rates are higher). 2. The practice of buying securities and then selling them quickly.

Round up. To increase a fractional figure to the nearest full figure.

Royalty. Money paid to an inventor, writer or the owner of land for the right to use their property, usually a specific percentage of sales, or a specific amount per sale.

RPI. Abbr. Retail price index.

RPM. Abbr. Resale price maintenance.

RRP. Abbr. Recommended retail price.

RSP. Abbr. Retail service provider.

RTGS. Abbr. Real-time gross settlement.

Rule. A statement that directs how people should behave.

Rulebook. A book which lists the rules by which the members of a union or self-regulatory organization must operate.

Run. 1. A period of time during which a machine is working. 2. A rush to buy something.

Runaway inflation. Very rapid inflation, which is almost impossible to reduce.

Run down. 1. To reduce a quantity gradually. 2. To slow down the business activities of a company before it is going to be closed.

Running costs. Money spent on the day-to-day cost of keeping a business going.

Running yield. A yield on fixed interest securities, where the interest is shown as a percentage of the price paid.

Run to settlement. A futures sale which runs until the actual commodity is delivered.

Rupee. A unit of currency used in India, Mauritius, Nepal, Pakistan and Sri Lanka.

S

S.A.E. Abbr. Stamped addressed envelope.

Safe deposit. A bank safe where you can leave jewellery or documents.

Safe deposit box. A small box which you can rent to keep jewellery or documents in a bank's safe.

Safeguard. To protect something or someone.

Safe investment. Something, e.g. a share, which is not likely to fall in value.

Safe keeping. The fact of being looked after carefully.

Safety. 1. The fact of being free from danger or risk. 2. To make something safe, to be safe.

Safety margin. A time or space allowed to make sure that something can be done safely.

Safety regulations. Rules to make a place of work safe for the employees.

Salaried partner. A partner, often a junior one, who receives a regular salary in accordance with the partnership agreement.

Salary. 1. A regular payment for work done, made to an employee usually as a cheque at the end of each month. 2. An amount paid to an employee, shown as a monthly, quarterly or yearly total.

Salary cheque. A monthly cheque by which an employee is paid.

Salary deductions. Money which a company removes from salaries to pay to the government as tax, National Insurance contributions, etc.

Salary reduction. The act of removing money from an employee's salary to put into a pension plan.

Salary scale. Same as pay scale.

Salary structure. The organization of salaries in a company with different rates of pay for different types of job.

Sale. 1. An act of giving an item or doing a service in exchange for money, or for the promise that money will be paid. 2. An act of selling goods at specially low prices.

Sale and lease-back. The sale of an asset, usually a building, to somebody else who then leases it back to the original owner.

Sales. 1. Money received for selling something. 2. Items sold, or the number of items sold.

Sales analysis. An examination of the reports of sales to see why items have or have not sold well.

Sales book. A record of sales.

Sales chart. A diagram showing how sales vary from month to month.

Sales curve. A graph showing how sales increase or decrease.

Sales drive. A vigorous effort to increase sales.

Sales forecast. An estimate of future sales.

Sales invoice. An invoice relating to a sale.

Sales ledger. A book in which sales to each customer are entered.

Sales literature. Printed information which helps sales, e.g. leaflets or prospectuses.

Sales mix. The sales and profitability of a wide range of products sold by a single company.

Sales mix profit variance. The differing profitability of different products within a product range.

Sales return. A report of sales made each day or week or quarter.

Sales returns book. A ledger giving details of goods returned by purchasers, including invoice number, credit notes, quantities, etc. Abbr. SRB.

Sales revenue. The income from sales of goods or services.

Sales slip. A paper showing that an article was bought at a certain shop.

Sales target. The amount of sales a sales representative is expected to achieve.

Sales tax. A tax which is paid on each item sold (and is collected when the purchase is made). Also called turnover tax.

Sales value. The amount of money which would be received if something is sold.

Sales volume profit variance. The difference between the profit on the number of units actually sold and the forecast figure.

Salvage. 1. The work of saving a ship or a cargo from being destroyed. 2. Goods saved from a wrecked ship, from a fire or from some other accident.

Salvage money. Payment made by the owner of a ship or a cargo to the person who has saved it.

Same-day funds. Money which can be withdrawn from an account the same day as it is deposited.

Sample. 1. A small part of an item which is used to show what the whole item is like. 2. A small group which is studied in order to show what a larger group is like.

Sampling. 1. The testing of a product by taking a small amount. 2. The testing of the reactions of a small group of people to find out the reactions of a larger group of consumers.

Savings. Money saved (i.e. money which is not spent).

Savings account. An account where you put money in regularly and which pays interest, often at a higher rate than a deposit account.

Savings certificate. A document showing that you have invested money in a government savings scheme. Also known as savings bond.

Scale. 1. A system which is graded into various levels. 2. To start in business with a small staff, few products or little capital.

Scale down. To lower something in proportion.

Scale up. To increase something in proportion.

Scam. A fraud, an illegal or dishonest scheme (informal).

Scarcity value. The value something has because it is rare and there is a large demand for it.

Scatter diagram. A chart where points are plotted according to two sets of variables to see if a pattern exists.

Scenario. The way in which a situation may develop, or a description or forecast of possible future developments.

Schedule. 1. A timetable, a plan of how time should be spent, drawn up in advance. 2. A list, especially a list forming an additional document attached to a contract. 3. A list of interest rates. 4. A form relating to a particular kind of income liable for Indian income tax.

Scheme. A plan, arrangement or way of working.

Scheme of arrangement. A scheme drawn up by an individual or company to offer ways of paying debts, so as to avoid bankruptcy proceedings. Also called voluntary arrangement.

Scorched earth policy. A way of combating a takeover bid, where the target company sells valuable assets or purchases unattractive assets.

Scrap. 1. Material left over after an industrial process, and which still has some value (as opposed to waste, which has no value). 2. Pieces of metal to be melted down to make new metal ingots.

Scrap value. The value of an asset if sold for scrap.

Screening. The act of evaluating or assessing new product ideas.

Screen trading. Trading using a monitor, as opposed to the old open outcry system.

Scrip. A security (a share, bond, or the certificate issued to show that someone has been allotted a share or bond).

Scrip issue. An issue of shares whereby a company transfers money from reserves to share capital and issues free extra shares to the shareholders (the value of the company remains the same, and the total market value of shareholders' shares remains the same, the market price being adjusted to account for the new shares). Also called free issue, capitalization Issue.

SDB. Abbr. Sales day book.

SDR. Abbr. Special drawing rights.

Sea freight. The transportation of goods in ships, or goods sent by sea.

Seal. 1. A special symbol, often one stamped on a piece of wax, which is used to show that a document is officially approved by the organization that uses the symbol. 2. A piece of paper, metal or wax attached to close something, so that it can be opened only if the paper, metal or wax is removed or broken.

SEAQ. A computerized information system giving details of current share prices and stock market transactions on the London Stock Exchange. Dealers list their offer and bid prices on SEAQ, and transactions are carried out on the basis of the information shown on the screen and are also recorded on the SEAQ database in case of future disputes. Full form Stock Exchange Automated Quotations system.

Search. An examination of records by the lawyer acting for someone who wants to buy a property, to make sure that the vendor has the right to sell it.

Season. A period of time when some activity usually takes place.

Seasonal. Which lasts for a season or which only happens during a particular season.

Seasonal demand. Demand which exists only during the high season.

Seat. Membership of a stock exchange.

SEC. Abbr. Securities and Exchange Commission.

Secondary industry. An industry which uses basic raw materials to produce manufactured goods.

Secondary market. A market where existing securities are bought and sold again and again, as opposed to a primary market, where new issues are launched.

Secondary mortgage market. A nationwide system organized by various federal mortgage associations for polling mortgages and selling them to investors.

Secondary products. Products which have been processed from raw materials (as opposed to primary products).

Secondary properties. Commercial properties which are not in prime sites and therefore are not as valuable.

Second-class. To a less expensive or less comfortable way of travelling.

Second half. A period of six months from 1st July to 31st December.

Second mortgage. A further mortgage on a property which is already mortgaged.

Second quarter. A period of three months from April to the end of June.

Second round. A new trance of venture capital raised for a new project after the start-up finance.

Secret. Which is deliberately kept hidden from people, or which is not known about by many people.

Secretary. 1. An official of a company or society whose job is to keep records and write letters. 2. A member of the government in charge of a department.

Secret reserves. Reserves which are illegally kept hidden in a company's balance sheet, as opposed to 'hidden reserves' which are simply not easy to identify.

Section. 1. A part of something. 2. One of the parts of an Act of Parliament.

Sector. 1. A part of the economy or the business organization of a country. 2. A section of a stock market, listing shares in one type of industry (such as the banking sector).

Sector fund. A fund which is invested in only one sector of the stock market.

Secured creditor. A person who is owed money by someone, and can legally claim the same amount of the borrower's property if the borrower fails to pay back the money owed.

Secured debt. A debt which is guaranteed by assets which have been pledged.

Secured loan. A loan which is guaranteed by the borrower giving assets as security.

Securities. 1. Investments in stocks and shares. 2. Certificates to show that someone owns stocks or shares.

Securities market. A stock exchange, a place where stocks and shares can be bought or sold.

Securities trader. A person whose business is buying and selling stocks and shares.

Securitization. The process of making a loan or mortgage into a tradable security by issuing a bill of exchange or other negotiable paper in place of it.

Securities. To make a loan into a security which can be traded (e.g. by issuing an IOU for a loan)

Security. 1. The fact of being protected against attack. 2. The fact of being kept secret. 3. A guarantee that someone will repay money borrowed. 4. A stock or share.

Seed money. Venture capital invested when a new project is starting up (and therefore more risky than secondary finance or mezzanine finance).

Segment. A section of a market defined by certain criteria.

Segmentation. The division of the market or consumers into categories according to their buying habits.

Self-employed. Working for yourself or not on the payroll of a company.

Self-financed. The project pays its development costs out of its own revenue, with no subsidies.

Self-financing. The financing of development costs, the purchase of capital assets, etc. by a company from its own resources.

Self-insurance. Insuring against a probable future loss by putting money aside regularly, rather than by taking out an insurance policy.

Self-regulation. The regulation of an industry by itself, through a committee which issues a rulebook and makes sure that members of the industry follow the rules.

Note: For example, the stock exchange is regulated by the Stock Exchange Council.

Self-regulatory organization. An organization, such as the Securities and Futures Authority, which regulates the way in which its own members carry on their business. Abbr. SRO.

Self-service banking. A situation where a bank's customers arrange transactions by themselves, without involving bank staff, e.g. by using ATMs for cash withdrawals.

Self-supporting. Which finances itself from its own resources, with no subsidies.

Sell. 1. To give goods in exchange for money. 2. To be sold.

Sell-by date. A date on a food packet which is the last date on which the food is guaranteed to be good.

Seller's market. A market where the seller can ask high prices because there is a large demand for the product.

Sell forward. To sell foreign currency, commodities, etc. for delivery at a later date.

Selling costs or Selling Overhead. The amount of money to be paid for the advertising, reps' commissions and other expenses involved in selling something.

Selling price. The price at which someone is willing to sell something.

Selling price variance. The difference between the actual selling price and the budgeted selling price.

Sell off. To sell goods quickly to get rid of them.

Sell out. To sell your business.

Sell up. To sell a business and all the stock.

Semi-fixed cost. Same as semi-variable cost.

Semi-variable cost. Money paid to produce a product which increases, though less than proportionally, with the quantity of the product made. Also called semi-fixed cost.

Senior. 1. To an employee who is more important 2. To an employee who is older or who has been employed longer than another. 3. To a sum which is repayable before others.

Senior capital. Capital in the form of secured loans to a company (it is repaid before junior capital, such as shareholders' equity, in the event of liquidation).

Senior debt. A debt which must be repaid in preference to other debts (such as a first mortgage over a second mortgage).

Seniority. 1. The fact of being more important. 2. The fact of being older or having been an employee of the company longer.

Senior manager or Senior executive. A manager or director who has a higher rank than others.

Senior partner. The most important partner in a firm of solicitors or accountants.

Sensitivity analysis. The analysis of the effect of a small change in a certain calculation on the final result.

Separable. Which can be separated.

Separable net assets. Assets which can be separated from the rest of the assets of a business and sold off.

Separate. Not connected with something.

Separate estate. The property of one of the partners in a partnership, as opposed to the property belonging to the partnership itself.

Series. A group of bonds or savings certificates, issued over a period of time but all bearing the same interest.

Service. 1. A piece of work done to help someone as a duty or a favor. 2. A form of business (e.g. insurance, banking, or transport) that provides help in some form when it is needed, as opposed to making or selling goods. 3. The fact of working for an employer, or the period of time during which an employee has worked for an employer. 4. The work of dealing with customers. 5. Payment for help given to the customer.

Service bureau. An office which specializes in helping other offices.

Service charge. 1. A charge added to the bill in a restaurant to pay for service. 2. An amount paid by tenants in a block of flats or offices for general maintenance, insurance and cleaning. 3. A charge which a bank makes for carrying out work for a customer. It is also known as bank charge.

Service contract. A contract between a company and a director showing all conditions of work.

Service industry. An industry which does not produce raw materials or manufacture products but offers a service (such as banking, retailing or accountancy).

Services. Benefits which are sold to customers or clients, e.g. transport or education.

Service sector. The part of an economy that consists of service industries.

Session. A period of time spent on a specific activity, especially as part of a larger event.

Set. Fixed or which cannot be changed.

Set against. To balance one group of figures against another group to try to make them cancel each other out.

Set aside. To decide not to apply a decision.

Setback. Something that stops progress.

Set off. To use a debt owed by one party to reduce a debt owed to them.

Sets. Abbr. Stock Exchange Electronic Trading System.

Settle. 1. To pay what is owed. 2. To place a property in trust.

Settled account. An arrangement between two parties who agree the accounts between them.

Settled property. Property which is held in trust.

Settlement. 1. The payment of an account. 2. An agreement after an argument or negotiations.

Settlement date. A date when a payment has to be made.

Settlement day. 1. The day on which shares which have been bought must be paid for (on the Bombay Stock Exchange the account period is three business days from the day of trade) 2. In the India, the day on which securities bought actually become the property of the purchaser.

Settle on. To leave property to someone when you die.

Set up. To begin something, or to organize something new.

Shadow director. A person who is not a director of a company, but who tells the directors of the company how to act.

Shakeout. 1. A reorganization in a company, where some people are left, but others go. 2. The process of revising prices on a stock market, usually at the end of a sharp rise or fall.

Shakeup. A total reorganization.

Shaky. Not very sure or not very reliable.

Share. 1. A part of something that has been divided up among several people or groups. 2. One of many equal parts into which a company's capital is divided.

Share account. An account with a credit union which pays dividends instead of interest.

Share at par. A share whose value on the stock market is the same as its face value.

Share buyback. An arrangement where a company buys its own shares on the stock market.

Share capital. The value of the assets of a company held as shares.

Share certificate. A document proving that you own shares.

Shareholder. A person who owns shares in a company.

Shareholders' equity. 1. The value of a company which is the property of its ordinary shareholders (the company's assets less its liabilities). 2. A company's capital which is invested by shareholders, who thus become owners of the company.

Shareholders' funds. The capital and reserves of a company.

Shareholding. A group of shares in a company owned by one owner.

Share incentive scheme. Same as share option scheme.

Share index. An index figure based on the current market price of certain shares on a stock exchange.

Share issue. An act of selling new shares in a company to the public.

Share option. A right to buy or sell shares at a certain price at a time in the future.

Share option scheme. A scheme that gives company employees the right to buy shares in the company which employs them, often at a special price.

Share premium. An amount to be paid above the nominal value of a share in order to buy it.

Share premium account. A part of shareholders' funds in a company, formed of the premium paid for new shares sold above par (the par value of the shares is the nominal capital of the company).

Share register. A list of shareholders in a company with their addresses.

Share split. The act of dividing shares into smaller denominations.

Share warrant. A document which says that someone has the right to a number of shares in a company.

Sharing. The act of dividing up.

Sharp. Sudden.

Sharp practice. A way of doing business which is not honest, but is not illegal.

Shell company. A company which does not trade, but exists only as a name with a quotation of the stock exchange.

Shipment. An act of sending goods.

Shipping company. A company whose business is in transporting goods or passengers in ships.

Shop. 1. A retail outlet where goods of a certain type are sold. 2. A workshop, the place in a factory where goods are made.

Shop around. To go to various shops or suppliers and compare prices before making a purchase or before placing an order.

Shopper. A person who buys goods in a shop.

Shoppers' charter. A law which protects the rights of shoppers against shopkeepers who are not honest or against manufacturers of defective goods.

Shopping. 1. Goods bought in a shop. 2. The act of going to shops to buy things.

Shopping cart. A software package that records the items that an online buyer selects for purchase together with associated data, e.g. the price of the item and the number of items required.

Short. 1. For a small period of time. 2. Not as much as should be.

Short bill. A bill of exchange payable at short notice.

Short-change. To give a customer less change than is right, either by mistake or in the hope that it will not be noticed.

Short credit. Terms which allow the customer only a little time to pay.

Short-dated bill. A bill which is payable within a few days.

Shortfall. An amount which is missing which would make the total expected sum.

Short position. A situation where an investor sells short (i.e. sells forward shares which he or she does not own).

Short-range forecast. A forecast which covers a period of a few months.

Short sale or Short selling. Arranging to sell something in the future which you think you can buy for less than the agreed selling price.

Short sellers. People who contract to sell a share in the future, expecting the price to fall so that they can it buy more cheaply before they have to close the sale.

Short-term. 1. For a period of weeks or months. 2. For a short period in the future.

Short-term forecast. A forecast which covers a period of a few months.

Short-terms. The fact of taking a short-term view of the market, i.e. not planning for a long-term investment.

Short-term loan. A loan which has to be repaid within a few weeks or some years.

Short-term paper. A promissory note, draft, etc. payable at less than nine months.

Short-term security. A security which matures in less than 5 years.

Short-term support. Support for a currency in the international market, where the central bank can borrow funds from other central banks for a short period.

SIB. Abbr. Securities and Investments Board.

Sight bill. A bill of exchange which is payable at sight.

Sight deposit. A bank deposit which can be withdrawn on demand.

Sight draft. A bill of exchange which is payable when it is presented.

Sight letter of credit. A letter of credit which is paid when the necessary documents have been presented.

Sight note. A demand note, a promissory note which must be paid when it is presented.

Sign. To write your name in a special way on a document to show that you have written it or approved it.

Signal. A warning message.

Signatory. A person who signs a contract, etc.

Signature. A person's name written by themselves on a cheque, document or letter.

Signature guarantee. A guarantee, such as a company stamp, that someone's signature is authorized as correct.

Silent partner. A partner who has a share of the business but does not work in it.

Silver. A precious metal traded on commodity markets.

Simple interest. Interest calculated on the capital invested only, and not added to it.

Single-entry bookkeeping. A method of bookkeeping where payments or sales are noted with only one entry per transaction (usually in the cash book).

Single-figure inflation. Inflation rising at less than 10% per annum.

Single-life annuity. An annuity which is paid only to one beneficiary, and stops when he or she dies (as opposed to a 'joint-life annuity').

Single premium policy. An insurance policy where only one premium is paid rather than regular annual premiums.

Sink. 1. To go down suddenly. 2. To invest money (into something).

Sinking fund. A fund built up out of amounts of money put aside regularly to meet a future need, such as the repayment of a loan.

Sister company. Another company which is part of the same group.

Slash. To reduce something sharply.

Sleeper. A share which has not risen in value for some time, but which may suddenly do so in the future.

Sleeping partner. A partner who has a share in the business but does not work in it.

Slide. To move down steadily.

Sliding scale. A list of charges which rises gradually according to value, quantity, time, etc.

Slow. Not going fast.

Slow down. To stop rising, moving or falling, or to make something go more slowly.

Slow payer. A person or company that does not pay debts on time.

Slump. 1. A rapid fall. 2. A period of economic collapse with high unemployment and loss of trade.

Slush fund. Money kept to one side to give to people to persuade them to do what you want.

Small business. A little company with low turnover and few employees.

Small businessman. A man who owns a small business.

Small companies. Companies which are quoted on the stock exchange, but which have a small capitalization.

Small investor. A person with a small sum of money to invest.

Small-scale. Working in a small way, with few staff and not much money.

Soar. To go up rapidly.

Social costs. The ways in which something will affect people.

Social investing. The practice of investing in companies which follow certain moral standards.

Social security or Social insurance. A government scheme where employers, employees and the self-employed make regular contributions to a fund which provides unemployment pay, sickness pay and retirement pensions.

Socio-economic. To social and economic conditions, social classes and income groups.

Socio-economic groups. Groups in society divided according to income and position.

Soft commodities. Foodstuffs which are traded as commodities (such as rice, coffee, etc.)

Soft currency. The currency of a country with a weak economy, which is cheap to buy and difficult to exchange for other currencies.

Soft landing. A change in economic strategy to counteract inflation, which does not cause unemployment or a fall in the standard of living, and has only minor effects on the bulk of the population.

Soft loan. A loan (from a company to an employee or from one government to another) at a very low rate of interest or with no interest payable at all.

Soft market. A market where there is not enough demand, and where prices fall.

Soft sell. The process of persuading people to buy, by encouraging and not forcing them to do so.

Sole agency. An agreement to be the only person to represent a company or to sell a product in a particular area.

Sole distributor. A retailer who is the only one in an area who is allowed to sell a product.

Sole owner. A person who owns a business on their own, with no partners, and has not formed a company.

Sole proprietor or Sole trader. A person who runs a business, usually by themselves, but has not registered it as a company.

Solvency. The state of being able to pay all debts on due date.

Solvent. Having assets which are more than your liabilities.

Source. The place where something comes from.

Source and application of funds statement. A statement in a company's annual accounts, showing where new funds came from during the year, and how they were used.

Special. 1. Better than usual. 2. To one particular thing.

Special drawing rights. Units of account used by the International Monetary Fund, allocated to each member country for use in loans and other international operations. Their value is calculated daily on the weighted values of a group of currencies shown in dollars. Abbr. SDR.

Specialist. 1. A person or company that deals with one particular type of product or one subject. 2. A trader on the BSE who deals in certain stocks for his own account, selling to or buying from brokers.

Special mention assets. Loans made by a bank without the correct documentation.

Special notice. Notice of a proposal to be put before a meeting of the shareholders of a company which is made less than 28 days before the meeting.

Special offer. A situation where goods are put on sale at a specially low price.

Specification. Detailed information about what or who is needed or about a product to be supplied.

Specimen. Something which is given as a sample.

Speculate. To take a risk in business which you hope will bring you profits.

Speculation. A risky deal which may produce a short-term profit.

Speculative share. 1. A share which may go sharply up or down in value. 2. A bond with a low credit rating.

Speculator. A person who buys goods, shares or foreign currency in the hope that they will rise in value.

Spend. To pay money.

Spending. The act of paying money for goods and services.

Spending power. 1. The fact of having money to spend on goods. 2. The amount of goods which can be bought for a sum of money.

Spin off. 1. A useful product developed as a secondary product from a main item. 2. A corporate reorganization in which a subsidiary becomes an independent company.

Split. 1. An act of dividing up. 2. A lack of agreement.

Split-level investment trust. An investment trust with two categories of shares: income shares which receive income from the investments, but do not benefit from the rise in their capital value; and capital shares, which increase in value as the value of the investments rises, but do not receive any income. Also called split trust, split-capital trust.

Split payment. A payment which is divided into small units.

Sponsor. 1. A company which pays part of the cost of making a TV programme by taking advertising time on the programme. 2. A person or company which pays money to help research or to pay for a business venture. 3. A company which pays to help a sport, in return for advertising rights. 4. An organization, such as a merchant bank, which backs a new share issue.

Spot. 1. A place. 2. A place for an advertisement on a TV or radio show. 3. The buying of something for immediate delivery adjective done immediately.

Spot cash. Cash paid for something bought immediately.

Spot market. The market for buying oil for immediate delivery.

Spot price or Spot rate. A current price or rate for something which is delivered immediately (also called 'cash price').

Spread. 1. Same as range. 2. The difference between buying and selling prices (i.e. between the bid and offer prices) to space something out over a period of time.

Spreadsheet. A computer printout showing a series of columns of figures.

Square. To balance your position by selling futures to balance purchases.

Stabilization. The process of making something stable, e.g. preventing sudden changes in prices.

Stabilization of the economy. Keeping the economy stable by preventing inflation from rising, cutting high interest rates and excess money supply.

Stability. The state of being steady or not moving up or down.

Stable. Steady or not moving up or down.

Staff incentives. Higher pay and better conditions offered to employees to make them work better.

Stag. 1. A person who buys new issues of shares and sells them immediately to make a profit. 2. A dealer in stocks who is not a member of a stock exchange.

Stage. A period, one of several points in a process of development.

Staged payments. Payments made in stages.

Stagflation. Inflation and stagnation happening at the same time in an economy.

Stagnant. Not active, not increasing.

Stagnation. The state of not making any progress, especially in economic matters.

Stake. An amount of money invested.

Stale. To a cheque which is so old, that the bank will not clear it unless it has been confirmed as correct by the payer.

Stale bull. An investor who bought shares hoping that they would rise, and now finds that they have not risen and wants to sell them.

Stamp duty. A tax on legal documents such as those used e.g. for the sale or purchase of shares or the conveyance of a property to a new owner.

Standard. The normal quality or normal conditions which other things are judged against.

Standard cost. A future cost which is calculated in advance and against which estimates are measured.

Standard deviation. The way in which the results of a sample deviate from the mean or average.

Standard direct labour cost. The cost of labour calculated to produce a product according to specification (used to measure estimates).

Standard of living. The quality of personal home life (such as amount of food or clothes bought, size of family car, etc.)

Standard rate. A basic rate of income tax which is paid by most taxpayers.

Standard risk. A normal risk on a loan which is likely to be repaid on time.

Standby arrangements. Plans for what should be done if an emergency happens, especially money held in reserve in the International Monetary Fund for use by a country in financial difficulties.

Standby credit. 1. Credit which is available if a company needs it, especially credit guaranteed by a euro note. 2. Credit which is available and which can be drawn on if a country needs it, specially credit guaranteed by a lender.

Standby loan. A loan which is available if needed.

Standing order. An order written by a customer asking a bank to pay money regularly to an account.

Standing settlement instructions. Instructions given by one bank to other banks as to the procedure to be followed when making payments to it. Abbr. SSI.

Standstill agreement. An agreement between a borrower and a lender that it is better to renegotiate the terms of the loan than for the lender to foreclose on the property used as security.

Starting. The act of beginning.

Starting salary. A salary for an employee when he or she starts work with a company.

Start-up. 1. The beginning of a new company or new product. 2. A new, usually small business that is just beginning its operations, especially a new business supported by venture capital and in a sector where new technologies are used.

State enterprise. A company run by the state.

Statement. 1. Something said or written which describes or explains something clearly. 2. A list of invoices and credits and debits sent by a supplier to a customer at the end of each month.

Statement of affairs. A financial statement drawn up when a person is insolvent.

Statement stuffer. An advertising leaflet enclosed with the monthly bank statement.

State monopoly. A situation where the state is the only supplier of a product or service.

Statistical discrepancy. The amount by which sets of figures differ.

Statistics. 1. Facts or information in the form of figures. 2. The study of facts in the form of figures.

Status. 1. The importance of someone or something relative to others, especially someone's position in society. 2. Legal position.

Status inquiry. An act of checking on a customer's credit rating.

Status quo. The state of things as they are now.

Statutory. Fixed by law.

Steadily. In a regular or continuous way.

Stimulate. To make something or someone become more active.

Stipulate. To state something specifically as a binding condition in a contract.

Stipulation. A condition in a contract.

Stock. 1. The quantity of goods for sale in a warehouse or retail outlet. 2. Shares in a company.

Stockbroker. A person who buys or sells shares for clients.

Stockbroker's commission. The payment to a broker for a deal carried out on behalf of a client.

Stock certificate. A document proving that someone owns stock in a company.

Stock code. A set of numbers and letters which refer to an item of stock.

Stock control. The process of making sure that the correct level of stock is maintained, to be able to meet demand while keeping the costs of holding stock to a minimum.

Stock controller. A person who notes movements of stock.

Stock depreciation. A reduction in value of stock which is held in a warehouse for some time.

Stock exchange. A place where stocks and shares are bought and sold.

Stock Exchange Electronic Trading System. The London Stock Exchange's electronic share trading system in major shares. Buyers and sellers are automatically matched by computer.

Stock exchange operation. Buying or selling of shares on the stock exchange.

Stockholder. A person who holds shares in a company.

Stockholding. The shares in a company held by someone.

Stock-in-trade. Goods held by a business for sale.

Stock jobber. A person who bought and sold shares from other traders on the stock exchange.

Stock jobbing. The business of buying and selling shares from other traders on the stock exchange.

Stock level. The quantity of goods kept in stock.

Stock market. A place where shares are bought and sold.

Stock market manipulation. The practice of trying to influence the price of shares by buying or selling in order to give the impression that the shares are widely traded.

Stock market manipulator. A person who tries to influence the price of shares in his or her own favor.

Stock market rating. The price of a share on the stock market, which shows how investors and financial advisers generally consider the value of the company.

Stock market valuation. A value of a company based on the current market price of its shares.

Stock mutual funds. Mutual funds where the money is invested in corporate stocks as opposed to bonds or government securities.

Stock option. A right to buy shares at a cheap price given by a company to its employees.

Stock picker. A person whose job is to choose which shares to buy.

Stock-purchasing loans. Loans from a company to members of staff to allow them to buy shares in the company.

Stock quote. A current price of a share on a stock exchange.

stocktaking. The counting of goods in stock at the end of an accounting period.

Stocktaking sale. A sale of goods cheaply to clear a warehouse before stocktaking.

Stock transfer form. A form to be signed by the person transferring shares.

Stock turnover. The total value of stock sold in a year divided by the average value of goods in stock.

Stock valuation. An estimation of the value of stock at the end of an accounting period.

Stop. A situation where someone is not supplying or not paying something.

Stop-go. An economic policy leading to short periods of expansion followed by short periods of squeeze.

Stop-loss order. An instruction to a stockbroker to sell a share if the price falls to a certain level.

Stoppage. A sum of money taken regularly from an employee's wages for insurance, tax, etc.

Store card. A credit card issued by a large department store, which can only be used for purchases in that store.

Straddle. 1. Spread, the difference between bid and offer price. 2. The act of buying a put option and a call option at the same time.

Straight bonds. Normal fixed-interest bonds which can be redeemed at a certain date.

Straight line depreciation. Depreciation calculated by dividing the cost of an asset, less its remaining value, by the number of years it is likely to be used.

Strength. The fact of being strong, or being at a high level.

Strong market. A market where prices are moving up.

Structure. The way in which something is organized.

Style. A way of doing or making something.

Sub-account. One of several separate investment accounts on which a variable annuity is based.

Sub-agency. A small agency which is part of a large agency.

Subcontract. A contract between the main contractor for a whole project and another firm who will do part of the work.

Subcontractor. A company which has a contract to do work for a main contractor.

Subscriber. A person who has applied for shares in a new company.

Subscription. 1. Money paid in advance for a series of issues of a magazine, for membership of a society or for access to information on a website. 2. Application to buy shares in a new company.

Subscription list. A list of subscribers to a new share issue.

Subscription price. A price at which new shares in an existing company are offered for sale.

Subsidiary company. A company which is more than 50% owned by a holding company, and where the holding company controls the board of directors.

Subsidize. To help by giving money.

Subsidized accommodation. Cheap accommodation which is partly paid for by an employer or a local authority.

Subsidy. 1. Money given to help something which is not profitable. 2. Money given by a government to make something cheaper.

Sub-underwriter. A company which underwrites an issue, taking shares from the main underwriters.

Success. 1. An act of doing something well. 2. An act of doing what was intended.

Supplementary benefit. Formerly, payments from the government to people with very low incomes. It was replaced by Income Support.

Supplier. A person or company that supplies or sells goods or services.

Supply. The act of providing something which is needed.

Supply and demand. The amount of a product which is available and the amount which is wanted by customers.

Supply price. The price at which something is provided.

Supply shock. A sudden rise in productivity which gives higher output and profits without inflation.

Supply-side economics. An economic theory that governments should encourage producers and suppliers of goods by cutting taxes, rather than encourage demand by making more money available in the economy.

Support. 1. Actions or money intended to help someone or something. 2. Agreement or encouragement.

Support level. A level below which a share, a commodity or the stock market will not fall, because of general support from investors.

Surcharge. An extra charge.

Surety. 1. A person who guarantees that someone will do something. 2. Deeds, share certificates, etc., deposited as security for a loan.

Surplus. 1. More of something than is needed. 2. An amount of money remaining after all liabilities have been met.

Surrender. The act of giving up of an insurance policy before the contracted date for maturity.

Surrender charge or Surrender fee. A charge levied when someone withdraws money invested before the date allowed (this is to deter early withdrawals)

Surrender value. The money which an insurer will pay if an insurance policy is given up.

Suspend. To stop doing something for a time.

Suspense account. An account into which payments are put temporarily when the accountant cannot be sure where they should be entered.

Suspension. An act of stopping something for a time.

Swap. An exchange of one thing for another.

Swap arrangement. An arrangement between central banks to allow each other credit in their respective currencies so as to make currency transactions easier.

Switch. To change, especially to change investment money from one type of investment to another.

Syndicate. A group of people or companies working together to make money.

Synergy. The process of producing greater effects by joining forces than by acting separately.

System. An arrangement or organization of things which work together

Systems analysis. The process of using a computer to suggest how a company can work more efficiently by analyzing the way in which it works at present.

Systems analyst. A person who specializes in systems analysis.

T

Table. 1. A diagram or chart. 2. A list of figures or facts set out in columns.

Table of contents. A list of contents in a book.

Tabulation. The arrangement of figures in a table.

Take. 1. The money received in a shop. 2. A profit from any sale. 3. To need a time or a quantity.

Take away. To remove one figure from a total.

Take-home pay. Pay received, after tax, etc., has been deducted.

Take off. 1. To remove or to deduct something. 2. To start to rise fast.

Take out. 1. To remove something. 2. To apply for and receive a patent.

Take-out. The act of removing capital which you had originally invested in a new company by selling your shares.

Take over. 1. To start to do something in place of someone else. 2. To buy a business by offering to buy most of its shares.

Takeover. 1. An act of buying a controlling interest in a business by buying more than 50% of its shares. 2. The act of starting to do something in place of someone else.

Takeover bid. An offer to buy all or a majority of the shares in a company so as to control it.

Takeover target. A company which is the object of a takeover bid.

Taker. A person who wants to buy something.

Take up. To accept an option which has been offered and put into action.

Take up rate. The percentage of acceptances for a rights issue.

Tally. A note of things counted or recorded.

Tally sheet. A sheet on which quantities are noted.

Tangible assets or Tangible fixed assets. Assets which have a value and actually exist (such as buildings, machines, vehicles and fittings).

Tangible asset value or Tangible net worth. The value of all the assets of a company less its intangible assets (goodwill, patents, etc.). It is shown as a value per share.

Tap. Same as tap stock. To get finance by borrowing from investors, lenders, etc.

Taper or Tapering relief. A new system of reducing capital gains tax payable when shares are sold, according to the length of time the shares have been held.

Target. Something to aim for.

Target company. Same as takeover target.

Target market. The market in which a company is planning to sell its goods.

Target price. A wholesale price within the certain products, such as wheat, which market management is intended to achieve; it is linked to the intervention price.

Note: Target prices are set in terms of fixed agricultural units of account, which are converted into different national currencies using adjusted exchange rates known as 'green rates'.

Tariff. A rate of charging for something such as electricity, hotel rooms or train tickets.

Tariff barrier. The customs duty intended to make imports more difficult.

Tax. An amount of money charged by government as part of a person's income or on goods bought.

Tax abatement. A reduction of tax.

Taxable. Which can be taxed.

Taxable income. Income on which a person has to pay tax.

Taxable items. Items on which a tax has to be paid.

Taxable supply. A supply of goods which are subject to VAT.

Tax adjustments. Changes made to tax.

Tax adviser or Tax consultant. A person who gives advice on tax problems.

Tax allowance. A part of the income which a person is allowed to earn and not pay tax on.

Tax assessment. A calculation by a tax inspector of the amount of tax a person owes.

Tax avoidance. The practice of legally trying to pay as little tax as possible.

Tax bill. An amount of tax (to be) paid.

Tax bracket. A section of people paying a particular level of income tax.

Tax break. An allowance which can be set off against tax.

Tax concession. An act of allowing less tax to be paid.

Tax credit. 1. A sum of money which can be offset against tax. 2. The part of a dividend on which the company has already paid tax, so that the shareholder is not taxed on it.

Tax-deductible. Which can be deducted from an income before tax is calculated tax has to be paid on these expenses.

Tax deductions. 1. Money removed from a salary to pay tax. 2. Business expenses which can be claimed against tax.

Tax-efficient. To an investment which helps avoid tax.

Tax evasion. The practice of illegally trying not to pay tax.

Tax-exempt. 1. To a person or organization not required to pay tax. 2. Which are not subject to tax.

Tax exemption. 1. The fact of being free from payment of tax. 2. The part of income which a person is allowed to earn and not pay tax on.

Tax-favoured investment. An investment which offers tax-reducing incentives.

Tax-filing program. Computer software to help draw up your income tax return.

Tax-free. With no tax having to be paid.

Tax haven. A country or area where taxes are low, encouraging companies to set up their main offices there.

Tax loophole. A legal means of not paying tax.

Tax planning. Planning how to avoid paying too much tax, by investing in, e.g., tax-exempt savings schemes or offshore trusts.

Tax relief. An allowance to pay less tax on certain parts of someone's income.

Tax shelter. A financial arrangement (such as a pension scheme) where investments can be made without tax.

Tax threshold. A point at which another percentage of tax is payable.

Teaser ad. An advertisement that gives a little information about a product in order to attract customers by making them curious to know more.

Teaser rate. A specially good interest rate on a new product, used to encourage savers to switch funds to that product. It is replaced by a normal rate when enough subscribers have invested in it.

Technical. 1. To a particular machine or process. 2. To influences inside a market (e.g. volumes traded and forecasts based on market analysis), as opposed to external factors, such as oil-price rises, wars, etc.

Technical analysis. A study of the price movements and volumes traded on a stock exchange.

Technical correction. (Stock Exchange) A situation where a share price or a currency moves up or down because it was previously too low or too high.

Technical decline. A fall in share prices because of technical analysis.

Telephone banking. A service by which a bank customer can carry out transactions over the phone using a password. It may involve direct contact with a bank representative or may be automated used the phone dial.

Telephone order. An order received by telephone.

Teller. A person who takes cash from or pays cash to customers at a bank.

Tenancy. An agreement by which a tenant can occupy a property.

Tender. An offer to do something for a specific price.

Tendering. The act of putting forward an estimate of cost.

Tender offer. A method of selling new securities or bonds by asking investors to make offers for them, and accepting the highest offers.

Tenor. A time before a financial instrument matures or before a bill is payable.

Term. 1. A period of time when something is legally valid. 2. Part of a legal or university year.

Term account. Same as term deposit.

Term assurance. A life assurance which covers a person's life for a period of time (at the end of the period, if the person is still alive he receives nothing from the insurance)

Term CD. A certificate of deposit which matures in more than twelve months.

Term deposit. Money invested for a fixed period at a higher rate of interest.

Terminal bonus. A bonus received when an insurance comes to an end.

Termination clause. A clause which explains how and when a contract can be terminated.

Term insurance. Same as term assurance.

Term loan. A loan for a fixed period of time.

Terms. The conditions or duties which have to be carried out as part of a contract, or the arrangements which have to be agreed before a contract is valid.

Term shares. A type of building society deposit for a fixed period of time at a higher rate of interest.

Terms of payment. The conditions for paying something.

Terms of reference. Areas which a committee or an inspector can deal with.

Terms of sale. The conditions attached to a sale.

Terms of trade. The ratio of a country's import prices to export prices.

Tertiary industry. An industry which does not produce raw materials or manufacture products but offers a service such as banking, retailing or accountancy.

TESSA. Abbr. Tax-exempt special savings account.

Thin market. A market where there are not many shares available for sale, so the price is distorted.

Third Market. Same as over-the-counter market.

Third party. A person other than the two main parties involved in a contract (i.e. in an insurance contract, anyone who is not the insurance company nor the person who is insured).

Third party insurance. Insurance to cover damage to any person who is not one of the people named in the insurance contract (that is, not the insured person nor the insurance company).

Third quarter. A period of three months from July to September.

Threshold. The point at which something changes.

Threshold agreement. A contract which says that if the cost of living goes up by more than a certain amount, pay will go up to match it.

Tie. To attach or to link something to something.

Tied loan. A loan which involves a guarantee by the borrower to buy supplies from the lender.

Tie in. To link an insurance policy to a mortgage.

Tier. A level.

Note: The British stock market is said to have two tiers: the first is the London Stock Exchange, with its listed securities. The second tier (which is linked to the first) is the Alternative Investment Market (AIM) which has less strict criteria for admitting securities, and is often used as a first stage in obtaining a main stock exchange quotation.

Tier One (According to London Stock Exchange) A first level of core capital which banks have (covering basic equity capital and disclosed reserves) to conform to the guidelines of the Basle Agreement.

Tier Two. A second level of capital which banks have (this applies to undisclosed debts, and provisions against bad debts) to conform with the guidelines of the Basle Agreement.

Tie up. 1. To attach or to fasten something tightly. 2. To invest money in one way, so that it cannot be used for other investments.

Tie-up. A link or connection.

Tight. Which is controlled, which does not allow any movement.

Tighten. To make something tight, to control something.

Tighten up on. To control something more strictly.

Tight market. A market where there is only a small spread between bid and offer prices.

Tight money policy. A government policy to restrict money supply.

Time. 1. A period during which something takes place, e.g. one hour, two days or fifty minutes. 2. The number of hours worked. 3. A period before something happens.

Time and a half. The normal rate of pay plus 50% extra.

Time and method study. A process of examining the way in which something is done to see if a cheaper or quicker way can be found.

Time and motion expert. A person who analyses time and motion studies and suggests changes in the way work is done.

Time and motion study. A study in an office or factory of the time taken to do certain jobs and the movements employees have to make to do them.

Time bill. A bill of exchange which is payable at a specific time after acceptance.

Time deposit. A deposit of money for a fixed period, during which it cannot be withdrawn.

Time limit. The maximum time which can be taken to do something.

Time of peak demand. The time when something is being used most.

Time rate. A rate for work which is calculated as money per hour or per week, and not money for work completed.

Timescale. The time which will be taken to complete work.

Time share. A system where several people each own part of a property (such as a holiday flat), each being able to use it for a certain period each year.

Time-sharing. 1. Same as time share. 2. An arrangement for sharing a computer system, with different users using different terminals.

Timetable. A list of appointments or events.

Tin. A valuable metal, formerly traded on commodity markets at an artificially high international price managed by the International Tin Council to protect tin producers from swings in the price.

Tip. 1. Money given to someone who has helped you. 2. A piece of advice on buying or doing something which could be profitable.

Tip sheet. A newspaper which gives information about shares which should be bought or sold.

Title. A right to own a property.

Title deeds. A document showing who is the owner of a property.

Token. Something which acts as a sign or symbol.

Token charge. A small charge which does not cover the real costs.

Token payment. A small payment to show that a payment is being made.

Token rent. A very low rent payment to show that some rent is being asked.

Toll. A payment for using a service (usually a bridge or a road).

Toll free. Without having to pay a charge for a long-distance telephone call.

Top. The highest point or most important place.

Top-ranking. In the most important position.

Top management. The main directors of a company.

Top official. A very important person in a government department.

Top-slicing. The practice of selling part of a holding in a share which is equivalent to the original cost of the investment, leaving another part still held which represents the gain made.

Top up. To add to something to make it more complete.

Total. Complete or with everything added together.

Total invoice value. The total amount on an invoice, including transport, VAT, etc.

Total return. The total capital growth and reinvested income on an investment at the end of any given period.

Touch. The narrowest spread between the buy and sell prices of a share.

Track. To follow someone or something; to follow how something develops, such as one of the stock market indices.

Tracker PEP. A PEP invested in funds which track a stock market index.

Tracking. The process of following a stock market closely.

Tracking unit trust. A trust which follows closely one of the stock market indices.

Track record. The success or failure of a company or salesperson in the past.

Example: The company has no track record in the computer market.

Trade. 1. The business of buying and selling. 2. A particular type of business, or people or companies dealing in the same type of product.

Trade agreement. An international agreement between countries over general terms of trade.

Trade association. A group which links together companies in the same trade.

Trade barrier. A limitation imposed by a government on the free exchange of goods between countries. Also called import restriction.

Trade bill. A bill of exchange between two companies who are trading partners (it is issued by one company and endorsed by the other).

Trade bureau. An office which specializes in commercial inquiries.

Trade commission. Same as broker's commission.

Trade counter. A shop in a factory or warehouse where goods are sold to retailers.

Trade credit. A credit offered by one company when trading with another.

Trade creditors. Companies which are owed money by a company (the amount owed to trade creditors is shown in the annual accounts).

Trade cycle. A period during which trade expands, then slows down, then expands again.

Trade deficit. The difference in value between a country's low exports and higher imports. Also called balance of payments deficit, trade gap.

Trade description. A description of a product to attract customers.

Trade Descriptions Act. An act which limits the way in which products can be described so as to protect customers from wrong descriptions made by manufacturers.

Trade directory. A book which lists all the businesses and business people in a town.

Trade discount. A reduction in price given to a customer in the same trade.

Traded options. Options to buy or sell shares at a certain price at a certain date in the future, which themselves can be bought or sold.

Trade fair. A large exhibition and meeting for advertising and selling a specific type of product.

Trade in. To give in an old item as part of the payment for a new one.

Trade-in. An old item, e.g. a car or washing machine, given as part of the payment for a new one.

Trademark or Trade name. A particular name, design or symbol which has been registered by the manufacturer and which cannot be used by other manufacturers. It is an intangible asset.

Trade mission. A visit by a group of businesspeople to discuss trade.

Trade-off. An act of exchanging one thing for another as part of a business deal.

Trade price. A special wholesale price paid by a retailer to the manufacturer or wholesaler.

Trader. 1. A person who does business. 2. A person who buys or sells stocks, shares and options.

Trade surplus. The difference in value between a country's high exports and lower imports.

Trade terms. A special discount for people in the same trade.

Trade-weighted index. An index of the value of a currency calculated against a basket of currencies.

Trading. 1. The business of buying and selling. 2. An area of a broking house where dealing in securities is carried out by phone, using monitors to display current prices and stock exchange transactions.

Trading account. An account of a company's gross profit.

Trading area. A group of countries which trade with each other.

Trading company. A company which specializes in buying and selling goods.

Trading estate. An area of land near a town specially for building factories and warehouses.

Trading firm. A stock broking house.

Trading limit. The maximum amount of something which can be traded by a single trader.

Trading loss. A situation where a company's receipts are less than its expenditure.

Trading partner. A company or country which trades with another.

Trading pattern. A general way in which trade is carried on.

Trading profit. A result where the company's receipts are higher than its expenditure.

Trading screens. Computer monitors listing stock market prices.

Trading session. One period (usually a day) during which trading takes place on a stock exchange.

Trainee. A person who is learning how to do something.

Training. The process of being taught how to do something.

Transaction on the stock exchange. A purchase or sale of shares on the stock exchange.

Transfer. An act of moving an employee to another job in the same organization.

Transferable. Which can be passed to someone else a document such as a bearer bond which can be passed to someone else.

Transfer of property or Transfer of shares. The act of moving the ownership of property or shares from one person to another.

Transferred charge call. A phone call where the person receiving the call agrees to pay for it.

Transfer value. The value of a pension when it is moved from one scheme to another.

Transit. The movement of passengers or goods on the way to a destination.

Transit letter. A letter sent with cheques or drafts, listing what is being sent.

Translate. To change something into another form.

Transparency. The fact of being clear about making decisions and being open to the public about how decisions are reached.

Travelling expenses. Money spent on travelling and hotels for business purposes.

Treasurer. 1. A person who looks after the money or finances of a club or society, etc. 2. The main financial officer of a company.

Treasurer's account. An account of a club or society with a bank.

Treasury. A government department which deals with the country's finance.

Treble. To increase three times, or to make something three times larger.

Trend. A general way in which things are developing.

Trend line. A line on a graph or chart which shows which way a trend is going.

Trial. 1. A court case to judge a person accused of a crime. 2. A test to see if something is good.

Trial balance. The draft calculation of debits and credits to see if they balance.

Tribunal. An official court which examines special problems and makes judgments.

Trigger . A thing which starts a process.

Trigger point. A point in acquiring shares in a company where the purchaser has to declare an interest or to take certain action.

Note: If an individual or a company buys 5% of a company's shares, this shareholding must be declared to the company. If 15% is acquired it is assumed that a takeover bid will be made, and no more shares can be acquired for seven days to give the target company time to respond.

There is no obligation to make a bid at this stage, but if the holding is increased to 30%, then a takeover bid must be made for the remaining 70%. If 90% of shares are owned, then the owner can purchase all outstanding shares compulsorily. These trigger points are often not crossed, and it is common to see that a company has acquired 14.9% or 29.9% of another company's shares.

Trillion. One million millions.

Triple. To become three times larger, or to multiply something three times.

Triplicate. With an original and two copies.

Trophy hunter. An investor who looks for cheap shares.

Troubleshooter. A person whose job is to solve problems in a company.

Trough. A low point in the economic cycle.

Troy weight. A system of measurement of weight used for gold and other metals, such as silver and platinum.

True and fair view. A correct statement of a company's financial position as shown in its accounts and confirmed by the auditors.

True copy. An exact copy.

Truncate. To operate a simplified banking system by not returning physical cheques to the paying bank.

Truncation. A simplified banking system, where actual cheques are not sent to the paying bank, but held in the receiving bank which notifies the paying bank by computer of the details of cheques received.

Trust. 1. The fact of being confident that something is correct or will work. 2. A legal arrangement to pass goods, money or valuables to someone who will look after them well. 3. The management of money or property for someone. 4. A small group of companies which control the supply of a product.

Trust company. An organization which supervises the financial affairs of private trusts, executes wills, and acts as a bank to a limited number of customers.

Trust deed. A document which sets out the details of a private trust.

Trustee. A person who has charge of money in trust.

Trust fund. Assets (money, securities, property) held in trust for someone.

Turkey. A bad investment, an investment which has turned out to be worthless (informal).

Turn. 1. A movement in a circle, or a change of direction. 2. A profit or commission.

Turn down. To refuse something.

Turnkey operation. A deal where a company takes all responsibility for constructing, fitting and staffing a building (such as a school, hospital or factory) so that it is completely ready for the purchaser to take over.

Turn over. 1. To have a specific amount of sales. 2. To pass something to someone.

Turnover. 1. The amount of sales of goods or services by a company. 2. The number of times something is used or sold in a period, usually one year, expressed as a percentage of a total. The term is also known as sales volume.

Turnover of shares. The total value of shares bought and sold on the stock exchange during the year.

Turnover tax. Same as sales tax.

Turn round. 1. To make a company change from making a loss to become profitable. 2. The value of goods sold during a year divided by the average value of goods held in stock. 3. The action of emptying a ship, plane, etc., and getting it ready for another commercial journey. 4. The act of making a company profitable again

Twenty-four-hour trading. Trading in bonds, currencies or securities that can take place at any time of day or night.

Note: Twenty-four-hour trading does not involve one trading floor being open all the time, but instead refers to the possibility of conducting operations at different locations in different time zones.

24-hour banking. A banking service provided during the whole day (e.g. by cash dispensers in the street and online services).

24-hour service. help which is available for the whole day.

24-hour trading. Trading in bonds, securities and currencies during the whole day.

Note: 24-hour trading is now possible because of instant communication to stock exchanges in different time zones; the Tokyo Stock Exchange closes about two hours before the London Stock Exchange opens; the New York Stock Exchange opens at the same time as the London one closes.

Two-tier market. An exchange market where two rates apply (usually one for tourists and a commercial rate for businesses).

Two-way market. A market where there is active buying and selling.

U

UBR. Abbr. Uniform business rate.

Ultimatum. A statement to someone that unless they do something within a period of time, action will be taken against them.

Umbrella organization. A large organization which includes several smaller ones.

Unacceptable. Which cannot be accepted.

Unaccounted for. Lost without any explanation.

Unanimous. Where everyone agrees or votes in the same way.

Unanimously. With everyone agreeing.

Example: The proposals were adopted unanimously.

Unauthorized. Not permitted.

Unauthorized unit trust. A private unit trust operated by a stock broking firm for its clients.

Unbalanced. To a budget which does not balance or which is in deficit.

Unbundling. 1. The process of separating companies from a conglomerate (the companies were independent in the past, and have been acquired by the conglomerate over a period of time). 2. The practice of charging separately for each different service provided.

Uncalled. To capital which a company is authorized to raise and has been issued but for which payment has not yet been requested.

Unchanged. Which has not changed.

Unchecked. Which has not been checked.

Uncollected. Which has not been collected.

Uncollected funds. Deposits which have not yet cleared through the clearing system and so cannot be drawn on.

Unconditional. With no conditions or provisions attached.

Note: A takeover bid will become unconditional if more than 50% of shareholders accept it.

Unconditionally. Without imposing any conditions.

Uncontrollable. Which cannot be controlled.

Uncovered bear. A person who sells stock which he does not hold, hoping to be able to buy stock later at a lower price when he needs to settle.

Uncrossed cheque. A cheque which does not have two lines across it, and can be cashed anywhere.

Undated. With no date indicated or written.

Undated bond. A bond with no maturity date.

Under. 1. Lower than or less than. 2. Controlled by, according to.

Under. Less important than or lower than.

Underbid. To bid less than someone.

Under bidder. A person who bids less than the person who buys at an auction.

Undercapitalized. Without enough capital.

Undercharge. To ask someone for too little money.

Undercut. To offer something at a lower price than someone else.

Underemployed. With not enough work.

Underemployed capital. Capital which is not producing enough interest.

Underestimate. An estimate which is less than the actual figure.

Underlying inflation rate. The basic inflation rate calculated on a series of prices of consumer items, petrol, gas and electricity and interest rates.

Underlying value. The basic value of a company, including its assets, goodwill, etc.

Under perform. To perform worse than the rest of the market.

Underperformance. The fact of performing worse than others.

Underrate. To value someone or something less highly than they should be.

Under react. Not to react strongly enough to a situation.

Undersell. To sell more cheaply than someone.

Undersigned. A person who has signed a letter.

Under spend. To spend less than you should have spent or were allowed to spend.

Understanding. A private agreement.

Understate. To make something seem less than it really is.

Under subscribed. To a share issue where applications are not made for all the shares on offer, and part of the issue remains with the underwriters.

Undertake. To agree to do something.

Undertaking. 1. A business. 2. A promise, especially a legally binding one.

Under valuation. The state of being valued, or the act of valuing something, at less than the true worth.

Undervalued. Not valued highly enough.

Underwater. Which has lost value.

Underwater loan. A loan which is worth less than its book value, as when an item bought with a loan loses its value on the market.

Underwater option. An option which has no value.

Underweight. Not heavy enough.

Underwrite. 1. To accept responsibility for something. 2. To insure, to cover a risk. 3. To agree to pay for costs.

Underwriter. A person or company that underwrites a share issue or an insurance.

Note: When a major company flotation or share issue or loan is prepared, a group of companies (such as merchant banks) will form a syndicate to underwrite the flotation: the syndicate will be organized by the 'lead underwriter', together with a group of main underwriters; these in turn will ask others ('sub-underwriters') to share in the underwriting.

Underwriting. The action of guaranteeing to purchase shares in a new issue if no one purchases them.

Underwriting fee. A fee paid by a company to the underwriters for guaranteeing the purchase of new shares in that company.

Underwriting syndicate. A group of underwriters who insure a large risk.

Undistributed profit. A profit which has not been distributed as dividends to shareholders.

Unearned income. Same as investment income.

Uneconomic. Which does not make a commercial profit.

Uneconomic rent. A rent which is not enough to cover costs.

Unemployment. The state of not having any work.

Unemployment rate. The number of people out of work, shown as a percentage of the total number of people available for work. Also called rate of unemployment.

Unencumbered. To property which is not mortgaged.

Unfair competition. The practice of trying to do better than another company by using techniques such as importing foreign goods at very low prices or by wrongly criticizing a competitor's products.

Unfavorable balance of trade. A situation where a country imports more than it exports.

Unfavorable exchange rate. An exchange rate which gives an amount of foreign currency for the home currency which is not good for trade.

Unfulfilled orders. Orders received in the past and not yet supplied.

Uniform business rate. A tax levied on business property which is the same percentage for the whole country. Abbr. UBR.

Unincorporated. To a business which has not been made into a company (i.e. which is operating as a partnership or a sole trader).

Un issued capital. Capital which a company is authorized to issue but has not issued as shares.

Unit. 1. A single product for sale. 2. A single share in a unit trust.

Unitary regulator. A single regulator, where before there were several.

Unit cost. The cost of one item, i.e. the total product costs divided by the number of units produced.

Unitize. To form investments into units which are sold to the public.

Unit-linked insurance. An insurance policy which is linked to the security of units in a unit trust or fund.

Unit of account. A standard unit used in financial transactions among members of a group.

Unit price. The price of one item.

Unit trust. An organization which takes money from small investors and invests it in stocks and shares for them under a trust deed, the investment being in the form of shares (or units) in the trust. The terms is also called as mutual fund.

Note: Unit trusts have to be authorized by the Department of Trade and Industry before they can offer units for sale to the public, although unauthorized private unit trusts exist.

Unlawful. Against the law, not legal.

Unlimited. With no limits.

Unlimited liability. A situation where a sole trader or each partner is responsible for all a firm's debts with no limit on the amount each may have to pay.

Unlisted company. A company whose shares are not listed on the stock exchange.

Unlisted securities. Shares which are not listed on the stock exchange.

Unlisted Securities Market. Formerly, the market for buying and selling shares which were not listed on the main stock exchange, now replaced by the Alternative Investment Market (AIM). Abbr. USM.

Unload. 1. To take goods off a ship, lorry, etc. 2. To sell shares which do not seem attractive.

Unlock. To sell undervalued assets and so increase the value of a company to its shareholders.

Unpaid. Not paid.

Unpaid balance. A balance of a loan or invoice which still has to be paid after a part payment or installment payment has been made.

Unpaid cheque. A cheque which has been deposited but which is bounced by the bank on which it is written, so the account of the person who should receive is not credited.

Unpaid invoices. Invoices which have not been paid.

Unprofitable. Not profitable.

Unquoted shares. Shares which have no stock exchange quotation.

Unrealized. Not sold to make a profit.

Unrealized capital gain. An investment which is showing a profit but has not been sold.

Unrealized profit. Same as paper profit.

Unredeemed pledge. A pledge which the borrower has not claimed back because he has not paid back his loan.

Unregistered. To a company which has not been registered.

Unsecured creditor. A creditor who is owed money, but has no security from the debtor for the debt.

Unsecured debt. A debt which is not guaranteed by a charge on assets or by any collateral.

Unsecured loan. A loan made with no security.

Unsettled. Which changes often or which is upset.

Unstable. Not stable, changing frequently.

Unsubsidized. With no subsidy.

Unsuccessful. Not successful.

Un weighted. Without giving any extra value to a certain factor.

Up. Preposition in or to a higher position.

Upcoming. Which will come in the near future.

Update. To revise something so that it is always up to date.

Up front. In advance.

Uplift. An increase.

Up market. A stock market which is rising or is at its highest level.

Upscale. Aimed at customers at the top end of the socio-economic ladder, who are well-educated and have higher incomes.

Upset price. The lowest price which the seller will accept at an auction.

Upside potential. The possibility for a share to increase in value.

Upstream. To the operations of a company at the beginning of a process (as drilling for oil as an operation of a petroleum company).

Upswing. An upward movement of share prices.

Up tick. A price of a share sold, which is higher than the previous price.

Upturn. A movement towards higher sales or profits.

Upward. Towards a higher position.

Upwards. Towards a higher position.

Use. A way in which something can be used.

User. A person who uses something.

User-friendly. Which a user finds easy to work.

User's guide or User's manual. A book showing someone how to use something.

Usual. Normal or ordinary.

Utilization. The act of making use of something.

Utility. A public service company, such as one that supplies water, gas or electricity or runs public transport.

V

Vacant possession. Being able to occupy a property immediately after buying it because it is empty.

Valuable. Which is worth a lot of money.

Valuation. An estimate of how much something is worth.

Value. The amount of money which something is worth.

Value added. The amount added to the value of a product or service, being the difference between its cost and the amount received when it is sold. Also called net output.

Value added tax. Full form of VAT.

Value investing. Basing investment strategy on the value of a company rather than simply on its share price.

Value investor. A person who buys shares for the value of the company.

Value-priced goods. Goods which are good value for money.

Value stocks. Shares which provide a good return on investment.

Variable. Which changes something which varies.

Variable annuity. An annuity based on funds invested in common stock, which varies with the value of the stock, as opposed to a fixed annuity.

Variable costs. Production costs which increase with the quantity of the product made, e.g. wages or raw materials.

Variable rate. A rate of interest on a loan which is not fixed, but can change with the current bank interest rates. Also called floating rate.

Variance. The difference between what was expected and the actual results.

Variation. The amount by which something changes.

VAT. A tax on goods and services, added as a percentage to the invoiced sales price. Full form Value Added Tax.

Vault cash. Cash held by a bank in its vaults, used for day-to-day needs.

VC. Abbr. Venture capitalist.

VCT. Abbr. Venture capital trust.

Velocity of money. The rate at which money circulates in the economy, usually calculated as the GNP shown as a percentage of the stock of money supply.

Vending. Selling.

Vendor. 1. A person who sells something, especially a property. 2. A company selling its shares on a stock market for the first time.

Vendor placing. The act of arranging for an issue of new shares to be bought by institutions, as a means of financing the purchase of another company.

Venture. A commercial deal which involves a risk.

Venture capital. Capital for investment which may easily be lost in risky projects, but can also provide high returns. Also called risk capital.

Venture capital fund. A fund which invests in finances houses providing venture capital.

Venture capitalist. A finance house or private individual specializing in providing venture capital. Abbr. VC.

Venture capital trust. A trust which invests in smaller firms which need capital to grow. Abbr. VCT.

Verification. The process of checking if something is correct.

Verify. To check to see if something is correct.

Vertical communication. Communication between senior managers via the middle management to the workforce.

Vertical integration. Same as backward integration.

Vested interest. A special interest in keeping an existing state of affairs.

Viability. The fact of being viable or being able to make a profit.

Viable. Which can work in practice.

Videoconference. A system linking video, audio and computer signals from different locations so that distant people can talk and see each other, as if in the same conference room.

View. A way of thinking about something.

Virtual credit card. A technology that allows a user to set up a new credit account with a bank on the Internet and then use this account number to purchase goods, also on the Internet.

Virtual tokens. Banking technology that allows a user to transfer money from their normal bank to an Internet bank and then use this credit to purchase goods on the Internet.

VISA. Trademark a trademark for an international credit card system.

Visible. Referring to real products which are imported or exported.

Visible exports. Real products which are imported or exported, as opposed to services.

Visible trade. Trade involving visible imports and exports.

Voicemail. An electronic communications system which stores digitized recordings of telephone messages for later playback.

Void. Not legally valid.

Void able. To a contract which can be annulled.

Volatile. To a market or price which is not stable, but which rises and falls sharply.

Volatility. The fact of being volatile.

Volatility rating. A calculation of how volatile a share is, by calculating how much its performance is different from the normal pattern.

Volume. 1. A quantity of items. 2. The quantity of shares traded on a stock market.

Volume discount. The discount given to a customer who buys a large quantity of goods.

Volume of business. The number of items sold, or the number of shares sold on the stock exchange during a day's trading.

Volume of sales. 1. The number of items sold. 2. An amount of money produced by sales. It is also called as turnover.

Volume of trade. Same as volume of business.

Volume-weighted prices. Prices which are calculated according to the volume of turnover.

Voluntarily. Without being forced or paid.

Voluntary. 1. Done freely without anyone forcing you to act. 2. Done without being paid.

Voluntary liquidation. A situation where a company itself decides it must close and sell its assets.

Voluntary organization. An organization which has no paid staff.

Voluntary redundancy. A situation where the employee asks to be made redundant, usually in return for a large payment.

Vote. The act of marking a paper or holding up your hand, to show your opinion or to show who you want to be elected.

Voting rights. The rights of shareholders to vote at company meetings.

Voting shares. Shares which give the holder the right to vote at company meetings.

Voucher. 1. A piece of paper which is given instead of money. 2. A written document from an auditor to show that the accounts are correct or that money has really been paid.

W

Wage. The money paid to an employee in return for work done, especially when it is paid weekly and in cash.

Note: The plural wages is more usual when referring to the money earned, but wage is used before others. The term 'wages' refers to weekly or hourly pay for workers, usually paid in cash. For employees paid by a monthly cheque, the term used is 'salary'.

Wage adjustments. Changes made to wages.

Wage claim. An act of asking for an increase in wages.

Wage differentials. Same as pay differentials.

Wage-earner. A person who earns a wage.

Wage-earning. People who have jobs and earn money.

Wage indexation. The linking of increases to the percentage rise in the cost of living.

Wage-price spiral. A situation where price rises encourage higher wage demands which in turn make prices rise.

Wages and prices freeze. A period when wages and prices are not allowed to be increased.

Wage scale. Same as pay scale.

Wages policy. A government policy on what percentage increases should be paid to workers.

Walk-in. A person who approaches an organization for a job, without knowing if any jobs are available.

Wall of money. A large amount of money ready to be invested on the stock market (especially, money from new investment funds, or foreign investors) Similar to the weight of money.

Wallpaper. Shares issued in large numbers during a takeover bid where the purchasing company offers them in exchange for the shares in the company being bought.

Wall Street. 1. A street in New York where the stock exchange is situated. 2. The US financial centre.

Warehouse. A large building where goods are stored.

Warehouse capacity. The space available in a warehouse.

Warehousing. 1. The act of storing goods in a warehouse. 2. An illegal act where someone buys shares in a company on behalf of another company and holds them in readiness to be surrendered when the second company makes a takeover bid.

Warning. A notice of possible danger.

Warrant. An official document which allows someone to do something.

Warrantee. A person who is given a warranty.

Warrant holder. A person who holds a warrant for shares.

Warrant premium. A premium paid to buy share warrants, above the price of the shares it entitles you to.

Warranty. 1. A legal document which promises that a machine will work properly or that an item is of good quality. 2. A promise in a contract. 3. A statement made by an insured person which declares that the facts stated by him are true.

Wasting asset. An asset which becomes gradually less valuable as time goes by (e.g. a short lease on a property).

Watchdog. A person or group that examines public spending or financial deals, etc.

Weak. Not strong, not active.

Weak currency. A currency which is trading at a low level against other currencies.

Weak market. A share market where prices tend to fall because there are no buyers.

Web. Same as World Wide Web.

Website. A position on the web, which is created by a company, organization or individual, and which anyone can visit.

Weight. A measurement of how heavy something is.

Weighted average. An average which is calculated taking several factors into account, giving some more value than others.

Weighted index. An index where some important items are given more value than less important ones.

Weighting. Additional salary or wages paid to compensate for living in an expensive part of the country.

Weight of money. A large amount of money ready to be invested on the stock market (especially cash available in pension funds).

Wheeler-dealer. A person who lives on money from a series of profitable business deals.

White-collar. Referring to office workers.

White knight. A person or company which rescues a firm in financial difficulties, especially one which saves a firm from being taken over by an unacceptable purchaser.

Whole-life insurance Or Whole-life policy. An insurance policy where the insured person pays a fixed premium each year and the insurance company pays a sum when he or she dies (also called 'whole-of-life assurance').

Wholesale. Referring to the business of buying goods from manufacturers and selling them in large quantities to traders who then sell in smaller quantities to the general public.

Wholesale banking. Banking services between merchant banks and other financial institutions (as opposed to retail banking).

Wholesale dealer. A person who buys in bulk from manufacturers and sells to retailers.

Wholesale market. An inter-bank money market, where banks and other financial institutions deal with each other.

Wholesale price. The price charged to customers who buy goods in large quantities in order to resell them in smaller quantities to others.

Wholesale price index. An index showing the rises and falls of prices of manufactured goods as they leave the factory.

Wholesaler. A person who buys goods in bulk from manufacturers and sells them to retailers.

Wholly-owned subsidiary. A subsidiary which belongs completely to the parent company.

Will. A legal document where someone says what should happen to his or her property when he or she dies.

Note: A will should best be drawn up by a solicitor; it can also be written on a form which can be bought from a stationery shop. To be valid, a will must be dated and witnessed by a third party (i.e. by someone who is not mentioned in the will).

Windfall. A sudden winning of money or a sudden profit which is not expected.

Windfall profit. A sudden profit which is not expected.

Winding up. Liquidation, the act of closing a company and selling its assets.

Window. A short period when something is available or possible.

Window dressing. 1. The practice of putting goods on display in a shop window, so that they attract customers. 2. The practice of putting on a display to make a business seem better or more profitable or more efficient than it really is.

Window of opportunity. A short period which allows an action to take place.

Window shopping. The practice of looking at goods in shop windows, without buying anything.

Wind up. 1. To end a meeting. 2. To put a company into liquidation.

WIP. Abbr. Work in progress.

Wipe off. To remove something completely.

Wire transfer. A transfer of money from one account to another by telegraph.

Witching hour. A critical moment on a stock exchange, where several options expire at the same time.

Withdraw. 1. To take money out of an account. 2. To take back an offer.

Withdrawal. The act of removing money from an account

Withholding tax. The tax which removes money from interest or dividends before they are paid to the investor (usually applied to non-resident investors).

With-profit bond. A bond which guarantees a capital return plus the profits which have accumulated during its lifetime.

With profits. To an insurance policy which guarantees the policyholder a share in the profits of the fund in which the premiums are invested.

Work. 1. Things done using the hands or brain .2.A job, something done to earn money.

Worker. A person who is employed.

Worker director. A director of a company who is a representative of the workforce.

Workforce. The total number of employees in an organization, industry or country.

Working capital. Capital in the form of cash, stocks and debtors (less creditors) used by a company in its day-to-day operations. Also called circulating capital, floating capital, net current assets.

Working conditions. The general state of the place where people work (e.g. whether it is hot, noisy, dark or dangerous).

Working partner. A partner who works in a partnership.

Working week. The usual number of hours worked per week.

Example: Even though he is a freelance, he works a normal working week.

Work in progress. The value of goods being manufactured which are not complete at the end of an accounting period. Abbr. WIP.

Work permit. An official document which allows someone who is not a citizen to work in a country.

Works committee Or Works council. A committee of employees and management which discusses the organization of work in a factory.

Work-sharing. A system that allows two or more part-timers to share one job, each doing part of the work for part of the pay.

Works manager. A person in charge of a works.

Workspace. The memory or space available on a computer for temporary work.

Workstation. A desk with a computer terminal, printer, telephone, etc., at which an employee in an office works.

World Bank. A central bank, controlled by the United Nations, whose funds come from the member states of the UN and which lends money to member states.

World rights. The right to sell the product anywhere in the world.

World Trade Organization. An international organization set up with the aim of reducing restrictions in trade between countries. Abbr. WTO.

Worldwide. Everywhere in the world.

World Wide Web. An information system on the Internet that allows documents to be linked to one another by hypertext links and accommodates websites and makes them accessible. Also called web.

Worth. Having a value or a price.

Worthless. Having no value.

Write down. To note an asset at a lower value than previously.

Write-down allowance. An allowance for the depreciation of an asset over a period of years.

Write off. To cancel a debt, or to remove an asset from the accounts as having no value.

Write-off. 1. The total loss or cancellation of a bad debt, or the removal of an asset's value from a company's accounts. 2. Something which is so badly damaged that it cannot be repaired (informal).

Write out. To write something in full.

Written-down value. A value of an asset in a company's accounts after it has been written down.

WTO. Abbr. World Trade Organization.

XYZ

Xc. Abbr. Ex-capitalization.

Xd. Abbr. Ex-dividend.

Year. A period of twelve months.

Yearbook. A reference book which is published each year with updated or new information.

Year end. The end of the financial year, when a company's accounts are prepared.

Yearly. Happening once a year.

Yen. A unit of currency used in Japan.

Yield. The money produced as a return on an investment, shown as a percentage of the money invested to produce an amount or percentage as interest or dividend.

Yield curve. A graph showing the yields on different types of investment.

Yield to maturity. A calculation of the yield on a fixed-interest investment, assuming it is bought at a certain price and held to maturity.

Yuan. A unit of currency used in China.

ZDPS. A bond which pays no dividend, but has a fixed term and a fixed redemption price, which is a little higher than the redemption price on similar gilts though the redemption price is not in fact guaranteed. Abbr. Zero dividend preference shares.

Zero inflation. Inflation at 0%.

Zero-rated. To an item which has a VAT rate of 0%.

Zero-rating. The rating of an item at 0% VAT.

Zinc. A metal which is traded on commodity markets, such as the Bombay Stock Exchange.

Zone. An area of a town or country for administrative purposes to divide a town into different areas for planning and development purposes.